CUES

CUES

Master the Secret Language of
Charismatic Communication

VANESSA VAN EDWARDS

PORTFOLIO / PENGUIN

PORTFOLIO / PENGUIN

An imprint of Penguin Random House LLC

penguinrandomhouse.com

Most Portfolio books are available at a discount when purchased in quantity for sales promotions or corporate use. Special editions, which include personalized covers, excerpts, and corporate imprints, can be created when purchased in large quantities. For more information, please call (212) 572-2232 or e-mail specialmarkets@penguinrandomhouse.com. Your local bookstore can also assist with discounted bulk purchases using the Penguin Random House corporate Business-to-Business program. For assistance in locating a participating retailer, e-mail B2B@penguinrandomhouse.com.

Image credits: pages 9, 11, 17, 19, 29, 38, 54, 56, 70, 75, 101, 129, 132, 158, 204, 212, 218, 219, 224, 225, 228, 236 by Science of People; pages 42, 43 by Brian Dean; pages 63, 64, 66, 68, 86, 102, 106, 108, 123, 124, 149, 151, 153 by Maggie Kirkland; pages 115, 171, 172, 194, 237, 238 by Vanessa Van Edwards.

Library of Congress Cataloging-in-Publication Data

Names: Edwards, Vanessa Van, author.

Title: Cues: master the secret language of charismatic communication / Vanessa Van Edwards.

Description: New York: Portfolio, [2022] | Includes bibliographical references and index.

Identifiers: LCCN 2021048764 (print) | LCCN 2021048765 (ebook) | ISBN 9780593332191 (hardcover) | ISBN 9780593332207 (ebook)

Subjects: LCSH: Interpersonal communication. | Social interaction. | Body language.

Classification: LCC BF637.C45 E32 2022 (print) | LCC BF637.C45 (ebook) | DDC 153.6—dc23/eng/20211202

LC record available at https://lccn.loc.gov/2021048764

LC ebook record available at https://lccn.loc.gov/2021048765

Printed in the United States of America

4th Printing

BOOK DESIGN BY TANYA MAIBORODA

To my husband, Scott,
and my daughter, Sienna.
I love your cues.

Cues
noun, plural

the powerful verbal, nonverbal, and vocal signals
humans send to one another.

Contents

The Signals That Are Secretly Shaping You

Have you ever shared a great idea only to find that others didn't get it?

You're not alone.

This was exactly what happened to mogul and entrepreneur Jamie Siminoff, the founder of Ring. His video doorbell company made headlines when it was acquired by Amazon in 2018 for over $1 billion. But before Ring was installed on millions of front doors around the world, it was almost derailed by a single bad pitch on *Shark Tank*, a TV show where entrepreneurs talk up their company to a panel of investors.

In fact, when Jamie went on the show in 2013 to pitch his company (then called Doorbot), *every single Shark passed on the opportunity to invest*—despite strong early sales and traction.

What happened?

The answer lies not in the information Siminoff presented but in *how* he presented it. Virtually every tiny signal, or *cue*, Siminoff shared—through his body language, vocal modulation, and pitch—undermined his credibility. He all but told the Sharks to stay away.

Siminoff had a great idea with huge potential, but with the wrong cues, it crashed and burned. Those *cues* spoke even louder than his billion-dollar idea.

Let's go through Siminoff's pitch step by step so you can see exactly where his cues went wrong.

Siminoff began his pitch with a knock on the door to the Shark Tank. "Who's there?" tech investor and Shark Mark Cuban asked. Siminoff replied from behind the closed door: "It's Jamie?"

This was Siminoff's first cue, or miscue. Instead of *stating* his name, he *asked* it. This is an example of a **question inflection**, also known as uptalk. Research has found that when the question inflection is accidentally used in a statement, it signals low confidence and insecurity. When the question inflection is used with a statement, it causes the listener's brain to question the speaker's credibility. The brain says, "If you aren't confident in what you just said, why should I be?"

Making things worse, Siminoff used the question inflection a second time: "Here to pitch?" Repeating this cue reinforced his lack of confidence—and he hadn't even started the pitch yet! Not a great first impression.

When the door finally opened, Canadian entrepreneur Robert Herjavec gave Siminoff a cue of his own: a fake smile. A genuine smile reaches all the way to the upper cheeks, activating the crow's-feet on the sides of your eyes. A fake smile appears only on the bottom half of the face. Herjavec's fake smile should have signaled Siminoff to change tack. If he'd caught it, he could have worked to build rapport with Herjavec. He didn't, and Herjavec passed on the idea.

When Siminoff finally began his official pitch, things seemingly moved back in his favor. He fielded questions from the Sharks on everything from market size to pricing. Mark Cuban even gave him a "Good for you!" when Siminoff shared that he'd had over a million dollars in sales. Throughout, however, the cues passing back and forth told a very different story about Siminoff's chances.

Three minutes in, Cuban pulled the corners of his mouth down into what looks like a frown but is actually a **mouth shrug**. This cue signals disbelief or doubt. It's a sign that someone feels disconnected or indifferent.

Researchers believe this is because the position of the mouth makes it impossible to speak. It's a nonverbal way of indicating a lack of interest

Shark Tank

in responding and therefore a bid to terminate the exchange of information. Cuban was telling Siminoff, "I'm done here."

Instead of seizing that moment to address Cuban's disbelief, Siminoff barreled along obliviously. If he'd registered Cuban's cue, he could have addressed his doubt with a simple acknowledgment: "Mark, I see that you're skeptical. Let me share some data with you." But Siminoff could only hear the words—"Good for you!"—and missed the underlying nonverbal message. A few minutes later, Cuban pulled out of the deal.

Of course, Siminoff wasn't just blind to the Sharks' negative cues during his pitch. He was also sending dozens of his own. For example, when he mentioned the price of his product, he showed a **one-sided shoulder shrug**, yet another low-confidence signal. Five minutes in, challenged on a crucial point about the future of smart devices, Siminoff gulped a **deep swallow**, a cue conveying nervousness. While all of this is completely understandable—who wouldn't be anxious defending years of work in front of skeptical billionaires on a TV show—these cues completely undermined the clear and confident words he actually spoke. **A strong idea cannot stand alone. It needs to be accompanied by strong cues.**

Siminoff slipped yet again when he tried to convince the Sharks he didn't face any serious competition in the space. His answer started strong, but then he leaked a **halt cue:** "We do not have any direct competitors. When I say direct [pause], we're [pause] the first video doorbell built for the smartphone." As you can see, a halt cue is when someone adds an out-of-place pause in the middle of a sentence. Liars halt. So do the very nervous. Since our brains can't tell the difference, we protectively and instinctively worry that someone is being dishonest. Halting can also occur when someone switches from a spontaneous answer to a rehearsed one. This is probably what happened to Siminoff. Having realized mid-sentence that he'd prepped for this question, he switched over to his script. Even though the substance of what he was saying was faultless, the choppy delivery undermined his credibility yet again.

Siminoff made the classic mistake many smart people make: **He focused too much on the *content* and not enough on the *cues*.** Cues could have supported his message, but instead they undermined it. In the end, it was Siminoff's failure as a communicator, not as an entrepreneur, that scuttled his pitch and sent him home empty-handed.

What Good Is a Brilliant Idea If No One Listens?

Every day I meet brilliant, creative, strategic thinkers held back, unwittingly, by their cues. Aspiring leaders, ambitious professionals, and entrepreneurs like Siminoff are not sending the right signals and are missing the signals being sent to them.

They have ideas but don't know how to share them persuasively. They are underpaid and don't know how to prove their worth to a boss or client. They leave a meeting feeling as if it went badly, but they aren't sure why . . . or worse, they finish an interaction thinking it went well only to be blindsided by negative feedback later.

Hundreds of subtle signals are being sent to you every day. Humans are social animals. We evolved to get along in groups, so we're constantly telegraphing information—about our social status, our potential as mates, and our intentions. Similarly, we're constantly alert to social information others are sending to us.

When you uncover the cues being *sent to you*, everything becomes clearer. You won't miss hidden emotions. You know who and what information to trust. You can communicate authentically and assertively.

When you learn to *send* the right cues to others, people start listening to you, find you engaging, and are more interested in what you have to say. You'll also feel more confident going into your interactions.

The right cues can take a lackluster conversation, meeting, or interaction and make it memorable. Send the wrong cues and potential opportunities are missed, doubted, and overlooked.

Researchers have long known about the power of cues, and most people have some inkling that body language is important. But what most people *don't* know is how well cues predict behavior, personality, and achievement with surprising accuracy. For instance:

- We can predict a leader's charisma based solely on five seconds of exposure.
- Want to know who will get divorced? One single cue can predict with 93 percent accuracy which couples will split—sometimes years ahead of time.
- We can predict which doctors will get sued more often by listening for specific cues hidden in their voice tone.
- When jurors exhibit this one nonverbal cue, it can completely change a criminal's fate.
- Researchers observing speed daters can predict who will trade numbers at the end of the night simply by observing their silent nonverbal cues.
- Want to know who will win an election before it happens? Researchers found that voters decide who is more dominant in just one minute of political exchange, and that predicts their vote.

If cues can be used to predict the outcomes of critical events like elections, marriages, and malpractice lawsuits, imagine what mastering them can do for you in your day-to-day life. My goal with this book is to make these normally invisible signals visible, whether it's in person, on phone calls, in video calls, and even on email and chat. Armed with the knowledge of how cues work, you will be able to amplify your message and increase your impact. And you'll never be underestimated, overlooked, or misunderstood again.

Why Cues?

Twelve years ago, I made a discovery that profoundly changed the way I communicate. I discovered that there was an invisible language being spoken all around me. It explained why people so often dismissed my ideas. Why I had a hard time building relationships—both professional and social. It's why I felt so uncomfortable, bored, and awkward in so many interactions.

I was sending the wrong cues . . . and missing the ones being sent to me. Learning to decode and *control* my cues changed my life and my career. Now I would like to share that knowledge with you.

I've had the privilege to lead hundreds of corporate workshops, at companies like Amazon, Microsoft, PepsiCo, Intel, and Google, to name just a few. I've been fortunate enough to help millions of students level up their people skills in my courses, and 36 million more have watched my YouTube tutorials on communication. And now I'm very, *very* excited to bring that knowledge directly to you in this book.

My secret sauce is to combine the latest research (including original research my team conducted at Science of People), real-life case studies of success, and fascinating examples of notable figures, including Lance Armstrong, Oprah Winfrey, Richard Nixon, and Britney Spears, with practical strategies you can start using immediately.

I have grouped cues into four different channels: **Nonverbal, Vocal, Verbal,** and **Imagery**. And this is how the book is organized.

First, we will learn about nonverbal cues. Researchers find that nonverbal signals account for 65 to 90 percent of our total communication, yet most of us have no idea how to use our body language to communicate effectively. This is the largest section in the book because it constitutes the biggest channel in our communication. You'll learn to project confidence without having to say a word (which also helps you *feel* more confident too), to quickly build trust, and to have a powerful presence in any setting. I'll show you which hand gestures make you look smart and how to spot hidden emotions.

Next, in the Vocal Cues section, you'll learn how to sound powerful. Believe it or not, leaders actually use vocal cues to influence others. We'll also dig into why our brains associate vocal charisma with leadership, and how you can build trust on phone calls, on video calls, and in person.

In the Verbal Cues section, I'll show you how to make your emails, chats, and profiles more impactful. Ever wonder why certain people respond slowly to your emails? We'll dive into how to be more verbally engaging and how to communicate with charisma both online and offline.

In the final section, you will learn how Imagery Cues matter more than you think. I'll show you what your clothes, your desk, and the colors you wear say about you . . . whether you want them to or not.

Let's dive in!

CHAPTER 1

Cue for Charisma

Who is the most charismatic person you know?

This is one of my favorite questions to ask audiences. People immediately shout out their answers. "My dad!" or "My teacher!" or "My best friend!"

The next question is where things get more interesting. I ask, "What *makes* someone charismatic?"

Typically, I hear crickets. People rack their brains to come up with the answer. They venture, "Well, it's, you know, that feeling?" **Why is it that we struggle to define charisma, even though we immediately recognize it in others?**

In a groundbreaking study from Princeton University, researchers found that highly charismatic, likable, compelling people demonstrate a special blend of two specific traits: warmth and competence. It's a simple equation:

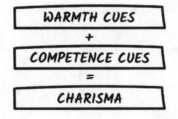

This formula is a powerful blueprint for every interaction. And it can completely change the way you communicate if you know how to use it.

According to the research, warmth and competence cues account for 82 percent of our impressions of others.

First, we quickly assess someone's warmth, answering the question: **Can I trust you?**

Then we look for competence, answering the question: **Can I rely on you?**

And this formula isn't just at play when making a first impression. Any time people interact with you, they continuously scan for cues to gauge your warmth and competence. And you do the same to others. Whether you are in a business meeting, on a date, with your boss, or with new friends, managing these two traits is essential for your effectiveness.

Highly charismatic people exhibit the perfect blend of warmth and competence. They immediately signal trust and credibility. We see them as friendly and smart, impressive and collaborative. They earn both our respect and admiration.

Here's the problem: **Most of us have an imbalance between these two traits.** It's often the hidden cause of our social difficulties, missed potential, and miscommunications.

We need this balance to succeed. Highly charismatic people use both warmth and competence cues to communicate successfully. We love being around people who make us feel like we are in both safe *and* capable hands. We like our leaders to be both highly effective and very approachable. We look for partners we can trust with our deepest secrets and call in an emergency. We want to work with people who are both friendly and productive.

We're always on the lookout for people who hit the sweet spot of both warmth and competence—the quadrant that has the star on the Charisma Scale on the following page. This Charisma Scale helps us map our communication.

Where do you think you fall on the scale? Are you more warm (upper left quadrant) or more competent (lower right quadrant), or do you strike a perfect balance and land in the Charisma Zone? Not sure? You might not show enough cues at all, putting you in the Danger Zone.

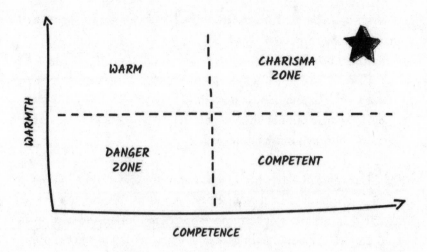

Consider where *others* might *place you* on the scale. Do a quick test below by choosing which column sounds more like you:

COMPETENT	WARM
Impressive	Trustworthy
Powerful	Collaborative
Smart	Kind
Capable	Compassionate
An Expert	A Team Player
Effective	Open

Be sure to take your official Charisma Diagnostic
in your digital bonuses at scienceofpeople.com/bonus.

Higher in Warmth

If you are highly warm, you have a strong desire to be liked. This can be good—you strive to be friendly and personable—but it can also be challenging. Highly warm folks are often people pleasers and struggle to say no and set boundaries. **Your desire to be liked can get in the way of your need to be respected.**

You might be seen as:

- Trustworthy but not always powerful
- Compassionate but not always competent
- Friendly but not always impressive

If this is you, you likely have good relationships with your colleagues but you find it hard to pitch yourself or your ideas. You might even get interrupted in meetings or feel underappreciated for all the hard work you do. In social or casual settings, people enjoy talking to you but might not ask for your business card.

You're likely higher in warmth if people tell you things like:

- I always feel so comfortable around you!
- You're such a sweetheart.
- I feel like I have known you forever.
- You have a trustworthy face.

Steve Wozniak is a good example of a business leader who is known for being jovial and kind but doesn't get as much credit for his accomplishments as his former partner, Steve Jobs, who was known for high competence.

Higher in Competence

If you are highly competent, you have a strong desire to be seen as capable and impressive. People take you and your ideas seriously, but you might have a harder time building rapport. You could be seen as:

- Smart but not always approachable
- Dependable but not always collaborative
- Important but not always kind

People might even be intimidated by you. They may tell you that you're hard to talk to or come across as cold. In business settings, this can be a double-edged sword. You're taken seriously as a leader, but you may have a harder time working with teams.

Clients, customers, or colleagues may find you credible but might not feel comfortable telling you all their needs. Researcher Susan Fiske found that **"competence without warmth is likely to leave us feeling suspicious."** In social settings, this means you're often perceived as important, but it takes you longer to build deeper connections and make friends.

You're likely higher in competence if people tell you things like:

- I never know what you're thinking.
- You can be a little intimidating!
- You're hard to read.
- You must be the one in charge here.

Business leaders like Mark Zuckerberg, Anna Wintour, and Elon Musk are examples of people who have had success with high competence but have been criticized for being harsh, hard to read, and unemotional.

You might notice that highly competent people will often partner with highly warm folks to balance them out. Many famous duos include a highly warm character and a highly competent character. This is a good way to think about how these traits play off each other.

- Captain Kirk (warm) and Spock (competent)
- Warren Buffett (competent) and Charlie Munger (warm)
- Ernie (warm) and Bert (competent)
- Sherlock Holmes (competent) and Dr. Watson (warm)

Put together, these duos often hit the sweet spot.

The Danger Zone

The last part of the quadrant is the one you need to work hard to avoid: the Danger Zone.

Researchers have found that if you rank low in both warmth and competence, you are more likely to be overlooked, dismissed, pitied, and undervalued.

The Danger Zone is also where I would have placed Jamie Siminoff during his *Shark Tank* pitch. His idea wasn't bad, he simply didn't send enough warmth and competence cues. As a result, the Sharks didn't believe him.

You can have the best *content* in the world, but if it's not shared with the right charisma *cues*, it doesn't land.

Siminoff's low competence and low warmth cues undermined his message. He addressed every single one of the Sharks' verbal questions with logical answers but missed critical nonverbal feedback cues from them. He prepared his numbers and created a helpful demo, but his Danger Zone cues sabotaged his credibility every step of the way.

Here's the key: You might be the most competent, warmest person in the world, but if you don't show it, people won't believe you.

The good news is that even if you fall into the Danger Zone, you don't have to stay there. Siminoff's idea was so successful that he was invited to come back to *Shark Tank* five years later *as a Shark*! When he walked into the tank as an investor, it was like seeing a different person. His cues transformed him. He strode into the room, made broad gestures, smiled, and shook hands with each of the Sharks. He even sounded different.

Sure, Siminoff had one bad pitch, but he bounced back. Everyone can improve their cues.

Why Charisma Matters

Golden Globe–winning actress Goldie Hawn is known for her beauty, her humor, and her talent in front of the camera. But in 2003 she decided to set her sights on a very different goal—creating a mindfulness program in schools. She decided to call the program MindUp and set out to create a mental fitness program for children that could be used in classrooms. But she had a problem. She worried that people wouldn't take her and the program seriously.

Hawn was keenly aware that she is known for her warmth but not necessarily for her competence. In her own words, "It's hard enough being me, being Goldie, who has been known for all these decades as being funny and sometimes bubble headed," said Hawn.

To help give her idea credibility, she brought in neuroscientists and psychologists and launched a massive study to validate the program. Hawn intuitively knew that she had to balance out her warmth with competence to get people to *trust* and *rely* on the program. And it worked!

Hawn and her team have grown the program to help over seven million students in fourteen countries and trained over 175,000 teachers. Eighty-six percent of the children who go through the MindUp program report being able to boost their well-being, and 83 percent show improvements in positive social behaviors.

Hawn isn't the only one embodying the balance of warmth and competence. If you visit the MindUp website, you will see it has a powerful blend of warmth cues—smiling kids, a laughing Goldie, and great stories— right alongside competence cues like statistics, social proof, and data. Brands, websites, social profiles, and companies also need to hit the sweet spot of warmth and competence.

No matter who you are or what you've achieved, balancing warmth and competence is key to your success. A famous study published in *The Journal of the American Medical Association* looked at how patients rated doctors on their warmth and competence. Researchers wondered, do *both* of these perceptions really matter? Isn't competence more important for doctors? Shouldn't years in school be enough?

Nope.

The researchers found that doctors who were rated poorly for warmth, rather than for their actual medical mistakes, were more likely to be sued for malpractice. Doctors who don't use enough warmth cues are unable to get across their competence and are sued more often.

If you can't showcase your warmth, people won't believe in your competence.

Too often I see people stuck in one part of the scale. I run into brilliant engineers who focus so much on technical skills that they are disliked and avoided in the office. They can't get buy-in on their innovative ideas, feel disconnected from the team, and wonder why they're always doing all the heavy lifting on projects.

Or I meet generous office managers who worry so much about being liked that they can't speak up in a meeting or get the respect they deserve. They wish for more social assertiveness so they can feel empowered to say no to toxic people and stand up for themselves.

Often it seems the kinder someone is, the less they are appreciated and respected. On the other hand, the more skilled someone is, the more they might struggle with their colleagues and teams.

Whether you're starting a new project, pitching ideas to a team, or trying to reset your reputation at work, we need *both* likability and respect. The right charisma cues can help.

PRINCIPLE

Balance warmth and competence cues to be charismatic.

Flavors of Charisma

When I ask audiences to name the most charismatic people they know, two names frequently come up: queen of talk Oprah Winfrey and the former prime minister of the United Kingdom, Margaret Thatcher.

Both of these women are considered successful, well respected, and charismatic. Yet their charisma feels completely different. How can this be?

One study examined Winfrey's and Thatcher's communication styles and found they use very different cues.

Thatcher was known for her control. She "stood leaning against the parliamentary podium, elbow out as if she owned it. Her head tilted upward. Her voice strong, loud, and with controlled pauses . . . Her body and face still," explained the researchers.

Winfrey is known for her expressiveness. She "moves with gusto—her arms are long and she gestures broadly. Her facial expressions carry every feeling—she cries, and laughs. . . . She sits and stands and moves all around," explained the researchers.

Winfrey and Thatcher both fall into the Charisma Zone, but they have different leanings. And that's good! We don't want everyone to look the same or mimic cues like robots.

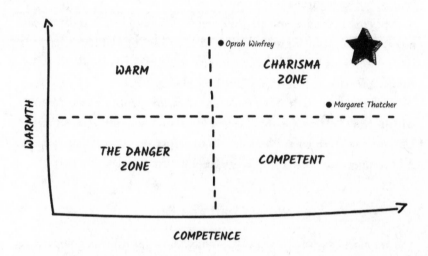

Winfrey leans toward warmth but grounds her warmth with enough competence cues to be taken seriously. This is clear in every episode of her show. She cries with people, touches their arms, but also listens intently and asks challenging questions. She laughs freely and pairs heartfelt stories with hard-hitting perspective.

Thatcher leans toward competence but shows enough warmth cues to be seen as trustworthy. In her speeches, Thatcher spoke with clarity and precision, rarely using flowery language, but she imbued her words with passion. She used fewer gestures but would frequently tilt her head toward the sky in a nonverbal gesture of warmth and optimism. Does it surprise you that the "Iron Lady" showed warmth cues? You can demonstrate warmth and still be seen as serious. In fact, you need both elements to communicate effectively.

Yes, there is one formula to charisma—warmth cues plus competence cues. **But each of us has our own special balance.** As long as you're in the Charisma Zone, you're showcasing enough warmth and competence to be perceived as credible and trustworthy.

Compare TV hosts and chefs Jamie Oliver (higher in warmth) with Gordon Ramsay (higher in competence). Both are considered very charismatic but have different flavors.

My goal is to give you the full menu of cues. Then you can *choose* how much of each ingredient you need to hit your unique charisma sweet spot. This is how we communicate authentically inside the Charisma Zone. You can add cues as you need them.

And the best part? **The most charismatic people move *flexibly* within the Charisma Zone.** Need a little more warmth in a situation? Use more warmth cues. Need to inject competence into an interaction? Add competence cues. You can use the Charisma Scale like a dial.

Your Charisma Dial

You are most charismatic when you adjust your warmth and competence based on the situation and person you're with—while still staying in the Charisma Zone. Take, for example, billionaire founder of Amazon Jeff Bezos. In one early interview with *60 Minutes Australia,* Bezos uses warmth cues as he casually takes a reporter around the office—he smiles, laughs, and gestures freely. The reporter even says, "The thing that strikes you first and most profoundly about Jeff Bezos is his laugh." He was incredibly likable in the interview because he leaned into warmth but still balanced his communication with competence cues—speaking with credibility about his company's growth, sharing impressive statistics and goals in between laughs.

In a later interview with *Business Insider,* Bezos got asked more serious questions about his legacy as a leader.* In response, Bezos dialed up

---

* Watch both interviews in your digital bonuses.

his competence cues. He sits expansively and makes purposeful eye contact with the interviewer, and if you listen carefully, you will hear that Bezos even uses a lower tone of voice than in the earlier interview. But Bezos still uses enough warmth cues to stay in the Charisma Zone (his famous chuckle kept the audience laughing with him).

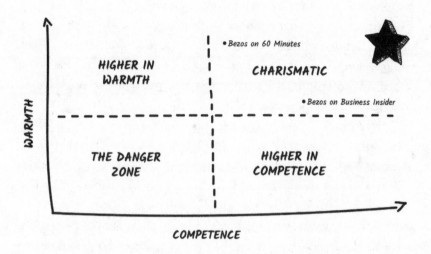

The number one way to improve your interactions is to send clear cues based on your goals.

When you need more credibility or to be taken seriously, as in negotiations, pitches, and important interviews, dial up competence. Additionally, if you're with someone who appreciates highly intelligent, capable, efficient people, use more competence cues.

If you want to build more collaboration and trust, dial up warmth. If you're with someone who values connection, rapport, and empathy, you should generate warm cues.

PRINCIPLE

The most charismatic people move flexibly within the Charisma Zone.

How to Solve Your People Problems

Every day we interact with people who fall into different zones of the Charisma Scale. This can create all kinds of disconnects and miscommunications. Let's say, for example, that you're a little higher in warmth. But your client or customer (or boss or colleague) is a little higher in competence. This can cause a connection problem.

You, as a highly warm person, love rapport. When you start a meeting, you feel that chitchat is essential for a successful interaction. When you present an idea, you value great stories, case studies, and examples. When you make decisions, you often go with your gut. You place a lot of confidence in recommendations by referrals.

Your client, as a highly competent person, loves information. When they start a meeting, they want to get right to business. They don't want to waste time with unproductive catch-ups. They prefer presentations with lots of data, research, and facts. If they doubt what you're saying, they *will* fact-check you on Google. They don't really care about social proof (it's only one person's opinion!) and they prefer hard numbers. Oh, and nothing drives them crazier than going off agenda on an unrelated tangent. They say things like "I need to do my own due diligence."

So what happens? You try to bond, while they try to be productive. You try to build trust, while they try to get informed. You feel your presentation is inspiring and they find it disorganized. You give them testimonials to close the sale, but they want more proof and data. You try to cultivate warmth and they try to harvest competence.

Neither of these approaches or preferences is right or wrong; they are just *different*. Remember, people have their own unique flavors of charisma, and that's good. Warm and competent folks have different talents, and we need *both* on a team. I will teach you how to spot these differences and even make them work for you.

Mismatches in charisma explain so many problems you might face:

- Why you just can't click with your boss.
- Why your presentations or ideas sometimes don't land.

- Why you've been passed over for a promotion or dismissed by a potential friend.
- Why you sometimes feel awkward or disliked.

Know you need more trust, collaboration, and openness with someone? Dial up your warmth cues.

Know you're interacting with someone who is higher in competence? Dial up your competence cues as a sign of respect.

We can use these cues to be more successful in every area of our life—face-to-face chats, social media profiles, voicemails, slide decks, presentations, and even in our offices. I'll teach you cues for each area of the Charisma Scale so you can use them purposefully, in the right situations, with the right people.

CHAPTER CHALLENGE

To help you get the most out of this book, we have created an official **Charisma Diagnostic.** This will help you identify exactly where you are on the scale. Take the official quiz and get your results at:

scienceofpeople.com/bonus

This is also where you'll find all the digital goodies, videos, and extras in this book.

CHAPTER 2

How Cues Work

I n 1498, Leonardo da Vinci finished painting *The Last Supper*. It would become one of the most famous paintings in the world. It is a beautiful, historic piece of art, but when you look deeper, you can see a new dimension: Da Vinci hid nonverbal cues in plain sight.

The painting depicts Christ's final meal with his twelve apostles before he finds out he has been betrayed by Judas.

What cues is da Vinci showing? First, take a look at Christ's hands. He's depicted with his arms held wide, palms open toward the viewer.

This is a universal cue of openness. Seeing another person's palms tells our brain they have nothing to hide. Christ also holds one palm facing down, and this is unusual. Typically, Christ is depicted with *both* his palms open toward the viewer. Why this difference?

The **palm up cue** is a signal of openness and trust. It's a high warmth cue, best used when trying to get people to be more collaborative and open. When I get to the question-and-answer part of my presentations, I always use the palm up gesture to invite questions.

The **palm down cue** is a signal of power and dominance. It is a high competence cue.

The palm down cue is best used when giving directives, commands, or instructions in situations that don't call for questions or feedback. It is most often used by people in positions of power.

Christ is depicted exhibiting both of these cues. Put together, they hit the perfect blend of warmth and competence.*

The next cue is in Christ's overall posture compared to the figures of the twelve apostles. Christ is depicted in the most expansive pose of any figure in the painting. It appropriately signals his outsize importance in relation to the others at the table. And it's another competence cue. The more space someone takes up, the more confident they look and feel. Da Vinci was able to signal Christ's importance with this **expansion cue**.

Da Vinci balanced this expansive competence cue with the ultimate warmth signal—a head tilt. A **head tilt** is a universal sign of engagement. We literally tilt our head to the side when trying to hear someone better, giving one of our ears a better chance to hear what is being said.

You'll notice a few of the apostles use expansion cues without head tilts or head tilts without expansion cues. **Christ is the only figure with the balance.** Unwittingly or not, da Vinci used the perfect balance of cues so Christ could be viewed as both highly competent (powerful) and highly warm (trustworthy).

The corollary to an expansion cue is a **contraction cue**. People who contract their body and take up as little space as possible signal low con-

---

* Some religious scholars believe that the one palm up and one palm down cue can also represent judgment in the afterlife. This might be an additional signal for religious onlookers.

fidence. Who has the most contracted pose? Judas, of course. The apostle who betrays Christ.

Judas is also showing a **blocking cue**: he has his arm in front of his torso. Blocking protects our body by putting something between us and another person. It can be as simple as crossing our arms or holding props in front of us like a laptop, clipboard, or sofa pillow. Whereas Christ is completely open, with nothing blocking our view of him, Judas is depicted as the only apostle in a contracted blocking pose. Others hold up their hands in innocence or point or gesture, but only Judas blocks. It's a clever way for da Vinci to signal Judas's guilt. Someone guilty of a crime is more likely to feel the need to nonverbally protect themselves by blocking.

Judas is depicted looking behind him. Can you guess why? This is an interesting **distancing cue**. When we try to get away from something or someone, we need to physically distance ourselves, sometimes literally pulling back. Liars often jerk their head back, scoot backward, or look away when confronted with their guilt. The phrase "watch your back" has some nonverbal truth to it. This is another cue signaling Judas's betrayal and shame.

Judas has one more illustrative cue. He is clenching his right fist. Not only does this conceal one of his palms from us—which makes him look more closed off—but it also signals that he is hiding something. A **fist** is a unique nonverbal cue. Sometimes it's positive—a signal of unshakable determination. And sometimes it's negative—a signal of concealment and anger. Researchers find that our hands evolved to make fists for punching. We make a fist right before we punch someone. This is another clever hint to Judas's anger and attack on Christ.

Cues give us the full picture *behind* this painting. Da Vinci's masterful use of cues allowed him to tell a richer story in a single image. **When you read cues, you see hidden meanings, understand more, and everything has more clarity.**

Luckily, our brain is hardwired to look for hidden meaning in cues. It's always scanning our real-life interactions in real time to provide us with additional social information. You probably picked up on some of these cues in *The Last Supper* without even realizing it. Let's hone that power.

Your Secret Superpower

Imagine this: You're interviewing for a job. On paper, it's a match made in heaven, and the interviewer seems happy with your answers. But halfway through the interview, you get a nagging sense that you're not getting an offer. Why?

Or you give a presentation and you have a sinking sensation that people are tuning out. Where did it go wrong?

Or your partner tells you, "I'm fine," but you know with absolute certainty that things are not, in fact, FINE.

You've certainly experienced these sensations before. They often come to us in the form of "intuition" or "gut feelings." But what's really happening is that your brain probably saw a cue from the Danger Zone of the Charisma Scale it didn't like. This ability, this spidey sense, is our secret superpower. **Learning to decode cues gives a name to your intuitive hits.**

Whether you know it or not, you have a sophisticated cue reading machine inside your head. Our brains have dedicated neural tools for handling and managing social signals. One part of the brain reads and identifies emotions displayed on another person's face within thirty milliseconds!

Though our brain is incredibly skilled at picking up these subtle signals, far too often this superpower is left untapped. While your lizard brain is great at picking up on social cues, your human brain often has trouble making sense of everything.

Culturally, we emphasize language as communication, and children are taught to express themselves verbally, which means our cue decoding skills atrophy. But cues remain one of the most powerful communication mechanisms we have. In this chapter, I'll share the fundamental rules of how cues work and why.

Your Cues Are Contagious

"I'm getting anxiety just being here," admitted Karamo Brown. Brown is one of five hosts on the hit Netflix show *Queer Eye*. And he's working to make over "Anxious Activist" Abby Leedy. After only a few hours with her, he admits to "catching" her anxiety.

In the show, the hosts (nicknamed the Fab Five) help make over one "hero" by giving them a refreshed look and a newfound sense of confidence. And Leedy certainly needs the boost! There isn't a moment on-camera when Leedy isn't in the Danger Zone. She leaks nervous cues—wringing hands, hunching shoulders, anxious pacing, and biting nails.

Fellow host Antoni Porowski even asks her, "Why do you look anxious in your own kitchen?" And then, "Are you an anxious person?"

Leedy cowered. "Ah, yeah . . . I would . . . I've been told that I seem anxious. Um, I think that is probably because I yeah . . . I am . . . yeah, pretty anxious," she admitted.

We watch her anxiety slowly spread through the Fab Five. Luckily, in true TV show fashion, by the end of the episode, Leedy uncovers her true source of confidence and promises to work on herself more.

What the Fab Five experienced is called **emotional contagion**.

> **EMOTIONAL CONTAGION**
>
> **When one person's emotions and related behaviors directly trigger similar emotions and behaviors in others.**

Have you ever been excited by someone else's good news? Or felt sad after being with someone going through a tough time? When your brain identifies an emotion in others, it primes your own brain to feel the same way. Your cues don't just influence your emotions, they also influence other people's emotions. This is why we can often "catch" a bad mood.

In one experiment, researchers split students up into small "salary committees." Each group was tasked with allocating a share of company funds to imaginary employees. But there was a catch. Each group was assigned an actor who was told to show one of four different moods: "cheerful enthusiasm," "serene warmth," "hostile irritability," and "depressed sluggishness."

Through projecting a simulated disposition, the one actor was able to completely change the decisions of the entire committee. When the actor was cheerfully enthusiastic and serenely warm, the groups got along better, had less conflict, cooperated more, performed better on the task, and *distributed raises more fairly* than the negative groups. **One person's mood can affect both the mood of others and an entire group's collaboration and decisions.**

Here's the thing: None of the other committee members could pinpoint exactly why their meeting changed directions. We are grossly unaware of our power to infect others—both positively and negatively.

Another study found that as soon as we see another person's facial expression, the muscles in our own face activate and subtly mimic it. This in turn causes us to *feel* the emotion they are transmitting. Researchers found that people caught moods within only *five minutes* of being near one another—even when working on different projects.

Simply moving our facial muscles in the positions of expressions like tiredness, fear, and happiness **activate our autonomic nervous system to feel the simulated emotion.** Another person's nonverbal cues can change *our* hormone levels, cardiovascular function, and even immune function.

Luckily, learning cues is one of the best ways to prevent their negative contagion. How? **Labeling.** UCLA neuroscientist Matthew Lieberman found that the moment we label a negative cue, it disengages the amygdala. In one experiment, researchers showed participants photos of an angry face while in an fMRI. Just seeing the angry face activated the fear center of participants' brains—we don't like to see people who are angry, it makes us nervous (and we don't want to catch it!). But here's the key: When participants were asked to label the emotion they saw, it immediately disengaged their amygdala, and their fear subsided.

Labeling negative cues reduces their impact. Learning cues will help you spot and stop negative cues being sent to you and be more in control of the cues you send to others.

Your cues can also help you influence for good and be positively contagious. Leaders can learn to spread productive feelings to others. When you project warmth, people are more likely to be warm with you. When you project a competent, confident calm, others are more likely to follow suit. Your charisma cues can flip others' negative ones. We just need to model the cues we want to inspire in others.

The Cue Cycle

When most people think about communication, they think about decoding cues.

Decoding is how we read and interpret social signals from others. Social signals help us decipher everything about a person—their intentions toward us, their trustworthiness, their competence, even their personality. Too often we miss cues and then wonder why people act the way they do. Decoding cues is essential for accurately reading emotions, predicting behavior, and solving your people problems. As you become more adept at decoding cues, you'll be able to figure out the difference between what people say they are feeling and what they actually feel.

But decoding is only a part of the equation. What about the cues we *send* to others? This is called **encoding**.

Encoding is how we send social cues. We send some cues purposefully—we stand with good posture to show confidence, or we smile to show friendliness. But many of our cues are accidental. We can't control every cue we send—it's almost impossible to alter your blink rate, for instance—but we can influence our most important cues.

Purposeful encoding puts you in control of how others perceive you. This helps you feel more confident, make stronger first impressions, and create a more memorable presence. You'll also avoid sending signals that are at odds with your relationship goals, like wanting to impress people but sending out too many warmth cues or seeking rapport but encoding competence cues that shut down bonding.

That fateful day in the tank, Jamie Siminoff missed the mark on *both* decoding and encoding. Even though he had a great product, he didn't encode the right cues to hook the Sharks and build their confidence in him. He also failed to decode the cues that could have saved his pitch. A little decoding could have alerted Siminoff to their early doubt.

Internalizing is how cues influence your internal emotional state—your productivity, your success, and your mood. The cues we decode in the world change how we feel about the world. Every cue

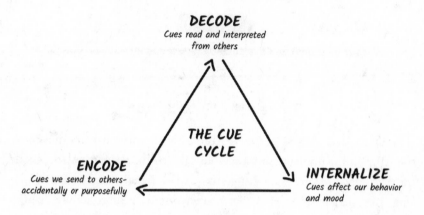

DECODE
Cues read and interpreted from others

THE CUE CYCLE

ENCODE
Cues we send to others-
accidentally or purposefully

INTERNALIZE
Cues affect our behavior and mood

we spot is internalized, which influences which cues we subsequently encode.

Imagine you're in a meeting and you experience a few negative cues from a colleague. They barely murmur hello; they roll their eyes at your comment and huff an exasperated sigh when you give your update. As you begin to contemplate what this might mean, something else happens in your body to help you figure it out. Researchers found that when we decode a cue of social rejection, **it actually increases our field of vision to see more, just in case another, perhaps more socially dangerous cue is coming our way.**

In other words, we spot certain cues, they are internalized, and then our body changes to adapt to what we think might come next. We decode cues, internalize their meaning, and then encode responses.

We don't realize that cues affect so many aspects of our success—not just the smoothness of our interactions and the clarity of our communication, but also our stress levels, our motivation, and even our feelings of inclusion at work. One MIT researcher observed that employees who receive positive cues from superiors and colleagues feel more included, engaged, and loyal and therefore become better performers. On the other hand, when employees receive negative cues, they feel excluded, devalued, and underappreciated. This in turn makes them less productive and connected and leads to lower morale.

PRINCIPLE

Cues trigger both positive and negative loops for you and others.

There's No Mute Button

Have you ever played poker? I think the hardest part of poker is bluffing. It's really hard to mute your cues to hide a particularly good or bad hand. In one fascinating study, MIT researchers studied bluffing. Researchers discovered that players often try to go "mute" while bluffing by going completely still and saying nothing. Players hope that if they conceal all gestures, no single gesture will give them away. **Muting** is a cue in and of itself. A bluffer's tell is that they try to show no tells at all.

I find many professionals also try to "go mute" to hide their emotions, neutralizing their face and using a sterile tone of voice in an attempt to become unreadable. Here's the problem: We really can't mute our cues. In fact, muting your cues sends you directly into the Danger Zone.

Muting is an attempt to be sterile. And sterile people are boring, forgettable, and cold. Concealing your cues is not the goal. Our mission is to align our cues with our professional and relationship goals.

CHAPTER CHALLENGE

Want to know how you are really coming across to others? The only way to accurately assess the cues you are encoding is to watch yourself on video (painful, I know!).

Try to record yourself in meetings or video calls where you can be as natural as possible—don't overthink your cues. We want to see what your starting point is.

Or dig up some old video call recordings or social media clips of you speaking or giving a toast. The more you have to study, the better.

As you learn each cue in the following chapters, revisit your videos to see which cues you use naturally.

PART ONE

Nonverbal Cues

CHAPTER 3

The Body Language
of Leaders

Growing up in Little Rock, Arkansas, Kofi Essel had two big dreams: become a doctor and go to the NBA . . . at the same time.

I met Kofi many years later while we were both studying at Emory University. From the moment I met him, I knew he would go on to do big things. While he didn't grace the NBA with his presence, he did go on to become a doctor, a professor of pediatrics, and an advocate for children's health.

Now working as a pediatrician at Children's National Hospital in Washington, DC, Dr. Essel has a tough job—he has to quickly connect, build trust, and show competence in the first few seconds of meeting his patients. And it's usually at least two different types of people at once—a child and a parent.

"When I think about connecting with my families . . . I have a few seconds to really make an impact. Make a statement. Because if not, I have lost them completely," said Dr. Essel.

To do this, Dr. Essel has an engagement protocol he uses with every family he sees: "First thing I tend to do is greet the child. Typically, I high-five the child. Then I try to drop down to the child's eye level. . . . I'll bend down or get down on my knees to really make sure I'm engaging them," explained Dr. Essel.

Dr. Essel has found that when he greets the child *first*, it wins over the parents. He noticed this by decoding facial cues. "I have noticed if the parents see that I engage with the child, it really takes the stress off of them. I see their face sort of changing. They seem more comfortable with me if I can engage with the child," said Dr. Essel.

Engagement is central to Dr. Essel's practice. **"People are always looking for appreciation, acceptance, and acknowledgment,"** he said. And his goal is to show this verbally and nonverbally.

Once the child feels welcome, Dr. Essel literally turns his attention to the parents, pointing his body and gaze toward them, making eye contact, and shaking hands. Dr. Essel has discovered that this small nonverbal cue is so important, he has created a way to do it even while taking notes on his computer. "I make sure I have a direct line of sight with the family," he says. "I don't like to have that divide there."

Dr. Essel finds that any kind of barrier puts up walls between him and his patients. He has a nonverbal trick for handling this: "To emphasize that I'm listening . . . I'll stop typing and turn my body all the way to them to let them know that I'm here." This communicates to the other person that "if you are sharing something with me that you need me to be completely and fully present for, I will do that."

Dr. Essel has a time-tested nonverbal protocol for interacting with his patients that makes him highly charismatic. Before we dissect the cues he uses, let's see why using nonverbal cues is a critical part of your charismatic communication.

The Power of Nonverbal

When most people think about communicating, they focus on one piece: verbal. While words matter, unfortunately, your words alone aren't enough. **Your nonverbal cues influence—by either enhancing or de-**

tracting from how your words are understood. The old cliché is true: "You hear what you see."

You can have the greatest story, the best piece of data, or the most impressive credentials, but if you don't share them with the right cues, they won't land.

You'll recall from the introduction that nonverbal cues account for 65 to 90 percent of our total communication. We're constantly sending or encoding nonverbal cues to others through our gestures, facial expressions, body movements, and posture. And of course in every interaction, cues are being sent right back to us. When you know how to accurately decode them, you get a sneak peek into someone's inner world.

Research finds that improving your ability to read nonverbal cues really pays off. Nonverbal prowess is a skill that is helpful in almost every area of life—socially, romantically, and professionally.

One study found that people with strong nonverbal cue recognition earn more money in their jobs. Why? Being able to quickly and accurately read emotions gives you an incredible advantage in the workplace. You can better predict behavior, spot hidden feelings, and get your ideas across more clearly. People who are adept at nonverbal skills "are considered more socially and politically skilled than others by their colleagues," explains the study's author.

Understanding nonverbal cues can help all of your relationships. Researchers found that students who made more errors decoding the emotions in facial expressions and tones of voice reported significantly less relationship well-being.

Researchers at the University of Victoria filmed real job interviews. They then showed the videos to a team of judges with the sound turned off. Simply by observing the candidate's nonverbal cues, judges were able to accurately assess their hireability *and* social abilities. Amazingly, the candidate with the highest ratings from the judges was the candidate who actually got hired. Just think about that for a moment! How much time have you spent thinking about and practicing your answers to the questions you know will come during an interview? But how much time did you spend thinking about how you were going to sit, how you were going to say hello, or what gestures you were going to use? *How* you say something is just as important as *what* you say.

We use nonverbal cues to assess everything—capability, social skills, and hireability. And nonverbal cues are either supporting your message or detracting from it.

In this chapter, I'll teach you the highly charismatic nonverbal cues leaders like Dr. Essel use to be nonverbally captivating. These special cues hit the sweet spot of both high warmth and high competence.

In chapter 4, I'll show you the highly warm cues that signal trust and openness.

Then, in chapter 5, we will go through the highly competent nonverbal cues that signal power and intelligence.

And in chapter 6, I'll show you the cues to avoid in order to stay out of the Danger Zone. These are the cues that trigger people's distrust, disrespect, and all the really bad *dis-* words you can think of—disengagement, disgust, and dislike.

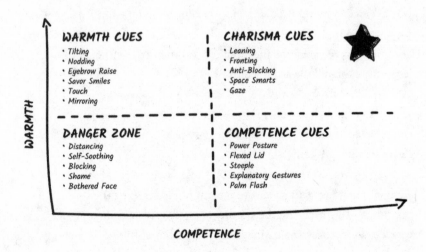

Using purposeful cues, Dr. Essel created a nonverbal protocol to build trust and rapport with his patients more quickly. Now let's create one for you.

Cultural Differences

While many of our nonverbal cues are universal, some, of course, have cultural influences.

Italians tend to use more hand gestures than Americans.

In India and Pakistan, people use nodding differently from Western cultures.

In certain Asian and Middle Eastern cultures, making eye contact with superiors is considered rude. In America, it is considered rude not to make eye contact with superiors.

Luckily, there are more similarities than differences in nonverbal behavior across cultures. Researchers conducted a meta-analysis of ninety-seven studies and found that emotions are universally recognized at better-than-chance levels across cultures.

Not surprisingly, people were more accurate at detecting emotions expressed by others in their same national, ethnic, or regional group. This tells us that you have an in-group advantage when you are decoding cues, and a distinct *disadvantage* when you are decoding cues of people outside it. All the more reason to get clear on cues and their meaning— so we can equalize our decoding abilities.

For the purposes of this book, whenever possible I will stick to universally recognized cues. If there is a strong cultural difference, I will note it.

CHARISMA CUE #1: Lean Like a Leader

Can we play a little mind game together?

Wherever you are right now—whether you're sitting or standing, would you mind leaning forward, please? Not too far, just a few inches. Go ahead and hold the lean for ten seconds.

How does it feel? Notice anything interesting?

This simple movement activates a specific part of your brain that makes you feel more motivated. In a fascinating experiment, researchers found that when they asked participants to lean forward, they had increased neural activation in the left frontal cortex. This is the part of our brain associated with desire and motivation—it creates an eagerness to move toward something. **The control group, who was asked to lean back, didn't exhibit any increased activation at all.**

When we lean in, we literally feel more motivation. When we lean back, we lose motivation.

Humans lean toward people, things, and ideas they like. When we lean, we're able to activate our five senses easier.

We lean in to **see** something more clearly.

We lean in when we need to **hear** something better.

We lean in when we're about to **touch** something.

We can lean in to **smell** something better.

We lean in when we want to pick up something and **taste** it.

If we like something, are interested in something, or want something, we want to get closer to it. So it makes sense that we decode leaning forward as a signal of interest. We like it when people lean toward us. And leaning in is the ultimate compliment because it makes *us* feel interesting and wanted. It doesn't take much—just a few inches will do the trick.

Lean cues are powerfully charismatic nonverbal signals because they both communicate interest to others and trigger internal interest.

In another study, researchers asked participants to look at photographs of people leaning forward or leaning back. They were then asked how much they liked or disliked each person. Results were clear: People seen leaning forward got much higher likability ratings.

Leaning in is the single fastest way to look (and feel) interested and engaged.

I think of leaning in as a nonverbal **boldface**. When you lean in, it bolds or highlights whatever has just been shared. I lean to show:

- **Emphasis:** If someone is saying something I think is important, I lean into them. If I'm saying something important, I lean in slightly.
- **Agreement:** If I agree with what someone is saying, I always bold it with a lean. It's to demonstrate to that person that *I'm so into what you're saying, I want to get closer to hear it better.* And it helps me feel even more motivated about understanding them.

- **Partnership:** If I'm feeling kinship with someone or want to show I'm on the same page, I will lean in toward them. This works especially well in the first few minutes of an interaction. Dr. Essel leans into and down to his patients' level to build rapport.

You can use leans while sitting or standing, on stages, and even on video calls.

One of the biggest misconceptions about leaning is that leaning back looks cool. Well, it is literally cool . . . as in cold. Leaning back or **slouching** is a Danger Zone cue.

One of the most uncharismatic things you can do is lean back, slouch, or recline while someone is sharing something that's important to them. Leaders make a point of leaning in.

PRINCIPLE

Lean in to show and stimulate interest, engagement, and agreement.

WHEN TO LEAN
- When you're talking to colleagues or partners and you want to show them how much you support them, are interested in their idea, and are engaged with them.

- When you want to call attention to someone else's idea and show you agree.
- When you are giving a presentation, to emphasize your most important points.

- When you disagree with others. In fact, withholding leaning is a great way to respectfully show someone you are *not* into what they're saying.
- When you need to create space or boundaries. Have a toxic person in your life? Do NOT lean in while stating your needs. Stand tall, stand firm.
- If you feel like you're bowing, you've leaned too far.

CHARISMA CUE #2: Open Body, Open Mind

Imagine if Christ in *The Last Supper* had been painted with his arms crossed. Or if the Statue of Liberty was clutching her torch in front of her chest, instead of proudly over her head, arm outstretched. These works of art wouldn't be as powerful, right?

A closed body signals a closed mind . . . and it inspires close-mindedness in others. I shared this phenomenon with my friend and famed online marketing expert Brian Dean. One day I was visiting his website and noticed his header had a photo of him with his arms crossed:

Knowing Brian's talent with data, I proposed a test. "Replace this picture with a photo of you with uncrossed arms. It will increase your website conversions," I told Brian. "It will make you look more open-minded and make people be more *open* to opt in to get your email updates."

Brian agreed to try this out and set up what's called a split test on his website. This means 50 percent of visitors to his site see the image of Brian with arms crossed and the other 50 percent see the open body version. Everything else on the website stayed exactly the same.

Split tests enable you to truly compare two versions of the same variable (in this case, body posture) with thousands of visitors. Over a period of ninety days, 237,797 people went through the test. And . . . the open posture won by A LOT. Simply switching to the open posture increased Brian's website conversions by 5.4 percent! That might not sound like much, but in terms of web traffic conversions, it's phenomenal. It translates to thousands more email subscribers from one tiny cue change.

Nonverbal cues don't just have an effect in situations where you are physically present. They also come across in your profile photos, websites, social media photos, and marketing materials. Researchers asked professionals to rate videos of people speaking in a business setting. It didn't matter whether participants watched the videos on mute or with the sound on. **Everyone with crossed arms was rated as more distant**

and defensive and less charismatic. And this happened with one or both arms crossed over their chest.

Humans don't like to have barriers between us and other people while trying to connect. Recall that in *The Last Supper*, Judas was depicted with his arm across his chest, exhibiting a **blocking cue**—which puts a barrier between ourselves and someone else. As I've discussed, this is most commonly done with crossed arms or with objects like a computer, purse, podium, clipboard, or pillow that we clutch or put in front of our torso.

Here's the problem: Most people *like* crossing their arms. Crossing our arms feels good because it makes us feel less vulnerable. With our arms across our chest, we protect our vital organs. But it comes at a cost. Your charisma is compromised for a little extra comfort. And many of us merely cross our arms out of habit. This small nonverbal cue creates a physical and emotional barrier between you and the people you're trying to connect with.

You might notice that when someone feels nervous in a meeting or on a date, they suddenly and often subconsciously cross their arms. This is an instinct to protect themselves from whatever is making them nervous. It's as if they're giving themselves a hug. When someone engages in sudden blocking behavior, I pay close attention to the behavior and make a mental note: they likely want to feel more secure.*

Dr. Essel makes a point of deliberately moving his computer to show he's removing a barrier. **He learned that any time our bodies aren't open, people are less likely to open up**.

Making a point of removing a barrier is an **anti-blocking cue**, a wonderful way to demonstrate charisma and get people to open up.

Evy Poumpouras is a former Secret Service agent who hosts Bravo's TV show *Spy Games*. In her life as a Secret Service agent she conducted interrogations and interviews to get people to open up. And she used a little nonverbal trick that involved anti-blocking. "When I would do in-

---

* Always be on the lookout for context explanations. For example, did the air conditioning just turn on? Someone might suddenly cross their arms when they're cold. We will talk more about context later.

terviews, I would take my phone. I would put that thing away. I would take my watch off. . . . I wanted that person, whoever it was, to know that I had nowhere to go. And all that mattered, in that moment, was them," she explained.

For Stage Presenters

If you present onstage, you often deal with microphones and podiums. Beware: These can cause accidental blocking. When handling a microphone, never, ever clutch it to your chest. People often make the mistake of tucking in their chin and contracting their body as they speak into the microphone. Hold it up and out. Or better yet, get a hands-free microphone!

Watch out for podiums. Physicist Neil deGrasse Tyson is frequently asked to speak to organizations, but the podium plagues him. "They always say, 'You've got to stay behind the podium,'" he says. But he likes using the whole stage to communicate. "What, you want me to stand here for two hours and talk? I say, No, I will use the entire stage," he explained. A podium limits stage movement, the fluidity of your gestures, and makes you look small.

Researchers have even found that a podium blocks presenters' ability to share new material. If you can help it, avoid standing behind a podium at all costs. It's a huge blocker to charisma.

Charismatic people also make a point to be as open and barrier-free as possible with the people they meet. Remember how our cues are contagious? **If you're open, it inspires openness.** When someone sees you're comfortable enough to be barrier-free, it encourages them to open up as well.

And openness is not just important as a social signal to others, it's also a critical signal for *yourself*. In a mind-blowing study, researchers in 2017 found that the way you hold your body changes the way you think. Participants were asked to complete creative tasks in different body postures. When participants sat in an open posture, they were significantly more creative! Bottom line: **Closed body posture makes us less creative and less open-minded.**

PRINCIPLE

To inspire openness, open up nonverbally.

WHEN TO BE OPEN

- **When you are in one-on-one interactions where you need to build rapport.** Make a show of removing all barriers between you and others. Clear the table in a client meeting. Push aside a computer in a brainstorming session. Move your clipboard to the side when talking to people. Scoot your coffee over on a date. Open body, open heart, open mind.
- **When you need to spark ideas.** Want to be more creative, open-minded, imaginative? Uncross your arms. Want others to be more creative, open-minded, or imaginative? Encourage them to uncross theirs. Hand them a cup of water, give them a pen to take notes, show them a photo of your family so they have to open up and lean in.
- **When you are presenting or pitching.** Always try to be barrier free—an open torso is the most charismatic. Use a remote instead of

sitting in front of your computer. Step away from the podium. Leave your arms loose by your sides so you can gesture easily and keep your torso open to the audience.

- **When you are choosing profile pictures**—especially for LinkedIn or dating app profiles. A closed body signals a closed mind and a closed heart.

- **When openness is not the right message.** Irish mixed martial artist Conor McGregor is often photographed with his arms crossed. And this makes complete sense for his brand. He doesn't *want* to be seen as open! It's better for his reputation to be seen as closed, intimidating, and tough. For him, crossed arms sends the right cues—he wants to be in the Danger Zone.
- **When you don't want to engage.** Is someone making you feel uncomfortable? Cross those arms! If you want to signal you're closed for business or aren't open to someone's ideas, block them out. This works well with close talkers or over-touchers.

CHARISMA CUE #3: Front Forward

John Stockton was a normal college senior playing basketball for Gonzaga University. Then, in June 1984, his entire life changed. Stockton was a surprise selection by the Utah Jazz in the first round of the 1984 NBA Draft. This was so shocking that when the announcement was made to 2,000 fans, "there was absolute silence. Pre-dinner blessings are noisier," reported the *Deseret News*.

Little did they know that Stockton would go on to play nineteen seasons for the Jazz, become a ten-time NBA All-Star and a member of the U.S. men's Olympic team, and be named one of the fifty greatest players of all time by the NBA.

What made Stockton so successful? One stat stands out. Despite retiring in 2003, he still holds the record for most assists of all time: 15,806, to be precise. (Jason Kidd comes in a distant second with 12,091 assists.)

In basketball, an assist is when one player makes a pass to a teammate that leads that teammate to score a basket. You've probably seen thousands of assists if you're a regular basketball watcher. What I bet you don't know though is that there is a critical nonverbal cue that makes assists successful. Stockton used it expertly: fronting.

Fronting is when you angle your body to signal attention. Specifically, we point our three T's—toes, torso, and top—toward whatever we're paying attention to. Our physical orientation cues others as to our mental orientation. Fronting is a great cue to know what someone is thinking about.

When someone is about to leave, they'll turn their toes toward the exit.

When two people are having a great discussion, their entire bodies align as if their toes, hips, and shoulders are on parallel lines.

When someone is hungry, they often front toward the buffet.

FUN TIP

Crushes and Bosses

When my team and I observed work holiday parties, we noticed most people's toes were angled toward the boss, the most important person in the room, even when people weren't speaking with her. Want to know who people really respect? Watch their toes.

People also tend to point their toes toward their crush. When our mind is on someone, our toes follow suit and are always at the ready to physically move toward them.

Conversely, people *don't* front when they *aren't* paying attention. When people are more interested in an email than in a presentation, they keep their body, feet, and head turned mostly toward their computer, only occasionally glancing up front. When someone isn't that into a conversation during a networking event or party, they angle their body out and point their feet toward the open room—in hopes of escape. On a bad date, people angle their bodies out and away.

The difference between the good and the great assisters of all time is their ability to signal to other players nonverbally before they even make a pass. Stockton used fronting to nonverbally communicate with his teammates. Stockton said this often came across as mind reading. "You throw crazy passes, and he catches them. People say, 'Wow. He must know what he's thinking,'" said Stockton, describing how he wordlessly threw expert passes to his teammate Karl Malone. Together they were known as the dynamic duo.

When you watch clips of Stockton's assists, you will notice that right before he makes a successful pass, he first turns his head toward his target, then angles his torso, and finally, if he has time and enough space on the court, points his toes in the direction of where he will pass the ball.

This method set him up for thousands of successful assists. And today Stockton is regarded as one of the greatest point guards of all time. Stockton cued other players to where he was going to send the ball. **His attention caught their attention.** Stockton nonverbally telegraphed to other players where the ball *would* be before he ever passed. Without realizing it, you might be doing the same.

How does fronting work in real life? From the top down.

When something first catches our attention, we turn our head toward it. Biologically it's easier and takes less energy to move just our head. If we're really interested, we turn our torso—all the better to be prepared to engage or embrace the object of our attention. And if we want to give it our full attention and maybe even get closer to investigate, we turn our toes as well.

With all the effort involved in physically reorienting ourselves, it's not surprising that fronting is a nonverbal cue for respect. It's a great way to make someone feel nonverbally engaged. Leaders give their full nonverbal attention to everyone they're with. They demonstrate with their body that *You're so important to me, I'm going to angle my entire body toward you.*

The fastest way to show someone that you're interested, present, and engaged is to fully square your body toward them. **The biggest mistake**

we make while attempting to build connection is giving only partial nonverbal attention.

- Someone is speaking to us and we barely glance their way. "Uh-huh," we murmur without taking our eyes off what we're doing.
- A colleague speaks up in a meeting, and we don't even bother to turn toward that person, focusing on the presentation slide deck at the front of the room.
- Our partner comes home with great news and our gaze stays locked on the TV instead of moving to them. "Great news," we call over our shoulder.

Want to show someone they matter? That you're listening? **Turning toward is tuning in.**

Dr. Essel showed his patients he was listening by actually turning toward each person in the room. In *The Last Supper*, Christ was depicted as the *only* figure "fronting" with the viewer. The apostles are gesturing or angled away from us. Only Christ is turned toward us from toes to top.

Fronting is one of the easiest cues to master, with the biggest payoff. It's a powerful charisma cue for two reasons:

1. Fronting makes it easy to encode and decode nonverbal cues. You can see someone from tip to toe and they can see you.
2. As we learned from the Cues Cycle, aligning ourselves physically makes it easier to get on the same page emotionally and mentally.

One of the best ways to use fronting is to make a point of turning toward someone and aligning with them. This is especially important when you're taking notes on a computer.

You immediately become more charismatic by fronting with someone. Do it while standing in the break room, while mingling at a bar or conference, or even when talking to your children. I notice that when I give my daughter my full nonverbal attention by angling toward her, she becomes calmer.

Inviting Fronting

Want to be approached at a bar or networking event? Stand against the bar or lean against a high table and front with as much of the room as possible. This shows you're open to connection and invites people to come speak with you.

Want to approach others? Look for open toes. When people are very engaged in conversation, they angle their entire body toward each other—so their feet are on parallel lines. Don't interrupt this kind of conversation! When people are open to interlopers, they stand with their feet angled out in an open-toe position, like a croissant. It's as if their toes are saying, "This is good, but there's room for one more. Come join!"

What about the opposite? Need to be "rescued" from someone who won't stop talking? Front toward a friend or host that can save you. This subtly cues them to come over and help.

And don't forget to front while seated. If someone down the conference table speaks up, rotate your chair and swivel your body to front with them.

> **PRINCIPLE**
>
> **If you want someone to feel heard, accepted, and respected, turn toward them.**

WHEN TO USE FRONTING

- **To signal respect and/or care.** Make sure your torso is turned toward people who matter to you. Greet your boss with full fronting when they come through the office doors, front with your partner when they're sharing good news, always swivel your chair toward the person speaking.

- **To see what others value.** Pay attention to where others are pointing their toes, torso, and top—it might give you a deeper understanding of where they're focusing.
- **At the office.** Make your office setup and furniture fronting-friendly. Move chairs and desks to make it easy for everyone to front. Circular boardroom tables are best. Swivel chairs make it easy.
- **When it's time to go.** Occasionally, I desperately need to escape a party early—my ambivert* self isn't the most charismatic after nine p.m. I casually indicate my desire to leave a conversation by fronting toward the door. You would be pleasantly surprised at how often people pick up on this subtle cue.

WHEN NOT TO FRONT

- **When you want to prevent distraction.** If I'm focusing intently on something and want to respectfully signal "I don't want to be bothered right now," then I do not front.
- **When someone is opening up too much.** Ever had someone verbally vomit all over you? Or share TMI—too much information? If you find someone is oversharing, stop fronting! You've given them too much engagement. Angling away is a nice way to cue them to slow down and back up.
- **When you don't have time or space.** John Stockton made thousands of successful passes without fully fronting first. Sometimes all he had time for was a quick look or turn of the head. And that can work too when you are pressed for time—it's certainly better than no turn at all!
- **When you need to be covert.** Some of Stockton's best assists were made on the sly, where he *deliberately* didn't front because he was sneaking a pass to someone. If you're trying to hide your attention and intentions, don't front.

---

* Ambiverts have the characteristics of both an introvert and an extrovert. Read my full guide on ambiversion in your digital bonuses at scienceofpeople.com/bonus.

"She wants to say hi. She's with her new boy[ ]
Seinfeld.

"What's he like?" asks Jerry's mom.

"He's nice. Bit of a close talker," said Jerry.

"A what?" she asks.

"You'll see," said Jerry.

A few minutes later Elaine's new boyfriend walks into Jerry's apartment and proceeds to stand six inches away from everyone he meets. While practically talking into people's mouths and breathing in their faces, the "close talker" is totally clueless to his social faux pas.

This episode of *Seinfeld* brings to light an incredibly important nonverbal cue: **space**.

Anthropologist and cross-cultural researcher Edward T. Hall found there are certain unwritten rules that lead individuals to maintain distances from one another. As humans, we navigate space based on how we feel about others in our environment. **The closer we feel to someone, the closer we allow them to come physically.**

Hall proposed that we use physical distance to cue intimacy. In other words, you can *decode* how someone feels about you based on how close to you they stand or sit. And you can *encode* how you feel about someone by how close to them you sit or stand.

People constantly enter or exit our personal space bubbles. Hall identified four space bubbles or zones. While every person and every culture have their own specific preferences concerning space, I have some averages for you on the following page. There are four areas around our body where we like to interact with different categories of people: (1) the intimacy zone, about zero to eighteen inches from our body; (2) the personal zone, about eighteen inches to four feet; (3) the social zone, about four to seven feet; and (4) the public zone, with anything beyond seven feet.

1. **Intimacy Zone:** We prefer to have only people we highly trust this close to us because it potentially makes our body vulnerable.

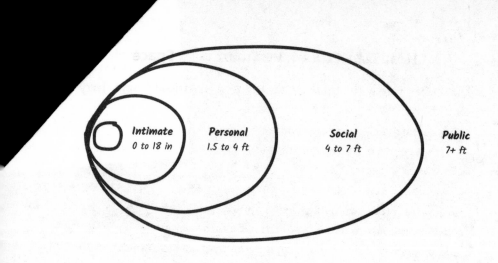

When someone is in this space, they can reach out and touch us, kiss us, punch us, or take something from us. We often feel uneasy when someone accidentally enters our intimate zone.

2. **Personal Zone:** This is the most commonly used zone. In this zone we can easily reach out and shake hands with someone. When we speak to colleagues, friends, or family members, this distance makes it easy to hear someone as well as exchange familiar gestures like arm touches or high fives.

3. **Social Zone:** This zone is most often used for business or professional interactions that don't require touch or deep conversation. It's often used at parties, when ordering at a bar, or sitting around a conference table in a meeting.

4. **Public Zone:** This zone gives us enough space to figure out someone's intentions before an approach. If you are seven feet from someone, you can see their entire body, their hand gestures and posture. Someone might wave, nod, or call out to us from the public zone before being invited closer.

Are you ever unsure how someone feels about you? This is an understandable worry. These days there are all different categories of relationship—online friends, Instagram friends, hometown friends,

friends of friends, frenemies, business friends. It's hard to know where you stand. Here's a little tip: Plant yourself and see how close the person comes to you. If they come right into your personal zone, they likely feel very comfortable with you and are excited to connect. If they stand or sit farther back, hanging out in the social zone (or even just waving or nodding from the public zone), then they likely need more time to warm up. If they come into your intimate zone, take note! They probably want to get *very* close physically or emotionally.

In one study, researchers directed a negative comment—something like "Your handwriting is messy"—toward a participant. They found that negative comments caused participants to pick seats farther away from the researcher who had insulted them. Not too shocking, right? We want to steer clear of people who we feel threaten us. In business we don't always know who has negative feelings toward us, but space can give us clues.

FUN TIP

Video Space

One of the biggest mistakes we make on video calls is getting too close to the camera—this is forcing yourself into someone's intimate space. Always be sure to be at least two feet away from your camera so your head, shoulders, and some hand gestures are visible. This will immediately help the other person feel more comfortable.

Da Vinci himself might have been subconsciously aware of these zones. He painted *The Last Supper* using space as a clue to allegiance. Religious scholars argue that the apostles who were closest to Christ are also placed closest to him at the table. Interestingly, da Vinci chose to have no one in Christ's intimate space.

If we loosely draw the four space zones over *The Last Supper*, we can see how the apostles rank in terms of intimacy.

This has modern applications as well. Think of your standard board-room or conference table. Where do you sit at a conference table?*

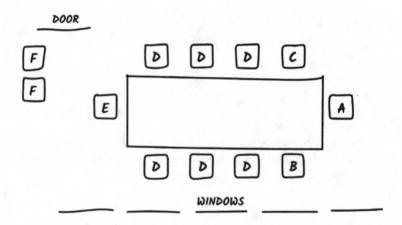

The physically closer to the boss you are, the more in the know you are. For example, typically the boss or leader of a meeting sits at the head of the table facing the door in position A. (Occasionally a leader will sit in position E at the head of the table facing a presentation or a white-

---

board.) This seat is inherently high in competence because it's the farthest away from everyone but also has the most visibility.

The people who sit in positions B and C are usually seen as the most supportive of the Power Player. In this way, these seats are high in warmth. Research from Cornell University found that **the closer you are to someone physically, the closer you feel to them**. When you are this close, you can lean into your boss's personal space, share documents, quietly share ideas in their ear, and even reach out for an arm touch or high five. In this seat, your opinion is more likely to be heard by the person sitting in the power seat, even if the group is talking all at once.

Dr. Richard Winters of the Mayo Clinic calls these the flanking positions. "When you sit in this position you can influence the flow of the meeting by assisting. You can draw attention toward or away from topics. You can prompt a speeding up or slowing down of the agenda," said Dr. Winters.

The farther away you sit from the leader of the meeting, the less you will be recognized or called on. Middle seats (position D) generate less eye contact and less floor time simply because of the nature of a boardroom table. **If you're sitting on the side, you're more likely to be sidelined**. But this isn't always a bad thing. If you want to simply listen or take notes in a meeting, a middle seat can be a great place to blend in and take it all in.

Special tip for middles: You especially need to use fronting and leaning. Be sure to swivel your body toward whoever is speaking to show respect and engagement. You can also lean in to show support. If you're forced into a middle seat, be prepared to speak up if you want to be heard.

What about sitting far away from the boss but in his or her line of sight? Position E (or the seat opposite wherever the boss is sitting) is an interesting choice. If you're sitting opposite your boss, you better have a lot to say. Yes, it's great to be close to the boss in seat B or C, but closeness isn't the only issue to consider. You also want to think about line of sight. Seat E is the only seat that allows for full fronting with seat A. If you want to stay front of mind for your boss or plan to say a lot, you might consider seat E.

Be aware that it's another high competence seat. If you choose it, be sure to dial up your warmth. Be more verbally and nonverbally supportive. Smile more, nod more, and give more supportive feedback.

Special tip: Sometimes if two people are running a meeting, they can take both ends of the table. This is a great way to physically show a balanced viewpoint, with info coming from both sides.

What about seat F? I call these sideline seats. Need to sneak out early? Don't want to be heard? Aren't a Power Player just yet? Then the sideline is for you. This is the seat farthest away from the action. If you don't want to be sidelined or plan to speak up in a meeting, I would avoid these seats. Speaking up from this seat makes it hard for others to front with you, often forcing them to crane their neck to see you. It is a seat of silence.

Bottom line: Be sure to choose your seat wisely. And do it with your social goals in mind. There are some meetings where I have a lot to say and want to be in people's personal space. Others, I want to hang back and observe, keeping my distance. Your seat can encode these goals.

You can also decode what someone's seat might mean. I find I can learn a lot about how someone feels based on their seat choice.

FUN TIP

Table Shape Matters

Researchers found that the shape of your table can affect how you make decisions! They asked 350 participants to sit at round or rectangular tables to evaluate advertisements.

Participants who sat at the circular table reacted more favorably to images that showed groups of friends and family members or conveyed a sense of belonging.

If participants sat in rectangular or square formations, they preferred ads portraying go-getters and competition.

It's essential to be aware of people's spatial needs in communal office spaces, bars, and parties. If you enter someone's space too quickly, you will put them on high alert. When someone violates our space needs, we become hypervigilant, our pulse races, and we might even flush under the threat.

How do you know when it's okay to move in? **Look for invitation cues or patience cues to determine someone's spatial needs.** We can also use these cues to encode *our* spatial comfort levels.

First, invitation cues nonverbally signal *Yes, please come closer!* These invitation cues might look familiar.

- **Fronting:** If someone is fronting us, it means they are fully engaged nonverbally.
- **Openness:** If someone has no barriers between you and them, it's a good sign they are open to you.
- **Leaning:** If someone is leaning into you, they're already working to get closer.

Other invitation clues include the warmth cues we will learn in the next chapter, which all signal friendliness and trust: smiling, nodding, mirroring, and eyebrow raises. If you want to *encode* closeness, show these invitation cues. If you want to know if you can go closer, *decode* these invitation cues.

On the other hand, always be on the watch for patience cues. Patience cues signal *I'm not ready yet.* Some common patience cues include:

- **Blocking:** If someone suddenly crosses their arms, holds a computer in front of their chest, or clutches their drink in front of them, they're trying to put a barrier between you and them. Back up.
- **Distancing:** If you take a step forward and they take a step back, you have come too close too fast.
- **Self-soothing:** Sometimes getting too close makes people anxious, so they engage in self-touch. You might see someone wring their hands, put their hand over their heart, or bite their nails.

Guess what? **You can use these patience cues to make a close talker back up.** If someone gets too close too fast, cross your arms or even put your hand out as a block.

And remember: When you see a patience cue, go slow and work to build more rapport.

Context is another important aspect that affects how we use space. For example, some contexts force people to get into intimate space quickly, like crowded bars, concerts, and dance clubs. This is one reason why these spaces often facilitate romance! They require people to get close quickly, and the heart follows.

FUN TIP

Small Spaces

We have unspoken spacing rituals for all kinds of public spaces. Ever been in an elevator? You don't talk, you don't make eye contact, and you keep your eyes straight ahead or look at your feet. This is how we show *I'm forced into your intimate space, but I don't want to get intimate.*

Dr. Essel has a unique space problem. He has to go from being complete strangers with a patient to checking their heart rate a few minutes later. This is a challenge for anyone in a career where touch is involved—dentists, masseurs, doctors, trainers, nurses, physical therapists, teachers, and healers all have to enter someone's personal space to do their job well.

Even reading about intimate space might be making some of you squirm. But fear not—I have an excellent nonverbal trick for dealing with quickly crossing space zones. I call it a **nonverbal bridge.** Nonverbal bridges help slowly bring you closer to someone by temporarily crossing into a more intimate zone.

Bridges are great warm-ups for intimacy because you aren't actually moving your feet or your body into someone's zone—which can be intimidating. A nonverbal bridge is just putting one limb or a part of your body into someone's intimate zone temporarily.

In Dr. Essel's protocol for listening, he first high-fives the child. This is the perfect example of a nonverbal bridge. It allows Dr. Essel to move quickly from public zone to personal zone to intimate zone and then back to personal zone. Then he bends down or gets on his knees in front of the child, so he is at their level. This genius move allows Dr. Essel to get closer in a less intimidating way. As he is talking to the child he leans in—another great nonverbal bridge.

Here are some of my favorites:

- **Leaning:** When we lean toward someone or lean across the table toward someone, we get closer to their next zone. It is a subtle way to warm up someone as you get to know them.
- **Leveling:** Have you ever tried to bond with someone while they're seated and you're standing? It's so hard! Try to get on the same level. I love signing books and meeting readers. But I often face one awkward problem—the table. It's weird to be sitting as someone is standing and opening up to you. For this reason, when I'm signing books, I try to use only high bar tables, so I'm standing *with* people as I sign. If I must use a standard table, I always stand to greet someone and shake their hand before sitting down to sign.
- **Gesture:** You can also use gestures to briefly enter someone's next zone. I frequently use the "you and I" gesture, in which my hand goes briefly toward them. I also might point or open palm gesture toward someone as I acknowledge them. This brings just my limb, not my whole body, closer to them.
- **Touch:** A touch is a way to temporarily cross into someone's intimate zone. You might be standing in someone's personal or social zone, but when you reach out and shake hands, touch their arm, give them a fist bump, or tap them on the shoulder, you're getting a short trial in their intimate zone. Remember, a touch is not a whole body move into their zone, just the extension of a hand or an arm, which feels safer.
- **Props:** When you hand someone a water, a handout, a clicker, a plate—any object they want or need—this is also an easy way to

cross into their zone temporarily. On the TV show *Shark Tank*, all the entrepreneurs start quite far away from the Sharks—in their social zone. My team and I spent countless hours coding 495 pitches on *Shark Tank* and found that the most successful pitchers use nonverbal bridges to get closer to the Sharks during parts of the pitch.* They offer samples, get Sharks to participate in demos, and pass out the product. Sometimes they even high-five or fist-bump with a Shark when they agree. This briefly allows entrepreneurs into the Sharks' intimate zone without being threatening. And it often helps a pitcher get a deal.

PRINCIPLE

Highly charismatic people leverage space to show and encourage intimacy.

HOW TO USE SPACE

- **Respect people's space boundaries** by moving physically closer as you feel more comfortable.
- **Try a side by side.** One way you might test the waters in someone's personal or intimate zone is to do it side by side. Fronting plus being in someone's intimate zone can be a little much—think pre-kissing. But sitting side by side in someone's intimate zone might be more comfortable for introverts or those slow to open up. This is why I love to go on hikes with new friends. I find walking side by side—in our intimate or personal zones but not always fronting—facilitates deep discussions more quickly. This might also be why people spill their life story while sitting side by side with someone at a bar, why teenagers often open up to parents when going somewhere in the car, and why some therapists have patients lie on a couch purposefully *not* fronting, to take away some of the intimacy pressure.
- **Use nonverbal bridges to slowly cross into others' inner space zones.** Give people handouts, snacks, or pens.

---

* Read more about our *Shark Tank* experiment in your digital toolbox.

HOW NOT TO USE SPACE

- **Don't ever go too close too fast.** Watch for invitation cues. Beware of patience cues.
- **Don't back someone into an actual corner.** Ever notice that people back themselves against a wall when you speak to them? You might be a close talker.
- **Never take a seat choice lightly.** Choose seats in meetings, bars, and restaurants that match your social goals.

CHARISMA CUE #5: Engage with Gaze

Can you read people's emotions just by looking at their eyes? Let's find out.

1. Which word best describes what the person in the picture is thinking or feeling?

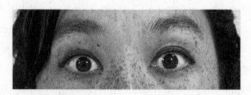

A. Surprised
B. Afraid
C. Anxious
D. Stressed

2. Which word best describes what the person in the picture is thinking or feeling?

A. Angry
B. Disappointed
C. Afraid
D. Confused

3. Which word best describes what the person in the picture is thinking or feeling?

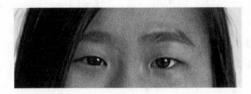

A. Bored
B. Sad
C. Confused
D. Contemptuous

How did you do?*

Over 15,000 people took this quiz.† Most struggled to identify the negative emotions—only 42.2 percent of people can correctly identify the contempt in question three (most people chose A. Bored). Only 41.3 percent of people can identify the anger in question two (most people chose C. Confused).

These are big mismatches! Anger is a completely different emotion from confusion—and should be treated differently as well. If we mistake scorn for boredom, we completely miss a negative cue (this happened to

---

* Answers: 1. A; 2. A; 3. D.
† Want to take the full test? Take the full RMET test in your digital bonuses.

Jamie Siminoff in *Shark Tank*). Don't worry, we will work on getting them right in chapter 6 on Danger Zone cues.

This quiz is based on the Reading the Mind in the Eye Test (RMET). The RMET was created by psychologist Dr. Simon Baron-Cohen (cousin of famed actor Sacha Baron Cohen) at Cambridge University. He found that humans are able to accurately identify people's inner states at above chance levels by just looking at their eyes.

Turns out the old cliché is true. Eyes are the window into the soul—or at least our emotional self. Infants as young as seven months are able to decode emotional cues from adult's eye cues. Eyes provide more information than any other part of the face. When researchers cut and pasted different facial parts together into one picture, participants always look to the eyes to identify the emotion. In other words, when people see angry eyes paired with a smile or a neutral mouth expression, they will always judge the entire face as angry.

Reading our eye cues became an especially important skill during the COVID-19 pandemic. When everyone wears masks, we have only the eyes and the eye regions to use when decoding emotion.*

Most of us have been told that eye contact is essential for connection. And it is! Study after study shows that making eye contact is one of the most important ways to build trust with others. The RMET gives us another critical reason: **Making eye contact helps you decode emotions.**

You'll notice this cue is about gazing, not about eye contact. That's because we gaze at more than just people's eyes. Most of us don't realize that when we're gazing at someone, we're actually taking in a whole range of different parts of the face. In the RMET, the muscles and areas around the eyes are just as important as the eyes themselves. "When we look at a face, our gaze quickly dances across the eyes, nose, mouth, chin, and forehead, to provide the pieces from which the whole face is assembled in our mind," said the researchers.

When you're gazing, look for eye clues to emotions. Here are the most important ones to know:

---

* During the COVID-19 pandemic we made a video tutorial on reading facial expressions even with masks on. The video quickly garnered thousands of views. If you would like to learn how to read faces with masks on, the video is in your digital bonuses.

- **Parallel lines:** A **furrow** is when we pull our eyebrows down and to-gether to form two parallel lines. If you see two parallel lines appearing between someone's eyebrows, it's usually an early sign of anger or irritation.

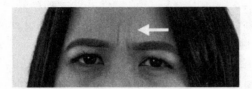

- **Eye crinkles:** You might be surprised to learn that the only true indicator of happiness is when those eye crinkles (also known as crow's-feet) appear on the sides of someone's eyes. When you see these, that person is feeling engaged and positive.

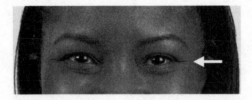

- **Droopy lids:** When we get sad, we droop our lids or even look down. Watch for suddenly droopy eyes—especially if they're accompanied by a look down. This is an early sign of sadness (and sometimes tiredness if accompanied by a yawn).

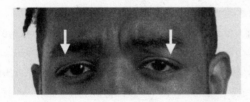

There is another big reason to make eye contact: oxytocin. Every time you lock eyes with someone, you both produce an important hormone for trust called **oxytocin**. Oxytocin has a number of incredible effects on our body—it helps us feel bonded and builds trust. But its most important effect is not as well known. **Oxytocin makes us better decoders.** Eye contact is not just great for connection; it also helps you spot and read others' cues better. Researchers even found that giving participants a nose spray full of oxytocin made them subsequently better at the RMET!

And yet another surprising benefit of mutual gazing: It helps us synchronize brain activity. Researchers used brain scans to look at neural activity while participants interacted. They found the greater the amount of mutual gazing, the more participants' brain waves synced up. Want someone to get on the same page as you? Gaze can literally help you sync up mentally. This is why, from birth, babies prefer to look at faces that engage with them in mutual gazing. When babies are four months old, their brain shows increased neural activity when they receive direct eye contact as opposed to seeing someone looking away.

FUN FACT

Gaze Direction

Have you noticed that many leaders use photos of themselves looking up and to the right? Researchers found that in Western cultures, looking up and to the right is associated with positive characteristics, like being upbeat, future-oriented, and successful. Want to look more like a hero? Gaze up and to the right in your photos.

Gaze is an attention cue. We look to gaze to see who or what someone is paying attention to. Are they looking at us? Great, that makes us feel important. In conversation, we pay attention to gaze direction to know whose turn it is to talk.

We also look to the gaze of others to see where *we* should be looking. My team and I have found that when we add gaze cues to our website, we can help users find their way around. For example, when we add a header image in which I am looking down, visitors of the website are encouraged to keep scrolling down and continue reading for their answers:

A few years ago, we started to offer visitors a free audio download on likability. We thought tons of people would love this, but after the first few weeks we were disappointed to see people weren't downloading it as much as we had hoped. Then a student told us they hadn't even noticed the new guide on the website! We added an image in which I pointed to and looked at the offer. It worked! This gaze cue helped cue people to look to the side and take notice of the new offer.

FREE AUDIO TRAINING

Be the most likable person in the room

Learn the skills I've taught 500k+ students to become more charismatic and successful—including:

- 5 phrases that will make you instantly more likable
- My secret likability strategy for introverts
- The #1 trick to never running out of things to say

Am I advising to simply make more eye contact with everyone, all the time? Certainly not. I want you to gaze with purpose.

HOW TO GAZE

- **Gaze with intent.** Don't just gaze, search. Looking for emotions gives your eye contact direction and purpose. When you're speaking with someone, search their face for clues about how they're feeling and what they're thinking. This is highly competent.
- **Gaze for oxytocin.** Avoid dead eyes and lifeless eye contact. Instead, try looking for eye locks. This is a moment where you and a conversation partner lock eyes—and it can be brief! Lock eyes when you agree, when you both laugh at the same time, or when you're intensely paying attention. This is a great way to produce oxytocin and reduces the pressure of having to make eye contact all the time. A few great eye locks will give you all the oxytocin you need. And that's a great way to add more warmth.

HOW NOT TO GAZE

- There are cultural differences concerning how much eye contact is appropriate. All humans benefit from oxytocin during gazing and use eye contact to decode behavior, but the amount of acceptable eye contact is different from culture to culture. Pay attention to invitation and patience cues to make sure you're making the right amount of eye contact.
- Be careful not to stare someone down! It's creepy. Watch for patience cues like blocking, self-soothing, or distancing.
- Are you dealing with an oversharer? A dominant colleague? An interrupter? You can subtly quiet a conversation hijacker by not making eye contact with them.

Lead with Your Body Language

We have just learned our five big charisma cues (and many little ones in between)—these are the nonverbal signals that can be used for both warmth and competence. Remember to front, stay open, lean in, use space, and gaze with purpose.

Dr. Essel uses all five of these cues to truly connect with his patients.

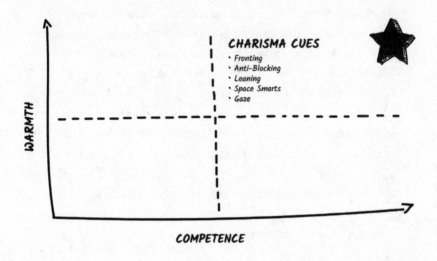

"I like to establish relationships with my families. One of the things I try to do is really make sure that my perspective and my posturing is right. I'm on a journey with them. I'm walking alongside them. I want to get to know who they are in and outside of the clinic," said Dr. Essel.

He signals his perspective nonverbally and verbally. "My positioning when I engage my families is key. I get at their level. I'm not standing above them and looking down upon them," explained Dr. Essel.

He wants them to know one thing: "I'm here to serve and be of assistance." When Dr. Essel keeps his body open, it encourages his patients to open up more. When he turns his body toward his patients and gets on their level, they feel they can level with him. Dr. Essel can help to the best of his ability, and patients get the help they need.

Truly charismatic leaders go into every interaction with cues that help them *and* the people they're with.

With each nonverbal cue, it's important to try it on to see how it feels. You can use this Cues Chart to track your learning. You will also find a full blank Cues Chart at the back of the book.

The Decode column is to track when you have *spotted* a cue. When learning new cues, I've found spotting is a fun way to see it in action before trying it yourself.

The Encode column is for you to challenge yourself to try the cue in your own life. Mark the date every time you try a cue, and try it at least three different times in three different scenarios. This will help you see if it truly works for you.

The Internalize column is for you reflect on how the cue makes you and others feel. Do you feel confident using it? Do you need to work on something? This is a good self-check. Below are some prompts for you to think about before you fill yours out.

The Cues Chart is a great way to keep track of each cue and its possible uses in helping you to meet your charisma goals.

CUE	DECODE	ENCODE	INTERNALIZE
Fronting	Do you notice who fully fronts with you? Who doesn't?	Try fronting with everyone who talks to you today.	How does fronting feel when someone does it to you? When you do it to others?
Anti-Blocking	Does anyone frequently block you with crossed arms or a computer?	Try using open body language with everyone who talks to you today.	How does it feel when someone blocks you? Does it feel better when you purposefully remove a barrier?
Leaning	Who leans in when you share?	Try using a lean when you agree with someone.	Do you like it when people lean into you?

CUE	DECODE	ENCODE	INTERNALIZE
Space Smarts	Pay attention to how the five most important people in your life use space. Which space bubbles do they use?	How can you signal your intentions with space? Try it when you sit at your next conference table.	What is YOUR personal space preference? Which zone do you prefer to use?
Gazing	Do you know someone who eye locks with you? How does it feel?	Try eye locking with someone. How does it feel?	Do you feel most comfortable with eye contact? It might explain a lot about where you fall on the Charisma Scale.

CHAPTER 4

The Wow Factor

In September 1953, two men had just two days to draw and draft a plan for a groundbreaking pitch that would one day become the happiest place on earth. In their proposal, Walt Disney and Herb Ryman wrote: "In these pages is proffered a glimpse into this great adventure . . . a preview of what the visitor will find in DISNEYLAND." Almost seven decades later, about 51,000 people visit Disneyland *every day*. There are now twelve different Disney parks around the world.

Disney's original goal of bringing people happiness is the underlying operational principle that carries on even today. Disney calls it the "Wow Factor."

Wowing guests is not only about meeting those high expectations but exceeding them. Every employee of Disney Parks operates under one main requirement: "Every guest be treated like a VIP—that is, a very important, very *individual* person."

How do they do this? Not only with a helpful can-do attitude, but also with a specific set of nonverbal behaviors. Yes, really. Disney University teaches every single person who works in Disney parks—from janitors to princesses—the specific nonverbal cues to use with guests. And they all embody the pinnacle of warmth.

These little warmth cues might seem small, but to Disney they are an important part of the wow experience—baked into the very essence of what it means to visit a Disney park. "It is this plethora of little wows, many of which seem fairly insignificant at the time, on which Quality Service depends. If the little wows are delivered consistently and continuously, they add up to a big WOW!" And so it is with the nonverbal warmth cues in our interactions as well.

Each warmth cue builds a little bit more trust with every single person, every single time you interact. Each warmth moment strengthens bonds between customer and company, clients and salespeople, manager and employee. For Disney, these little wows resulted in a customer return rate of 70 percent. Now that's magical.

Warmth cues create loyalty. We are drawn to people who wow us.

Warmth cues are also powerful because they create a **halo effect**. If you're warm *and* trustworthy, it makes people feel more trust for everything about you—from your personality to your office to your service to your mannerisms . . . even to your accent.

Researchers asked two groups of participants to watch a clip of a college professor teaching with an accent. One group saw the professor teach using lots of warmth cues. The other group saw the same professor teach the same content without warmth cues. They then asked the participants to rate the professor on his likability, his physical appearance, his gestures, and his accent.

It makes sense that the participants who saw the warmth video rated the professor as more likable. But they also rated his other aspects as more positive as well—they saw him as more attractive and liked his accent more. People who saw the video without warmth cues rated the same professor as less likable and attractive and even found his accent more irritating! Warmth cues created a halo effect, making everything about the professor better.

Warmth cues create a wow factor for everything about you. They signal trustworthiness, engagement, inclusion—all the warm and fuzzy feelings that make us feel close to others. Using tilts, nods, eyebrow raises, savor smiles, touches, and mirroring creates a halo effect around you.

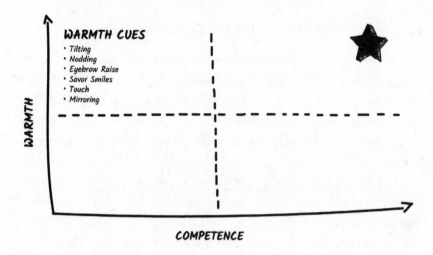

WARMTH CUES
* Tilting
* Nodding
* Eyebrow Raise
* Savor Smiles
* Touch
* Mirroring

WARMTH

COMPETENCE

And here's the best part: Dialing up your warmth doesn't just wow others. It also helps you *feel* more "wow" yourself.

Researchers from the University of Amsterdam had participants watch a short film and then describe it to research assistants. Half summarized the film to a positive listener—someone who smiled and nodded and had more open body language. The other half told their story to someone who exhibited a negative listening style: the person frowned more, slumped, and gave no positive head movement.

The participants with the positive listeners not only described the film differently but actually thought about it more creatively. They described characters' thoughts and emotions and included more of their own opinions about the film's deeper meaning. People with the negative listeners focused solely on facts and concrete details.

In other words, warm body language encourages more insight, big thinking, and creativity. **Warm listeners sparked the Cue Cycle, and inspired people to *feel* more wowed.** Cold body language caused people to withhold their ideas, think small, and be more close-minded.

Let's learn the warmth cues you can start using right now.

WARMTH CUE #1: Time Your Tilts

If I were to ask you, "Do you hear that?" what would you do?

Most people, when trying to hear something more clearly, tilt their head to the side to expose their ear. Because of this instinct, a **head tilt cue** shows interest and curiosity. People who tilt their head during conversations immediately increase their likability and thus their wow factor.

The head tilt is a literal indicator of "I really want to hear what you have to say." Or "Wow, that's interesting. Tell me more." It often accompanies a verbal "Wow."

Researchers even find that a head tilt is correlated with higher attractiveness ratings. Why? We like our potential partners to be good listeners (and of course it improves our self-image to boot).

Take a peek at your profile photos or headshots. Are you tilting? If you use dating apps, how many of your photos have a head tilt? When researchers asked people to pose for a photograph, nearly three-fourths of them tilted their head to one side! Instinctively, we know this makes us more approachable.

FUN FACT

Tilt and Smile

Do any of your pictures have an open mouth smile *and* a head tilt? In an analysis, Career Experts found that LinkedIn profile pictures that depict an open mouth smile with a slight head tilt were seen as the best pictures.

What do the famous paintings *Girl with a Pearl Earring* by Johannes Vermeer, *The Kiss* by Gustav Klimt, and *The Birth of Venus* by Sandro Botticelli all have in common? Yup, you guessed it—the leading ladies in all of these paintings are head tilting. One group of ambitious researchers examined 1,498 paintings from the fourteenth to the twentieth centuries looking for head tilts. They found head tilts in almost half of all the portraits.

And here's where head tilts get even more interesting. Researchers noticed differences between the head tilts in certain paintings. Specifically, **a person's social role predicted the degree of their head tilt.** The higher someone's social standing, the *less* they tilted. What does this tell us? While a head tilt is one of the fastest ways to show warmth, it also serves as a gesture of appeasement and an exhibition of conciliatory behavior. Why? Because the head tilt exposes a highly vulnerable part of our body: the carotid artery. This artery runs up the right and left sides of our neck and supplies our brain with blood.

Think of a head tilt as a heating blanket. It instantly warms you up, but too much can burn you. And it's a great way to warm up cold interactions.

Have to deliver bad news? Use the head tilt to show you're listening and you're there for them.

Been told you're cold, intimidating, or hard to talk to? The head tilt can soften you and encourage people to open up.

PRINCIPLE

Head tilts show interest, curiosity, and appeasement.

WHEN TO TILT
- To show someone you're interested and listening.
- To deliver bad news.
- To be seen as higher in warmth.
- To encourage someone to open up.

WHEN NOT TO TILT
- If you're trying to look powerful.
- If you want to discourage someone from talking. Ever been with someone who won't stop talking? Or won't end a meeting? Don't tilt!
- If you're already high in warmth, head tilting will make it hard to climb back into competence. Use it sparingly.

WARMTH CUE #2: Nod to Know

Major League Baseball player Alex Rodriguez, also known as A-Rod, played twenty-two seasons and earned a total of $441.3 million in the league. In 2007, he was accused of doping.

Rodriguez sat down for an interview with Katie Couric on *Eye to Eye* to answer questions about taking steroids. Couric asked Rodriguez, "For the record, have you ever used steroids, human growth hormone, or any other performance-enhancing substance?"

"No," said Rodriguez.

Couric pressed on. "Have you ever been tempted to use any of those things?"

"No," said Rodriguez.

Sounds pretty clear, right? Think again. Let's decode his nonverbal cues.*

SPEAKER	VERBAL	NONVERBAL
Couric	"For the record, have you ever used steroids, human growth hormone, or any other performance-enhancing substance?"	
Rodriguez	"No."	Head nod yes. Microexpression of contempt.
Couric	"Have you ever been tempted to use any of those things?"	
Rodriguez	"No."	Look up to the right. Head nod no.

The nods give Rodriguez away. An affirmative up-and-down nod is a nonverbal cue for yes. Liars often rehearse the verbal but forget about the nonverbal. And this is exactly what happened to Rodriguez. When asked about taking drugs he *says* no but his *body* says yes.

He also flashed a facial expression of contempt, exhibiting scorn or disdain. This is a one-sided mouth raise.

---

* To see a clip of the interview, check out your digital bonuses at scienceofpeople.com/bonus.

Rodriguez could have felt contempt for Couric, who was asking him hard questions. He could have felt it for himself. Liars often show contempt while lying because they know it can get them into trouble. Most people hate having to lie.

When Couric asks, "Have you ever been tempted to use any of those things?" Rodriguez looks up to the right and nods his head horizontally, a nonverbal cue for "no." This is true—he wasn't *tempted* to take drugs, he *did* take drugs.

A few years later, Rodriguez did come clean and admit to taking steroids.

So what's the takeaway here? Our emotions often leak into our nods and can reveal our true feelings. If you want to have more control over your message, controlling your nods is essential. The vertical nod meaning yes is for agreement and encouragement. The horizontal nod meaning no is for disagreement and discouragement.

Nodding is also one of the most underutilized persuasion tools. In the mid-nineties, attorneys began to notice that nodding was having an effect on their courtroom cases. They observed that expert witnesses often looked to jurors to see if they were nodding in an agreement. Moreover, they found if a juror nodded, agreement could actually become contagious and infect the opinions of jurors around them.

In 2009, researchers decided to test the idea that head nodding by mock jurors could change perceptions of expert credibility. The researchers instructed certain jurors to nod vertically only while the expert was speaking. Could this small nonverbal cue change opinions in the courtroom? Oh yes. Results showed nodding significantly affected whether expert witnesses were believed and how much the other jurors agreed with the actual testimony. **Nodding changed how jurors voted in trial.**

Nodding is a great way to inspire agreement. Most people make the mistake of hiding or stifling their feelings in meetings or interactions. If you agree with something, show it.

Here is another weird effect of nodding: When you nod yes, you get the other person to speak more . . . 67 percent more. Researchers observed applicants interviewing for civil service positions. They found that when the interviewer nodded, the duration of interviewees' speech increased by 67 percent.

What if you're on a phone call or someone can't see your body language? Nodding can still help. After one of my speaking events in 2015, I was approached by a lovely woman named Nicole Seligman. Seligman worked as an advocate for the National Domestic Violence Hotline. She talked to callers who are in traumatic or emotional situations. She said that advocates are trained to nod while listening to callers. "Even though the caller can't see your nodding, the way you speak and behave on the call will be more empathetic and warmer, while also encouraging callers to use this safe space to continue sharing their story and seek resources," she told me. Nodding created warmth for both the operators and callers.

Affirmative nodding is the ultimate warmth cue because it signals empathy and *triggers* empathy. If you nod while listening to someone open up, you will encourage them to open up more and feel more open yourself.

Don't just take my word for it; try it yourself the next time your partner is telling you something important, a colleague is sharing something personal, or you're deep in conversation with a friend.

Nodding is part of the wow factor because it's one of the fastest ways to show encouragement and agreement, and we like people who are encouraging and agreeable.

FUN TIP

The Male Nod

My male students have told me that guys have an unspoken nodding custom. If you see another guy you know, you nod up. This nonverbally says, "What's up?"

If you pass by a guy you don't know but want to acknowledge, you nod down. This nonverbally says, "Respect." Try this code for yourself: Nod up for friends. Nod down for strangers.

Know the Speed Limit

There is one aspect of nodding that's important to keep in mind when deploying the nod technique: speed. The best nods are slow and thoughtful. A slow triple nod is best. Fast nodding can actually look like impatience.

Try this exercise with me. Say the following three phrases slowly, about one per second, and nod with each one: "I hear you . . . I hear you . . . I hear you."

You should feel and sound empathetic, compassionate, and kind.

Now say all three in less than a second with a quick nod for each one. "I hear you. I hear you. I hear you."

This should feel and sound rushed, hurried, and impatient. The slow nod says, "Keep going, I have all the time in the world." The fast nod says, "I get it. Finish up quick."

FUN TIP

Beware of the Bobblehead*

Studies have found that women tend to nod more than men. A few years ago, I realized this was a big problem for me. I was nodding too much, which was overly warm. And it made me look like a bobblehead doll. It looked like I was agreeing with everything. If you have the bobblehead problem, try replacing your nod with a slight head tilt. It's still warm but more moderate.

PRINCIPLE

Nod yes to get more yeses.

---

* There are certain cultures in places like Bulgaria, India, and Pakistan where nods are used differently. Check your cultural norms.

- **Nod to greet.** Walk by someone in the hallway? Give 'em a nod and a smile. Hopped onto a team video call? Nod and wave hello.
- **Nod to encourage.** Is someone saying something you really like or agree with? Nod yes.
- **Nod to solicit.** Need to get someone to open up? Want someone to keep talking? Try a slow triple nod.

WHEN NOT TO NOD

- To subtly show disagreement or discontent, withhold your nods. This can softly signal you're not on the same page with someone.
- If you're already displaying too many warmth cues, don't nod. Or if you've been nodding a lot already, don't be a bobblehead.
- If you want someone to stop talking or when you need someone to wrap up, don't nod.

WARMTH CUE #3: Eyebrows Raise Expectations

On the TV show *Dating in the Dark Australia*, contestants are sent out on blind dates with random strangers . . . in complete darkness. Contestants can talk, touch, and even make out, but they can't see each other until the final episode, where they participate in a "reveal."

During the reveal each participant stands on opposite sides of a very dark room. Each contestant is lit up one at a time so they cannot see the other person's reaction to how they look. At home, we get to see both people with a special infrared camera. Then, later in the episode, the contestants decide if they want to be together after the show.

The best part of this show is seeing the natural body language reactions and expressions. Since participants are dating without being able to see each other, their nonverbal cues are purely instinctive.

In one episode of *Dating in the Dark Australia,* a promising couple enters the reveal room: Rob and Kim. They had wonderful dates, deep discussions, and lots of touch.

Rob is the first to be revealed. "I was so nervous. I was shaking like a leaf," he said. Then the light turns on.

Kim, his partner across the room, takes him in. She immediately raises her eyebrows and smiles. Then she covers her mouth and raises her eyebrows again. She grins sheepishly.

The light turns off Rob. Kim's eyebrows flash yet *again*.

Kim raised her eyebrows three times in the span of four seconds because she liked what she saw . . . and wanted to see more of it.

If you want to convey excitement, curiosity, and engagement in an interaction, raise your eyebrows. When we raise our eyebrows, we signal that we, like Kim, want to see more. It's as if we want our eyebrows to get out of the way to see something or someone better. As is true of all warmth cues, in professional, social, and romantic situations the eyebrow raise is a positive social cue that will increase your wow factor. Universally, the eyebrow raise is a sign of acknowledgment.

Researchers have found that we also raise our eyebrows to show an intention to communicate. This is because raising our eyebrows increases the distance at which it's possible for an observer to detect our gaze direction.

In short, **the eyebrow raise is a nonverbal shortcut**. It's the fastest way to communicate interest, curiosity, and attention. We can use it as a shortcut in many scenarios. For example:

- **When we're seeking confirmation**—we might raise our eyebrows in a soft question: "Does this make sense?"
- **When we're actively listening.** Researchers found that an eyebrow raise can be used to demonstrate agreement in conversation. This is especially useful on video calls where you are mute but still want to show engagement.
- **When we want to emphasize a point.** When *you* raise your eyebrows, others are cued to pay attention and are more likely to make eye contact with you. It's as if you're saying with your eyebrows, "Listen to this, it will wow you."
- **When we are wowed.** We often raise our eyebrows when we are positively delighted.

Neil deGrasse Tyson even uses the eyebrow raise to gauge what content he should include in his books. When writing *Astrophysics for People in a Hurry,* Tyson would share facts with people on airplanes and then take note when they raised their eyebrows. Unsurprisingly, the eyebrow raises guided him well—*Astrophysics for People in a Hurry* hit number one on the *New York Times* bestseller list when it debuted in May 2017.

Tyson found that even a little signal like a subtle eyebrow raise can reveal our inner preferences. By strategically utilizing the eyebrow raise, you too can both demonstrate and uncover warmth and enthusiasm quickly.

One thing to be aware of—this cue is an *eyebrow* raise, NOT an *eyelid* raise. When we raise our lids to show the whites of our eyes, it signals fear. This is a negative cue. Be sure when you eyebrow raise that it's *just* your eyebrows and not your lids too.

And remember that the eyebrow raise is a shortcut. You don't need to hold it for long. Most eyebrow raises are quick—less than a second. Keeping your eyebrows in the raised position too long will make you look permanently surprised—not a great look.

> **PRINCIPLE**
>
> The eyebrow raise is the fastest way to show interest and curiosity and capture attention.

WHEN TO EYEBROW RAISE

- To encourage someone to speak up. Do you work with or spend time with a serious introvert? Introverts may struggle with sharing their ideas. You can encourage them to share with an eyebrow raise in their direction. A quick raise shows them that you would like to hear from them without calling them out.
- Use an eyebrow raise any time you want to show curiosity or interest.
- Use it to greet someone you like.

- If someone is pushing your buttons, keep those eyebrows down. An eyebrow raise will only encourage them to keep doing what they're doing.
- Don't do it too often. You do not want to look permanently surprised.
- In Japan, the eyebrow raise is used to indicate romantic interest. Therefore, if you're in Japan, suppress it in professional situations.

WARMTH CUE #4: Savor Smiles

Here's something that won't surprise you at all: We're 9.7 times more likely to be seen as warm when we're smiling. A **smile** is a pure warmth cue.

But what might surprise you is that smiling is not just about warmth or happiness. It's also about engagement. **Smiling makes you more memorable.** Researchers put participants in an fMRI and asked them to remember people's names while looking at photos of them. Some of the faces they saw were smiling and some were not. When participants were trying to memorize the names of the smiling individuals, their orbitofrontal cortex, the reward center in the brain, activated. In plain English: Our brain likes smiling people and makes a greater effort to remember them. Smiles wow us because they wake up our *own* reward centers, and it's easier to remember people and things that make us feel good.

Our brain likes when *we* smile too. Researchers found that smiling increases blood flow to your brain. It's one of the few nonverbal cues that activates our entire nervous system by triggering a release of hormones that make us feel great. This gives you more energy and makes you feel more optimistic. Simply put, smiling creates an internal and external wow. **Smiling has internal benefits as well as social benefits.**

Does this mean I want you to walk around in a perma-smile? No! That'd be fake. And fake smiles aren't memorable anyway. There is a very important difference between real and fake smiles: A real smile reaches all the way up into someone's eyes. The best way to tell the difference between a real and a fake smile is that a real smile activates those eye crinkles, or crow's-feet, like so:

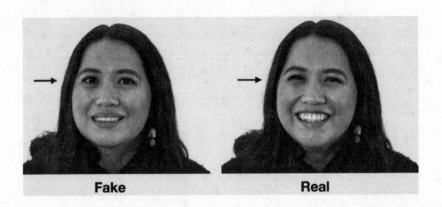

Fake   **Real**

Here's why a real smile is so important: Only real smiles actually have an impact on the people that see them. When we see someone else authentically smile, it activates our own smile muscles. In fact, researchers found that it's difficult to frown when someone is smiling at you.

Your warmth triggers others' warmth.

This is why Disney instructs: "Start and end every guest interaction and communication with direct eye contact and a sincere smile."

Note the word *sincere*. Even Disney, the world of happiness and magic, knows there is nothing worse than a fake smile.

Direct from their handbook: "Practices such as smiling, greeting, and thanking guests are well and good, but if these actions are restricted to rote, mechanistic behaviors, their effectiveness is severely limited." Smile only if you truly feel it. And if you can, try a **savor smile**.

Savor smiles are smiles that **take longer to spread across someone's face**. Researchers found that they are seen as more attractive. To get specific: a smile that takes longer than half a second gives the feeling that you are truly relishing someone's presence, idea, or story.

The best part of a savor smile? A real one will often lead to laughter, another warmth cue. Most people think of **laughter** as a humor cue—it signals that something is funny. But laughing *with* someone is also a great way to bond.

Researchers found that laughing with someone is one of the best catalysts for connection. This is because laughter is a shared positive experience that also stimulates feel-good endorphins. Laughter makes us more open *and* encourages us to open up.

FUN TIP

Honor Any Humor

Don't feel pressure to be funny. It's great if you can create humor, but it's even better if you can honor other people's humor. Always be ready to laugh. Think of a laugh like a compliment. It's telling someone you appreciate them.

PRINCIPLE

Smiles spread joy and create joy . . . but only when they're sincere.

- Don't perma-smile, **be smile ready.**
- Start and end on a savor smile. Smiles are most important when we first see someone (we want to know, "Are you truly happy to see me?") and when we're ending an interaction (we want to know, "Did you enjoy our encounter?").
- If you see someone smiling, see if you can jump in on the action.
- Match a smile. Don't smile behind closed doors or behind people's backs. Instead, save your smiles to enjoy with others. Don't just smile about someone, smile *with* someone. Smile once the Zoom camera pops on or the moment you lock eyes.

- If you're already too high in warmth, work on saving your smiles for the big moments.
- Need to show disproval? Want someone to back off? Don't smile.

WARMTH CUE #5: A Touch of Trust

Ever wondered why some teams have great chemistry?

One group of researchers at UC Berkeley wanted to find out and devised a clever way to watch basketball games in the name of science. The team watched the first three games of the NBA finals during the 2008–2009 season and counted every single time players were seen touching on-camera—from back pats to butt slaps to leaping shoulder bumps to arm drapes to head grabs. **They found the team who touched one another the most won the most games.**

The Mavericks had a total of 250 touches, making them almost twice as touchy-feely as the Miami Heat, who had only 134 touches. In those three games, the Mavericks had 82 percent more high fives.

The moment we touch someone or someone touches us, our chemistry changes. Touch creates the potent chemical oxytocin. As we have learned, oxytocin plays a complicated role in our body, but in interactions it increases trust, warmth, and rapport. **Even small touches—a** high five, a fist bump, or a pat on the back—produce oxytocin and encourage trust.

Oxytocin is the chemical of WOW. It feels like the warm and fuzzies. Ever been with someone and felt like you just clicked? That's the feeling of oxytocin.

Study after study shows that a subtle touch increases trust in all kinds of relationships, from social to romantic to professional. Touch has also been shown to make us feel closer to and more positive about the toucher, whether that person is a friend, a family member, a colleague, a stranger, or even a basketball teammate. When you trust your teammates, you play better, you pass more, you have faith that everyone is doing their job well.

Oxytocin also helps us read and decode others better. The basketball researchers found that the more teammates touch one another, the better they're able to read and predict their teammates' future behavior.

FUN TIP

My Secret Weapon

I'm a big, big fan of the high five. I high-five teammates on a job well done. I high-five friends whenever one of us makes a good joke. Take every opportunity to high-five—it's one of the fastest and easiest ways to touch mid-interaction.

Touch can also help you make more money. Researchers wanted to know if a simple touch could change how much a server got tipped. And this is not just for women. They found a light touch on the hand or arm increased female servers' **average tips by 23 percent and male servers' average tips by 40 percent**.

Even more interesting, touching increased the average tips of *younger* customers by 62 percent but only increased the tips of older customers by 15 percent. Those youngsters love that oxytocin rush!

Be Strategic, Not Creepy

Now, not all touch is created equal. Touch is a nonverbal cue that varies from culture to culture. One study even found that touch nuances are different among three otherwise closely related European countries— France, the Netherlands, and England. In some cultures, people greet each other with a cheek kiss; in others, they bow. In some cultures, friends of the same gender hold hands in public. In some cultures, the feet are considered no-touch zones and are off-limits.

How do we work with this? By thinking about touch in terms of zones. In Western cultures, the hands and forearms are usually safe zones and the least intimate, making handshakes and arm touches good warmth cues in professional situations. For friends, family, and other closer relationships, contacts with the upper arms, the shoulders, the upper back (back pats), and cheeks (cheek kisses) are usually accepted warmly.

As you interact, think about touch zones for yourself and the people in your life. What are your comfortable zones? Watch for their invitation and patience cues. If you touch too much, too quickly, or too intimately you will see patience cues. If your touch is welcome, you will see invitation cues.

FUN TIP

Liars Touch Less

Need another reason to touch appropriately? Liars have been found to touch less. Perhaps it's because they don't want to bond with the person they're lying to.

What about video calls? Sometimes just mentioning touch is enough to create warmth. When I get on video calls, I often say, **"Sending you a virtual high five,"** or **"Here's a little digital hug,"** and hug my camera. It always gets a chuckle and cues for warmth even though we can't actually touch.

What if you're in person but you can't touch? Say it's flu season, or an international pandemic hits. Dr. Kofi Essel said that during the COVID-19 pandemic, he gave his kids an elbow (for a quick elbow touch) because they couldn't shake hands. This always produced a little laugh and a little touch. Dr. Essel also says addressing the *desire* to bond is important.

"Sometimes I'll address them and say, I'm sorry I can't shake your hand. I really want to. But it's very nice to meet you today," explained Dr. Essel.

He also uses air fives and air hugs. Even the thought of touch adds warmth.

WHEN TO TOUCH

- When you want to trigger warmth, closeness, and trust.
- At the start, middle, and end of an interaction. Don't just start with a handshake and end it there. Instead, high five during conversation, arm touch to emphasize a point, and end with a hug if it feels comfortable.

WHEN NOT TO TOUCH

- When you don't feel comfortable with someone or they don't look comfortable with you. If you see patience cues, take it slow.
- Beware of a belittling touch. We don't like being patted on the head—it reminds us of our parents.

WARMTH CUE #6: Mirroring Makes You Magnetic

It was four a.m. and my husband and I were groggily getting ready for our flight. Half asleep, we dragged our bags into the lobby of our hotel and clomped over to the checkout counter.

"Good morning!" the receptionist chirped. "Happy, happy day," she singsonged.

I peered at her through blurry eyes. Did she fancy herself a Disney princess? This was a little much for four a.m.

Then she went into hyperdrive. "Did you have a lovely stay? We sure hope you did! Can't wait to have you come again. Any suggestions for us?" Before we could reply, she asked, "Can I get someone to help you with your bags?"

"Yes, please," my husband said.

Then she turned to the open lobby. "George?! Geooooooorge?!" she shouted.

"Actually, we're good. Thanks, but we can get them."

She flashed us a practiced smile and waved broadly, almost knocking over my paper cup of coffee. We ducked, grabbed our bags, and rushed toward the door. "Hope you come again!" she yelled after us.

"Wow," my husband said to me once we escaped outside. "That was a LOT."

There's a big myth about wowing people. Wowing someone is not about showcasing the highest energy possible. Wowing someone doesn't mean knocking them off their feet. (Who really wants to be knocked off their feet anyway?) **Wowing someone is meeting them where they're at.** It's showing someone nonverbal respect by going to *their* level instead of forcing them to come to yours.

Warmth is about making someone feel welcome. This might mean being calm and serene for someone who is very stressed. Or bringing out the excitement for someone who's enthused. Or even being contemplative and empathetic for someone who needs advice.

Even Disneyland, the happiest place on earth, recognizes the need for "appropriate," or measured, warmth. If a mom can't find her child in the park, it wouldn't make sense for a Disney employee to be all smiles and cheer. Instead, Disney employees take the far more helpful and wow-inducing route: nodding in understanding and leaning in to get more information and be as competent and efficient as possible.

Dr. Essel is keenly aware of this with his patients as well. Sometimes he's meeting a family for a routine checkup, so he keeps it positive and light—makes small jokes and smiles more. If a child is sick or there is a difficult diagnosis, he changes his nonverbal behavior, energy, and tone completely to match the seriousness of the situation.

"I really match the behaviors that families are making. If the mood in the room is very solemn and sad, I'm careful not to come in all spunky. I'll try to calm it down and acknowledge everyone," explained Dr. Essel.

This nonverbal practice is known as **mirroring**, or **mimicry**. We mirror nonverbally with our body language and facial expressions. We can mirror vocally, with our volume, tone, and pitch. And we can mirror verbally with the kinds of words we use.

Luckily, we *already* mirror in our interactions. In chapter 2, I talked about how our cues are contagious—that we often "catch" the mood and nonverbals of people we are with. Studies find that humans begin to synchronize their blink rate, arm movements, breathing, and body movements without even realizing it.

The Magic Mirrors

There are many, many benefits to mirroring the people you are with.

First, **mirroring earns you more money and helps you feel better about it**. Researchers from MIT tracked the amount of mirroring in real salary negotiations of midlevel executives transferring to a new company. They found that the more a new hire mirrored during the negotiation, the more they earned in their final salary by 20 to 30 percent. Negotiations with mirroring were also rated to be more pleasant by the mirrorer and the mirroree!

Second, **mirroring makes you more likable and persuasive**. People who've been mirrored—even when they haven't consciously noticed—later reported having a more favorable impression of the person doing the mirroring.

In one experiment, a team of researchers had an actor stop people in the street and ask them to take a survey. Half of the time the actor subtly mirrored the survey takers' nonverbal behavior. A lean got a reciprocal lean, an arm cross triggered an arm cross, a slumped posture was met with a slumped posture. The other half of the time the actor stood normally.

Later, the researchers asked survey takers how they felt about the person who gave them their survey. Even though they had no idea they were being mirrored, the people who were mirrored reported feeling more emotionally close with the survey giver!

Third, **mirroring helps you emotionally sync up with someone by enabling your empathy**. In one study, participants watched videotaped couples arguing. Participants then had to guess the emotion of the couples. Researchers found that the participants' physiology began to sync up to the people they were watching. And here is where it gets even more interesting. The *more* a participant's body mirrored the couple's, the *better* they were at identifying the emotions of the couple. Again, here is the Cue Cycle at work: Spot a cue, internalize the information, encode it in our own bodies.

There is one more critical aspect of mirroring successfully: Mirror what you want to magnetize. Don't mirror negative body language; this will only highlight it. Effective mirroring is about matching and emphasizing positive, curious, engaging body language. This creates a positive feedback loop. They show openness, you show openness; they continue to catch your openness and you continue to catch theirs. And exponential openness is created!

Warning: Mirroring is so potent that only subtle mirroring is needed. Copy every cue and you will quickly stray into creepy territory. The key is to mirror subtly—no need to copy every gesture.

PRINCIPLE

Meet people where they're at by mirroring—match
the positive, transform the negative.

WHEN TO MIRROR

- Mirror any and all positive body language to show you're on the same page with someone.
- If you want to encourage warmth, mirror their warmth to highlight it. If you want to stimulate competence, mirror their competence cues to emphasize them.

- If you feel awkward or see a cue that doesn't feel natural to you, don't mirror it!
- Don't mirror negative cues lest you catch and encourage them.
- If you aren't on the same page with someone and want them to know it, don't mirror.
- If you feel like you're playing Simon Says, you're mirroring too much. The best mirroring is subtle.

Wowing Everyone You Meet

When you walk into a Disney park, you're greeted with big authentic smiles and waves. Cast members nod when you ask for help and head tilt when you ask questions. They match your enthusiasm for the new attraction. They raise their eyebrows when you tell them this is your first time in the park. They give your child a high five. And you think, *Wow, this is going to be a great day.*

Disney opens with warmth and then blows you away with know-how. Warmth cues are incredibly important for wowing people during your first impressions. My rule of thumb: **Show three warmth cues in the first three minutes of an interaction.**

Warmth cues can emphasize or even replace warm words. Here's my cheat sheet:

WARM WORDS	WARMTH CUE
"That's so interesting."	Eyebrow raise
"I agree."	Nodding
"I'm listening."	Head tilting
"This is exciting."	Leaning
"I respect you."	Fronting
"I trust you."	Touch
"I'm on the same page."	Mirroring

Let's expand our Cues Chart to put these warm cues into action.

CUE	DECODE	ENCODE	INTERNALIZE
Nodding	Do you notice who nods with you? Do you open up more with them?	Try a slow triple nod when you next want someone to open up.	When you're with a non-nodder, do you worry they aren't in agreement with you?
Tilting	Try to spot three head tilts in your next few conversations. What did someone want to hear more about?	Try tilting next time you have to deliver hard or bad news.	How does it feel when someone shows you a head tilt? Do you feel more open when you head tilt?
Eyebrow Raise	Try to spot three eyebrow raises in your next few conversations. What intrigued someone?	Try an eyebrow raise upon greeting. Then try one when you hear something interesting.	How do you feel when you eyebrow raise? Try a fast one and a slow one. Find your ideal speed.
Smiling	See if you can spot a fake smile in an interaction. Then try to understand why you didn't get a real one.	Try to show no fake smiles in the next week. Smile only when you mean it.	Do you feel more authentic when you only stick to real smiles? Do you wish you had more reasons to smile?
Touch	Think of the three people you see most. What are their touch maps?	What's your touch map?	What kind of touch makes you uncomfortable? Who makes you uncomfortable when they touch you? Set up boundaries.
Mirroring	Who mirrors you most? Least?	Try mirroring with someone you like. Try mirroring with someone you don't. Does it feel different?	Does mirroring make you feel more in sync with someone? Or does it distract you? Only use mirroring if it feels good to you.

CHAPTER 5

How to Look Powerful

Richard M. Nixon was experiencing a string of bad luck. Just weeks away from the first ever televised U.S. presidential debate against John F. Kennedy, Nixon slammed his knee on a car door and ended up in the hospital. Weeks later, he emerged twenty pounds lighter, frail and weak with the flu.

On Monday, September 26, 1960, Nixon arrived at the television studio with a low-grade fever and a bandaged knee. While emerging from the car, he banged his injured knee yet again, exacerbating the wound.

Unfortunately for Nixon, things only went downhill for the rest of the evening. In fact, his performance during the debate changed the entire course of the election, and it all came down to his negative cues.

The very first thing we see is both candidates seated on either side of the moderator Howard K. Smith. Nonverbally, they couldn't look more different.

1. **Runner's feet:** First, look at how both men have positioned their feet. Kennedy had his legs folded in a relaxed seated position. Nixon is displaying a cue called **runner's feet**. This is when people

pull one foot back as if they're about to sprint down a track—you see runners use this as their starting position. It's a cue that signals impatience. Imagine the message you send to prospective voters if you're telegraphing that you're about to run out on them! Now we know Nixon likely was in this position because he was nursing his injured knee. But he stayed in this distracting position throughout most of the debate. The ideal condition in this situation would have been to have relaxed, planted feet pointed toward the audience . . . like Kennedy.

His calm seated position made him look like he was reliable, sturdy, and confident.

2. **White knuckling:** Next, take a look at the candidates' hand positions. Kennedy held his hands calmly folded in his lap. Nixon had one hand gripping the chair arm in what looks like a fist. This is an immediate anxiety cue. At first glance, it looked like Nixon was holding on to that chair arm for dear life. That's because we **white knuckle** when we're highly anxious and trying to keep it together. We also clench our fists when we're very angry and trying to hold it in. It's a way we can focus our internal emotions externally without changing our overall appearance too much, and it's often done unconsciously. This white-knuckle cue made Nixon look both anxious and angry.

3. **Self-soothing:** Nixon's right hand was resting on the top of his thigh. This isn't a negative cue on its own; in fact, it's positive to have your hands relaxed and visible. However, during the debate Nixon consistently rubbed the top of his thigh in a **self-soothing gesture**. When nervous, we try to calm ourselves down with self-touch. We're physically telling our body that everything will be okay. We might wring our hands, rub the back of our neck, or, like Nixon did, run our hands along our legs or arms. This cue was not only distracting but also made Nixon look very nervous.

   You know why else we rub our hands over our thighs? When our palms are sweaty! Whether his palms were damp or not, it sure looked like he was drying his hands on his pants. Gross . . . and not very presidential.

   And all that happens in the first 1.2 seconds . . . before the candidates spoke a single word.

4. **Gaze direction:** Then, two seconds in, before the debate even started, things got worse. Nixon made a huge nonverbal mistake: He looked over to his right. Doesn't sound like a big deal, right? From a nonverbal perspective this was the kiss of charisma death.

   Remember how important gaze is for trust and attention? When Nixon looked away from the camera (and us), we immediately lost trust. But even more damaging, when Nixon looked over to the right, it makes *us* want to look where he is looking—and

jfklibrary.org

that's straight at Kennedy! Nixon was basically telling us nonverbally, "Don't look at me, look at my opponent."

And he held this pose for eleven seconds! He then continuously bounced between the cameras, Kennedy, the moderator, and reporters in the audience for the duration of the debate. At the time, Nixon had the nickname "Tricky Dick," so his shifty gaze unintentionally reinforced his shifty reputation.

Kennedy, on the other hand, stared directly into the cameras.

5. **Expressing contempt:** At one point, moderator Smith introduced Nixon and a close shot zoomed in on his face. We see a number of quick cues—first a jerky head motion. Nixon shifted his head from side to side and then up and down in a nod. Then he flashed a microexpression of **contempt**—a one-sided mouth raise. This negative cue signals disdain, scorn, and pessimism.

Then the camera panned to Kennedy. Kennedy stared straight ahead, kept his face calm, and gave a single slow affirmative nod toward the audience. The difference between the two men could not have been starker.

Over the next fifty-eight minutes, Kennedy looked more and more like a winner. Calm, confident, secure—everything you'd want in a leader. And Nixon encoded cue after cue that undermined his credibility.

Before this debate, Nixon was consistently polling well, but his debate performance changed the course of the entire election. Nixon learned from his mistake, fixed his cues, and went on to perform exceptionally well in the remaining debates. But it didn't matter. That one night still cost him the election.

Six weeks later, Kennedy won the popular vote 49.7 percent to 49.5 percent. Studies revealed that more than half of all voters had been influenced by the debates, and 6 percent stated that the debates alone were the sole deciding factors.

Nixon wasn't a bad candidate; he just had a bad night of cue signaling. In his memoir, Nixon later admitted, "I should have remembered that 'a picture is worth a thousand words.'"

Both of these men were powerful. But only one *looked* powerful.

What can we learn from the Nixon-Kennedy debate? The look of power. Kennedy expertly used many competence cues from the Charisma Scale to create a powerful, memorable presence that took him all the way to the presidency. Now it's your turn to learn how to use them to up your competence.

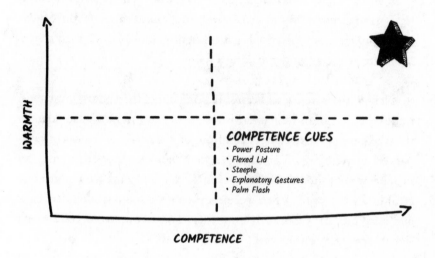

POWER CUE #1: Powerful Posture

Let's perform a posture diagnostic. Would you mind standing up for me? Please stand the way you would if you were talking to a professional acquaintance. If you can, grab two pens or pencils nearby and hold one in each hand (I'll explain why later). Put your arms by your sides. Now let's perform the evaluation by examining the three most essential parts of your posture.

1. **Your shoulders.** Relax them. Add inches between your shoulders and earlobes. I know this sounds weird, but anxiety causes us to tense our shoulders to protect our neck and "turtle" our head down. Want to immediately feel and look more confident? Pull your head up, shoulders down.
2. **Your feet.** Are they pressed tightly together? Are they wider than your hips? Place your feet three inches wider than you normally

would. Whether you're standing or sitting, you will feel instantly more grounded if you have your feet firmly, widely planted. If you're a leg crosser, that's fine. Just take a note from Kennedy and keep one foot firmly planted and the other relaxed. And if you can, angle them toward the person you're with.

3. **Your hands.** Relax them and create a little bit of space between your arms and your torso. Now take a look at the pens you're holding. First, are you gripping them tightly? Hold them loosely so you are not accidentally making a **fist**.

Next, if there were laser beams shooting out of the tops of your hands, would the laser beams intersect? Rotate your arms from the shoulders so that the pens point straight out in front of you, making the laser beams parallel to your hips. This changes your shoulder position by only an inch or two but should immediately make you look (and feel) more powerful in a subtle way. When we're confident, we roll our shoulders back and keep our arms loosely by our sides. This allows us to gesture and signals openness to the world.

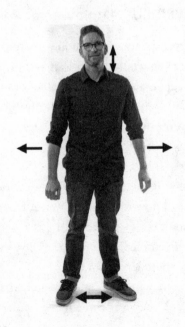

These areas are the three elements of your posture. And they matter. Your **posture** is the single most important cue for signaling confidence to others.

We like to be around people who feel confident because we want to share in that confidence and borrow some of it for ourselves! One 2016 study followed 144 speed dates and found that postural expansiveness was the most romantically appealing trait. **Participants who took up more space were 76 percent more likely to be chosen for future dates.**

Powerful posture isn't just important for your *perceived* confidence, it's important for your *actual* confidence.

Here's a simple rule: The more powerful you feel, the more space you take up, the more powerful you look. When we feel confident, we feel safe taking up space and are more comfortable with others noticing us.

When we feel powerless or anxious, we take up less space, so we're less noticeable to others and are less of a target to potential threats. We shrink up by hunching our shoulders and pinning our arms to our sides to protect ourselves and not expose vulnerable areas.

One study had participants sit in either a contracted or an expansive posture while writing about their own positive or negative traits. The participants in the expansive posture believed more strongly in what they wrote—no matter if it was positive or negative. They also found that participants in the contracted posture said they felt greater overall stress than participants who were in the expansive position. **Expansive posture helps you both look and feel more powerful.**

FUN TIP

Device Size Matters

When we use a computer or hunch over a phone, we're assuming the opposite of powerful posture. Researchers find that using bigger screens inspires more assertive confidence than working on small ones. If possible, get an external screen.

Does this mean you should walk into every room like Rocky? Stand at networking events like Superman? Please, no!

The best posture fixes are small—a few *inches* of movement. These tiny changes create a powerful shift, cuing others and yourself for more confidence.

Use confident posture to inspire confidence.

WHEN TO USE POWERFUL POSTURE

- Whenever you want to both look and feel more competent, use our easy posture fixes. Roll your shoulders down. Rotate your hands away from your body. Widen your feet just a smidge.
- When you check your phone! We tend to hunch down and tighten up when checking our phone. Be sure to pivot it up and keep your shoulders rolled out to maintain a powerful presence.
- One easy way to be more expansive is to lean on something. If it feels comfortable for you, try leaning forward on a desk, draping your arm on a chair, or leaning on a high table next to you.
- Pick the right chairs—in meetings, at social events, and at networking dinners. I love using chairs with armrests because these make it easier to create space between my torso and arms. But be careful not to encroach into others' space—that can be seen as socially aggressive.

WHEN NOT TO USE POWERFUL POSTURE

- If you want to show deference, humility, or regret. Or if you're apologizing to someone.
- If you want to calm someone down or show them you're not a threat. A social worker once told me that if someone is standing and shouting at you, sit down. This immediately takes up less space and shows the other person you don't want a conflict. It also encourages them to take a breather and take a seat as well.

- If you don't want to be noticed. I know you would never show up to a meeting unprepared (wink, wink), but if that ever were to happen, taking up less space will make you less noticeable.

POWER CUE #2: All Seeing, All Knowing

What do Dwayne "The Rock" Johnson, Blake Shelton, and John Legend all have in common?

They've all been named "Sexiest Man Alive" by *People* magazine. This highly anticipated annual issue publishes a list of the fifty sexiest men alive.

In the name of science, I recently picked up the latest issue and scanned the pages. I quickly noticed one specific nonverbal cue on almost every page.

Can you guess what almost every single one of the sexiest men did?

Along with their biceps, their lower lids were really hard.

Hardening our lower lid is sometimes called "flinty eyes," "steely eyes," or "narrowed eyes." This **flexed lid cue** is a signal of intensity, judgment, and scrutiny—it's the "look at me, I'm deep and thoughtful" stare. Tyra Banks calls it a smize.

This is an interesting cue because it's neither positive nor negative but rather a signal of one specific emotion: intensity.

When we want to see something better, we narrow our eyes by hardening our lower lids. We do this for an interesting biological reason.* When we widen our eyes, usually when experiencing emotions like fear and surprise, it allows us to see more. If we're afraid, we want to take in as much of our surroundings as possible to assess for potential threats or escape routes. When we narrow our eyes, it blocks out light so we can see greater detail.

Try this right now. See if you can spot a fleck on a wall nearby. Really try to see it. Do your lower lids harden as you try to see more? Do you

---

* Will Ferrell and Ben Stiller got the idea for the blue steel look in the movie *Zoolander* from Pierce Brosnan, who is known to harden his lower lids on the red carpet. See your digital bonuses at scienceofpeople.com/bonus for some hilarious examples.

feel like you're doing blue steel from *Zoolander*? Then you're doing it right.

This is one of my favorite cues because it's so easy to spot (and often missed). The moment you see someone flex their lower lids, it means they're trying to understand more deeply.

In social situations, someone might flex their lower lids while really trying to get to know you and understand you better. It's as if they're saying, "I want to really see you."

In romantic situations, it can demonstrate intense interest, which is why this cue is often seen on sultry photos of leading men.

In business scenarios, we like to see people laser focused and determined. A flexed lid shows powerful discernment and deep thought.

However, a lower lid flex can move from intense interest to confusion and then to suspicion rather quickly. I'm *always* on the lookout for a lower lid flex to see if someone is confused about what I'm saying. Then I can quell concerns immediately.

A sudden lid flex means someone has gone from just listening to scrutinizing.

It's a cue for you to pause. See a flexed lid? Try to:

- Take questions. Say, "Any questions so far?"
- Repeat the point you just made in a different way.

- Tell a story or give an example to demonstrate your point.
- Do a quick check-in. Ask, "All good?"

A major mistake presenters make is to skip decoding cues from their audience and to think only about encoding. They send all the cues of competence, warmth, and confidence, but then forget to see if their content is resonating and making *others* feel competent, warm, and confident. Even the most perfect presentation is going to be scrutinized by a savvy partner. Be ready for that scrutiny!

I was once giving a presentation on the science of leadership to a small group of executives. It was going great, lots of laughs and aha moments. But when I began talking about oxytocin as the chemical of connection, I noticed multiple lower lid flexes from the CEO. Since we were such a small group, I paused, looked directly at him, and asked, "Does this cue resonate with you, Greg? You look like you have some hesitations."

He immediately looked relieved and said he was confused—his only experience with oxytocin was when the doctors gave it to his wife to induce labor!

Cue laughter all around. Then I explained: "Yes, that's true! But in low doses, in social situations, it just makes us feel the warm and fuzzies. Oxytocin is a complicated chemical, but the bottom line is, it's essential for human bonding. Literally from the moment of birth."

This was a great learning moment. First, the CEO felt that I immediately addressed his concerns. He has asked me back for many trainings at many different levels of the company.

Second, it was a great learning opportunity for *me*. Now when I teach oxytocin I *start* with this caveat: "Oxytocin is a complicated chemical with many effects in the body. But for our purposes, we need to know . . ." I've become a better teacher because I learned a way to address confusion before it starts.

> **PRINCIPLE**
>
> **A lower lid flex shows contemplation, suspicion, and scrutiny—be ready for it!**

- When you want to show someone you're intensely focused on them and using your competence to listen.
- If you don't want to be interrupted, flex your lower lids to show you're sharply focused on a task.
- When you feel suspicious and want someone to expand on their point.
- Forgive me for this one: If you want people to think you could be on the cover of *People* magazine, give this cue a whirl. Many men and women find it very attractive. (This tip is only reserved for the most confident. If you feel silly, don't do it!)

- For longer than five seconds. That just cues people you have something in your eye. This is a quick flex, no need to hold it.
- If someone is really boring and won't stop talking. Flexing your lower lids will only make you look more interested.

POWER CUE #3: Smart People Steeple

German chancellor Angela Merkel does it. French president Emmanuel Macron does it. Former prime minister Theresa May does it. What do all of these powerful leaders use? The **steeple gesture**.

Steepling is when the palms of our hands are facing each other and we gently place just the tips of our fingers together to look like a church steeple. A steeple is a universal display of confidence.

In one study, participants were shown pictures of a leader using seven different hand positions. Steepled hands was chosen as one of the most positive gestures among the seven choices. This is because the steeple conveniently combines a few powerful cues:

- **It shows we're relaxed.** When we're anxious, we tend to make a fist or tense our grip. The steeple can be made only when our hands are nice and relaxed. The steeple cues others to our own calm state.
- **It shows confidence.** Remember from Power Cue #1: Powerful Posture, expansiveness shows confidence. The steeple is the most expansive hand gesture we can make. Our hands are up in front of us, fingers splayed and palms open. The steeple is like a power pose for your hands.
- **It keeps our palms visible.** Subconsciously, when we can see someone's palms, we're assured they aren't concealing something from us.

Steepling is a powerful gesture to convince others of your commitment to and confidence in what you're saying. It shows you're relaxed and open and they should be too.

In a study involving medical school teachers, researchers found the steeple gesture to be a great **complement cue** to teaching. A complement cue is a nonverbal signal that can be used to emphasize an idea. The steeple is a strong complement nonverbal cue when giving directives. It signals, "Let's think and consider this new information." Here are some other great complement cues:

- The head tilt when delivering hard news.
- The lean when sharing the most important point in a meeting.
- Fronting nonverbally encourages an introvert to speak up.

Not only does the steeple gesture indicate that *you* are a contemplative thinker, but it's also a great cue to encourage *others* to listen and think.

A steeple in front of the body is a great way to tell the audience it's time to ponder what you said.

On *Shark Tank,* the steeple is one of Kevin O'Leary's favorite gestures. When he is thinking about a deal, considering how to structure an offer, or waiting to counter someone, he often uses the steeple gesture. It cues pitchers that he is seriously considering something, and they should wait. It's also a clever signal to other Sharks to know he's intently considering taking the deal and they should take note too. The steeple also has the added bonus of making him look calm and collected to the audience at home—no matter what he's really thinking.

Special Note: The steeple can get dangerously close to **evil fingers**. If you don't want to look like you're hatching an evil plan, don't drum your fingers while steepling! This is a cue for scheming and should be avoided.

PRINCIPLE

The steeple is a power pose for your hands. Use it to show confident contemplation.

WHEN TO STEEPLE

- When you want to signal competence, contemplation, and confidence.
- To show you're listening and seriously considering what's being said and want others to do the same.
- **To anchor your hands and stop fidgeting**. Sometimes I tell fidgeters to steeple because it gives their hands something to do. It's hard to simply stop fidgeting. It's much easier to replace fidgeting with steepling.

WHEN NOT TO STEEPLE

- If you feel silly. **As with every single one of these cues, try them on, use them a few times, and adopt them only if they feel natural.**

- Don't feel like you have to hold the steeple gesture all the time. Continue to gesture, take notes, shake hands, and rest your hands in other positions. Steeple to highlight your contemplation.

POWER CUE #4: Excel at Explaining

Maria Konnikova had been playing poker for three straight days. The tournament started with 290 people and had dwindled down to just 62 players after fourteen hours of play on the first day.

By day three, Konnikova was sitting at the final table. She was up against Alexander Ziskin, a seasoned poker champion with two career titles who's won over $1.2 million. Meanwhile, Konnikova learned to play poker less than a year earlier. This was her first time at the tournament. The cameras were watching Konnikova closely—a novice player had never made it this far this fast.

After a few quick dramatic hands, Konnikova got her opponent to go all in and came out on top. She won the entire tournament for a take-home haul of $86,400.

Konnikova is not a professional poker player. She moved to the United States from Russia, attended Harvard and Columbia, and earned a PhD in psychology.

In 2017, she decided to spend one year learning to play poker and wrote a book about the experience. Despite her lack of poker knowledge, she had one big leg up: poker research. Before beginning her journey, Konnikova unearthed a little-known study that she felt could give her an edge over other seasoned players.

Before I tell you what it said, let's play a little thought experiment. Pretend I offered you $10,000 to watch a group of five people play poker. Your mission is to pick out the player with the best hand, but there's a catch. You have to choose which view you want to see to make your selection. Which would you choose?

A. **Head only:** You can see the players' heads but nothing below.
B. **Arms only:** You can't see the players' faces, heads, or lower bodies,

but you can see how their arms and hands move as they handle the chips and cards.

C. **Full body:** You can see the players' entire bodies.

Most people would choose C, full body—the more the better, right? Wrong. Researchers conducted this exact experiment and found that when they showed subjects full body clips of poker players, the subjects' guesses as to how good someone's hand was were no better than chance.

The next most popular guess would be A, head only. Facial expressions are telling, right? Nope. This answer is also surprisingly wrong.

"When subjects looked at faces, their judgments actually dropped to *below* chance levels," explained Konnikova. Skilled poker players are very adept at hiding telling facial emotions and head movements.

Your best bet is B, arms only!

How can this be? Do the hands leak some secret tell? Actually, yes, they do. One researcher found that confident players with winning hands have a fluidity of movement; they play smoothly.

There are two important cues we can learn from Konnikova. The first is the importance of **fluidity** and precision of movement. **Powerful and confident people don't waste energy on purposeless movement.** They move with intention. They don't hesitate. They don't stall. They aren't jerky. They know exactly what they want. People with clear thought take clear action. Researchers have found this to be true beyond the poker table as well.

When I show audiences the Nixon-Kennedy debate, the biggest difference consistently pointed out is Nixon's movement. He's jerky, he fidgets, he squirms. He wastes energy. It's distracting for viewers and makes Nixon look indecisive. Kennedy is still until it matters. He doesn't waste a single move. His precision makes him look confident, purposeful, and put together.

The second cue we learn from Konnikova is that the knowledge we gain from observing hands is underappreciated. People say that eyes are the windows to the soul, but I say hands are more telling. Powerful people intuitively know how important their hands are for effective communication.

We tend to think of powerful people as stoic, unmoving, unreadable beings. But this is not borne out by the research.

Researchers asked participants to rate photos of leaders using positive hand gestures, like a steeple, compared to leaders using no hand gestures. They found that "participants perceived the leader with no hand gestures to be distant, and the leader with positive hand gestures to be more immediate and attractive." Immediacy is defined as relatable, positive, and engaging—that's an immediate social win. In contrast, when leaders put their hands behind their back or in their pockets or had one or both arms crossed over their chest, they were rated as more defensive and distant.

This makes sense intuitively—our hands help us get things done. We grab with our hands, write with our hands, build with our hands. If they're out of sight or unavailable, we appear less likely to act.

Highly competent people signal power and capability with what I call **explanatory gestures**. These nonverbal cues help expand, explain, and expound upon verbal messages.

FUN TIP

Hands Are Honest

It's hard to lie with our hands. For example, try saying the number three out loud but holding up five fingers. Hard, right? We like to pay attention to hand gestures because intuitively we know they're used more by those who are telling the truth. Researchers found that liars tend to clasp their hands together to inhibit hand leaks. Liars often use no gestures because they're reciting memorized verbal information.

Researchers found that purposeful, confident gestures improve comprehension by 60 percent. And some gestures are so powerful that

they carry 400 percent more information! Gestures can convey importance, size, emotion, the direction of the conversation, and needs.

My team and I coded hundreds of hours of TED Talks looking for patterns. We wanted to know if there were any nonverbal differences between the most and least viewed TED Talks.

We found that hand gestures were key. The more popular TED Talkers used more hand gestures overall: an average of 465 gestures in eighteen minutes compared to 272 gestures by the less popular TED Talkers.

Second, we noticed that the more popular TED Talkers used explanatory gestures to help get their message across clearly. Here were the most common explanatory gestures you can use as well:*

1. **Numbers:** Any time someone mentioned a number, they nonverbally emphasized it by showing it on their hand.
2. **Big or Small:** We also noticed that TED Talkers helped their audience understand the size or importance of something with their gestures. If something was small or no big deal, they held up their fingers only an inch apart to emphasize just how small. If something was really important, they held their hands as if they were holding a beach ball.
3. **Me vs. You:** Really powerful speakers use their gestures to help *you* keep pace with their content. When they speak about their opinion or something personal, they often gesture toward themselves, sometimes even touching their own heart. When they're encouraging the audience or speaking about a call to action, they gesture toward the audience.

---

* In your digital bonuses we have fifty hand gesture ideas you can use!

4. **Thumb Pinch:** This is a favorite power gesture of politicians. The thumb pinch is when we make a loose fist with our thumb on top. It's a subtle thumbs-up gesture that in many Western cultures stands for "good" or "okay." This makes it a positive way to point or gesture toward someone or something and avoid the finger point (which we don't like).

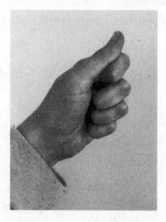

5. **Them vs. Us:** This is the most impressive gesture we noted. Highly competent speakers will show two different opinions or two different groups with their hands. For example, when talking about liberals, a politician might hold up his left hand; when talking about conservatives, a politico might hold up her right hand. By the end of a speech, all the audience has to do is look at which

hand is gesturing to know who the speaker is referring to. They're nonverbally providing us characters in their story, slowly ascribing meaning to their own body parts to use as shortcuts later on without having to repeat themselves.

Explanatory gestures represent competence because they lower the cognitive load of the speaker *and the listener.* Researcher Susan Goldin-Meadow has studied the power of gestures for decades. She finds that we better connect with those who gesture because it helps us track and understand content. Nonverbal gestures add depth to the verbal content we hear. This is what makes explanatory gestures a highly competent cue. **The better you know your verbal content, the more easily you're able to demonstrate it.**

Want to be a great communicator? Be able to explain anything to anyone? Speak to people on two tracks: **nonverbally and verbally.**

If you have a big idea, show your listeners just how big with your hands. If you have three great ideas, hold up one finger as you start the first one, two when you get to the second, and three at the final idea. This will help you stay on point *and* help your listeners track and remember each of the three.

FUN TIP

This Is Going to Be Good

One of my favorite cues as a presenter is the "this is going to be good" cue. Rubbing your palms together in excited anticipation is a great way to get an audience excited. Taking off one's glasses or rolling up your sleeves can also have the same effect, signaling that you're really getting into the material.

Gesturing also helps us express ourselves more clearly. Try this little experiment with me: Tell me about your favorite childhood memory out loud . . . while sitting on your hands. It's tough, right? Our hands are outlets for our thinking. The more we use gestures, the more fluent we are in our explanations and stories. Gestures don't just help your listener; they help you as the speaker.

When researchers coded people telling stories, they found that the participants used both explanatory gestures and beats as they narrated.*

PRINCIPLE

Explanatory gestures help you explain and others understand.

WHEN TO GESTURE

- When you want to explain something well and have it understood thoroughly.
- To show you have confidence in what you're saying and are competent about your topic.
- To be more engaging on video calls or onstage. Gestures add a new dimension to your explanations.

WHEN NOT TO GESTURE

- If you don't want people to look at you, don't gesture. For example, I work with many engineers and folks who have to explain highly tech-

---

* See this in action in a video in your digital toolbox.

nical concepts. They often show slides. When you want someone to look at your graphic, video, or demo and not you, don't gesture as much. Gesturing will distract the watcher.

- If people are staring at your hands while gesturing, you might be over-demonstrating. **Gestures are your backup dancers.** They're best kept in the background to emphasize your verbal points, but they shouldn't steal the show.
- If people are ducking out of the way when you gesture, you're gesturing too much. Try holding a pen, clicker, or cup of water to keep your hands under control. Ever played baseball? Try to keep your hands within the strike zone—under your shoulders, above your waist, and no more than a foot out from your body.

FUN TIP

Hands at Rest

Some researchers have noted a gesture called **humility hands**. This is when someone has their hands relaxed in front of their body at waist level. You can do this standing or sitting. Kennedy did this for the entire first minute of his presidential debate. This is a positive cue you can use while listening to others—it shows your hands are relaxed and calm while still keeping your torso open.

POWER CUE #5: Palm Power

María Eva Duarte was born out of wedlock, in a poor rural village in the heart of Argentina in 1919. Nicknamed Evita, at sixteen she fled to Buenos Aires to pursue her dream of becoming a star.

While working at a local radio station, she met her future husband, Juan Perón, a government official. Evita began to help him campaign for an even bigger position: president of Argentina. She organized rallies, gave speeches to workers, and led mass demonstrations on his behalf.

Quickly she became a star in her own right. Perón won the election and Evita began to take on an even larger role in the government. She spearheaded workers' rights and helped secure women the right to vote in Argentina. Her speeches were attended by thousands of avid fans.

She became known for a signature nonverbal cue: **the palm flash**. Watch clips of Evita's speeches and you'll see dozens of palm flashes— from waves to blowing kisses to holding her arms over her head.* She used her palms to guide the audience, to quiet them down or rile them up as necessary.

On October 17, 1951, over a million people gathered to hear one of Evita's final speeches. She had just been diagnosed with the cancer that would kill her just a few months later. The speech was given at a rally for workers. She called for change, spoke out against injustice, and then, in what would become an iconic picture, lifted her hands above her head, opened up her palms, and stretched up toward the sky.

The speech would go on to become one of the most famous speeches in history. It was dramatized by Madonna in the movie *Evita* and was the inspiration for the song "Don't Cry for Me Argentina" by Andrew Lloyd Webber. And, interestingly, whenever Evita's story has been told, it's often accompanied by that famous **palm flash**.

Our palms are our biggest attention grabbers, and to be powerful, you need to command attention. When we want someone's attention across the room, we wave at them. When we want teachers to call on us, we raise our hand, palm faced toward them. When we want someone to stop, we hold up our palm in front of our body.

Palm flashes are more than just explanatory gestures; they cue for attention. We love to see a palm, so we're always on the lookout for them.

When we can see someone's palms, we know they are not concealing anything from us. An open palm is the opposite of a fist, so it demonstrates that there's no hidden anxiety or aggression.

A palm is also how we nonverbally acknowledge people. Ever thought someone was waving at you, wave back, and then realized they were waving at someone else? This is an embarrassing but very human mistake. We love to be acknowledged, so we're always on the lookout to see

---

* See clips of Evita's iconic speeches in your digital bonuses.

if someone is waving at us, beckoning us over, opening their palm for a handshake, or gesturing toward us.

When you flash your palms, people pay attention. We're hypersensitive to palm cues because we know the hands are our deadliest weapon. Researchers found that when we raise our palms, we activate our limbic system, specifically the amygdala, which is the defensive area of the brain. In other words, palm flashes cue our emotions. The mere sight of someone flashing a palm-up gesture triggers our own mirror neurons to feel as the other person feels. Viewing a palm flash activates our limbic system as if we were doing it ourselves.

Many powerful people punctuate speeches in Evita's signature pose—arms above head, palms exposed. Russian president Vladimir Putin often holds his hands high with palms toward the audience while speaking. Pope Francis holds his palms high when offering blessings. Famous boxers like Mike Tyson, Muhammad Ali, and Floyd Mayweather held their hands up high, palms toward the audience, after winning a match. **Winners typically expose their palms and reach them toward the sky.**

Since we're subconsciously hyperaware of palm cues, let's use them purposefully. Here are the most common palm flashing gestures and what they mean:

- **Pre-Handshake:** Hold your hand out with a palm up in a greeting and you're asking for a handshake.
- **Pre-Hug:** Hold both hands out with palms facing toward the other person and you're asking for a hug.
- **Get Excited:** Hold your hands up with palms facing up and move your hands up and down toward the sky and you're asking people to get excited, stand up, or cheer. (Think about the "raise the roof" gesture.)
- **Calm Down:** Hold your hands out with palms facing down and move your hands up and down toward the ground and you're asking people to calm down, sit down, or quiet down.
- **Stop:** Hold your hand up and show someone your palm and it means stop. This can signal for someone to stop coming closer or stop talking.

- **Tell Me More:** Hold your hands out with palms up and gesture toward someone to tell them you're open and want to hear more from them.
- **Let Me Explain This:** Hold out one hand with a palm up and gesture while speaking to punctuate you're explaining something. It's as if you are holding the idea in your hand as you explain it.
- **Here's the Whole Story:** Rotate your forearms so that your palms are facing toward each other and move them in and out to show that you're explaining or presenting an idea.

The single best way to showcase your palms is to flash them instead of pointing. **An open palm is an invitation, while a finger point is an accusation.** If you want someone to look at your slides, refer to their handout, view a graph, or look at something, use an open palm point.

Special Note: Have you noticed some of these palm gestures might fall outside the ideal strike zone discussed in the last power cue? Here's my rule of thumb: **The bigger the room, the bigger you can gesture.** When you are in a meeting, on a date, or sitting with friends, the strike zone is ideal. In bigger spaces like conference rooms, ballrooms, or onstage, larger gestures are more acceptable. I doubt Evita used her iconic arms up, palms up gesture when having an intimate tête-à-tête with a diplomat. But onstage in front of thousands? It worked perfectly.

PRINCIPLE

Show your palm to cue attention.

These palm gestures are not hard to decode; in fact, many of them you probably recognized instinctively. My goal is to help you *encode* them more purposefully.

Palm cues can speak for you. Palm cues are the most powerful when used as a substitute for speech or to emphasize a verbal point. Here's how:

- **The "Call on Me" Cue:** You want to speak up in a meeting but can't seem to find an opening. Flash your palm to the group. This will subtly cue that you would like to say something so people turn toward you.

- **The "Giving" Cue:** You have a great idea for someone. In fact, it's so good, it's practically a gift of knowledge. You want them to know this. As you build up to your idea in a presentation, hold out one of your hands as if offering something to them and say, "Here's the idea I really want to share with you." It will spark their attention that something good is on offer.

- **The Hand Shrug Cue:** Someone is explaining something complex to you, but you want someone to slow down and clarify. Hold open both of your palms and shrug in a subtle but clear "I don't understand" gesture. This cues the other person that they need to clarify (and is much more polite than interrupting).

- **The "Let Me Explain This" Cue:** You have a highly technical pitch you're giving to a client or colleague. You have slides, charts, and graphs on a projector in the front of the room, but you also need to explain each one in depth. When you're speaking and want people looking your way, use explanatory gestures. When you want people to pay attention to the slides, open palm gesture toward the screen in front. This cues people to know exactly where they should be looking and when. It also makes you look highly competent and puts you more in control of the flow of information.

WHEN NOT TO PALM FLASH

- **If you're concealing something.** If you're trying not to be noticed and don't want to be questioned, hide your palms. It's a subtle signal to help people leave you be.

- **If you're all palms, all the time.** People love to see your palms, but constantly holding them up to the world might be inauthentic. Use palm flashes purposefully, not constantly.

POWER CUE #6: How to Nicely
Get Someone to Stop Interrupting You

Do people interrupt you? Or do you struggle with droners? Those people who just drone on and on and on . . . and never stop talking?

Powerful people are able to subtly and politely control the flow of conversation through nonverbal cues. Here are my favorite cues to get someone to stop talking, starting with the least aggressive and ending with some serious interventions.*

The Fish

Let's say you're talking to someone who just won't stop chattering. One way to get them to stop talking is to open your mouth about an inch and let it stay open for a few seconds, making a face like a fish. We intuitively know that when someone opens their mouth to say something, we should stop talking.

When you open your mouth, it indicates subtly that you have something to say and you're just waiting for others to pause. The simple act of slightly opening your mouth will often get people to wrap up and give you a turn to speak. You can also use the fish if someone interrupts you

---

* See my video demonstrating these techniques in your digital bonuses.

and you were not finished. When interrupted, we often snap our mouth shut in frustration. It's better to let it hang open for a few seconds to show them nonverbally you were mid-sentence or mid-thought.

The Bookmark

I have a frequent interrupter in my life. He looks for any opportunity to jump in with his thoughts. It became so bad that if I paused for a second to catch my breath, he interrupted. That made me rush to get out my thoughts, speaking faster and faster in the hopes of preventing his interruption. It was exhausting. Then I learned an easy little nonverbal cue: the **bookmark**.

When you're speaking to someone who you know interrupts but you need to pause for a breath or a thought, hold up your hand or finger, palm toward them. This subtle stop gesture is like adding a little bookmark to your thoughts. You're saying nonverbally, "Wait, I'm not done. Hold right there."

You can also do this with a droner. If they're talking incessantly, try holding up your hand in the bookmark pose. It's a nice way to ask them to pause so you can get a word in. The movement of your hand should also draw the other person's attention to you and get their thoughts off themselves, serving as a reminder that "someone else is in this conversation too!"

The bookmark works especially well when you pair it with the fish.

The Anchor Touch

Are they *still* talking? Let's turn it up a notch to what I call the **anchor touch**. Sometimes someone gets so into their story and in their head, they're literally in another universe. It's as if their head is in the clouds and you need to bring them back down to earth. To do this, you have to anchor them.

You can anchor someone by reaching out and slightly touching their hand, forearm, upper arm, or shoulder. It's a light touch as if to say, *I'm still here! My turn, please.*

This gesture pulls people out of their monologue, because while they may not pay attention to your facial expressions or gestures, they *will* notice if you touch them. Even people who love to talk will usually become silent for a moment when they're touched. Use that moment of silence to jump in and say your piece . . . or say goodbye.

FUN TIP

The Preview Technique

If you know you're about to have a conversation with a droner or an interrupter, you can discourage them from overtalking by telling them what you need to convey ahead of time. For example, if you have three points you need to make, tell them you have three things to say. Then hold up your fingers as you go through each one. You can also preview by saying something like "I want to tell you about a big idea, so it might take me a minute to explain it." This lets them know they need to give you a little more time to explain.

Create a Powerful Presence

If warm cues wow, power cues add that extra pow. Combined, they create a memorable presence.

Researchers in 2014 studied highly charismatic leaders and found they use nonverbal cues to move, inspire, or captivate others. And their presence is contagious. **Their confidence breeds confidence in others.**

They're also characterized by their ability to both **decode** the emotional needs of others and **encode** the right cues to inspire and spur emotion in others.

When the researchers showed videotaped speeches of leaders to participants and asked them to rate the speakers on their charisma, they found that the highest-rated speakers blended both competence cues and warmth cues. They:

- Used dynamic hand and body gestures.
- Showed more erect posture.
- Maintained eye contact, especially at the end of statements.
- Had a more open body and didn't engage in blocking behaviors.
- Nodded more.
- Were more emotionally expressive through their facial expressions, gestures, and tone of voice (there will be more on this in the section on vocal cues).
- Invited others to speak up.
- Sat at the head of the table.
- Had a greater repertoire of cues and strategies to express themselves.
- Touched themselves less but touched others more.

One of my clients—let's call him Dave—leads an international supply chain team of thousands. Every week he meets with his managers to talk about goals for the week. He told me these meetings had gotten stale. People straggled in late, leaving Dave stalling for time until people arrived. There wasn't much engagement when he asked for feedback on new projects. He suspected people were checking email while he presented important changes in the business.

Together, we watched a Zoom recording of a recent meeting he led. We immediately noticed a number of missed opportunities that could have reinvigorated these important gatherings.

At the start of the meeting, Dave slipped into the room, head bowed, laptop in front of his chest in blocking behavior. While waiting for people to arrive, Dave checked his phone in a low power posture. He didn't acknowledge people as they trickled in.

Once the meeting started, Dave quickly clicked through his slides, aiming his gestures back toward the slides behind him. Instead of looking at his audience, he barely glanced up, the glow of his laptop screen illuminating his face. When he wasn't clicking through slides, his hands were mostly hidden in his lap under the table.

And we counted, Dave smiled only once . . . for a colleague's birthday.

The meeting wasn't terrible, it was just boring and sterile. Dave's presence wasn't offensive or aggressive, it was forgettable.

He needed a presence reset. We identified some simple cues he could employ comfortably to reset these meetings.

We started by turning his forgettable entrance into a grand entrance. He was the person leading the meeting, so it needed to start when he entered. No more waiting. His lingering starts were encouraging people to show up late and cued low energy and low impact.

At the very next meeting, Dave walked in with his laptop *at his side* and waved to everyone as he walked in. He smiled broadly and said, "Good morning!"

As he passed people, he touched their shoulder and said hello. He made eye contact with those across the room and offered personal acknowledgments to all the participants.

Dave took his seat, plugged in his computer, and pushed it to the side—no longer blocking his view to everyone else in the room. "Today we have a few things on the agenda, but let's start with a quick update from everyone. Tell me how you're doing and what projects you're tackling this week."

We decided the best way to make purposeful eye contact would be to start with quick updates from each person. This worked on multiple levels. First, it would get everyone off their email. Second, if there were latecomers, they wouldn't miss anything crucial as everyone shared their updates. Third, it allowed him to gaze, lean toward, and front with each person as they spoke. Dave also felt comfortable in the steeple gesture as he listened to people's answers.

For the slides portion of the meeting, we got him a remote to switch his slides, so Dave was freer to gesture. He thought it would be too awkward to stand and present while everyone was sitting, so instead we had him roll his chair to the center of the table, so his computer was off to the side. This opened up his body language, allowed him to gesture more, and made it easy to turn and front with people as he delivered.

We added two surprise laughter moments into his slides: a funny meme to kick off and a customer service story to end. This created laughter for everyone. On a few technical slides we added some helpful explanatory gestures to aid in comprehension.

At the very end of the presentation, Dave invited people to ask questions. This usually didn't go very well. But this time he put down his clicker and opened up his palms to the room. "I'd love to hear from you."

Dave looked at one of his top engineers and asked, "Sarah, I would especially like to hear what you think about the new model. Anything I missed?" He raised his eyebrows and leaned in toward her.

This opened up a table-wide discussion on the issue, with Dave directing the conversation with open palm gestures and head tilts. He nodded to encourage one introverted colleague to keep going on an important issue. Overall, the meeting had a completely different feel. People shared more, discussed more, and stayed off their laptops. Most important, Dave *felt* more empowered as a leader. He knew exactly what he needed to do to encourage his team and inspire confidence. He stopped second-guessing himself. He knew where to put his hands, where to stand, and how to engage people—especially his introverts. His own confidence inspired their confidence.

After the meeting, one of his engineers messaged him, "That was a GREAT meeting. Loved it!" This had never happened before. It was the start of many great meetings to come.

How's your presence? Do you inspire competence? Warmth? Charisma? You now have a portfolio of cues to use to hit your charisma sweet spot.

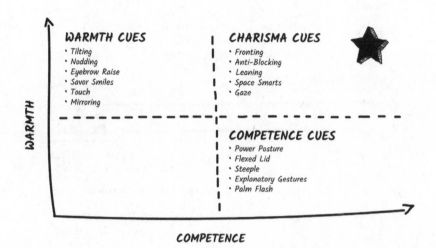

CHAPTER CHALLENGE

Let's expand our Cues Chart to put these competence cues into action.

CUE	DECODE	ENCODE	INTERNALIZE
Power Posture	Do you notice certain people get smaller around you? Bigger?	Try standing a few inches wider. Try rolling your shoulders down. Do you feel more confident?	Do certain people, places, or topics make you contract in anxiety? Expand in confidence? Stick to what gives you confidence.
Lower Lid Flex	Try to spot three lower lid flexes in your conversations or media. What were they trying to understand better?	Try a lower lid flex to encourage someone.	When you use the lower lid flex, does it make you feel more curious or more judgmental? Try to keep it positive.

CUE	DECODE	ENCODE	INTERNALIZE
Steepling	Does anyone in your life steeple their hands? Do any of your favorite characters use the steeple on TV or in movies?	Try to steeple in at least three different situations— maybe on a video call, with a friend, or in a meeting. How does it feel?	Does steepling make you feel silly or strong? You decide if it works for you!
Explanatory Gestures	Who in your life over-gestures? Who under-gestures?	Try to add more purposeful gestures to your elevator pitch.	Are you overly conscious of your hands when you speak? Don't be! It's enough to find a few gestures you like and then keep it natural.
Palm Flashing	Can you think of any pop culture examples of people flashing their palms?	Do you use the palm flash? Try to do three this week.	Does exposing your palm make you feel vulnerable or powerful? Find the palm flashes that work for you.

CHAPTER 6

How to Spot a Bad Guy . . .
and Not Be One Yourself

On August 25, 2005, Tour de France champion cyclist Lance
Armstrong appeared on *Larry King Live* to convince the public
he wasn't doping. I listened to his words, watched his quasi-
sincere expressions, and thought, *This guy is hiding something.*

I didn't know why I had that feeling at the time, but Armstrong was
leaking all kinds of negative nonverbal cues and my gut was picking up
on them.

A few minutes into the interview, Armstrong told a bald-faced lie
about his use of performance-enhancing drugs. "That's crazy," he said. "I
would never do that . . . that's . . . no. No way." And he then pressed his
mouth into a hard line forming a cue called a **lip purse**.

A lip purse indicates suppressing or hiding one's true feelings. When
we're hesitant to say something, we press our lips together as if to force
ourselves to "keep it in!"

Eight years later Armstrong finally admitted to his massive undercover doping scheme dating back to the nineties.

The lip purse cue falls squarely in the Danger Zone. Cues in the
Danger Zone are red flags indicating the possibility of something nega-

Larry King Live, CNN

tive. If you see them, they warrant further investigation. They signal anxiety, boredom, confusion, defensiveness, close-mindedness, incompetence, or aggression. Always be on the lookout to **decode** and address these cues, while also making sure not to **encode** them yourself.

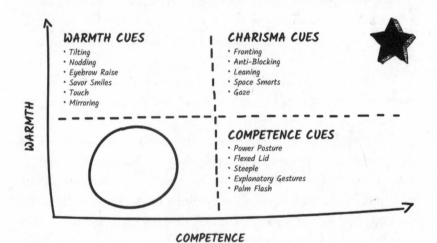

Lie to Me

Have you ever wondered what happens to your body language when you lie? If you leak any tells? Now's the time to find out.

Let's play a little game I call Lie to Me. You'll need five minutes and a way to film yourself.

Sit in a well-lit spot so your camera can record your face, hands, and upper body clearly. Open the camera on your phone or computer and hit record.

STOP HERE UNTIL YOU'RE READY TO RECORD. DO NOT PREVIEW THE QUESTIONS BEFORE HITTING RECORD.

Ready? Okay, please look at your camera and answer the following questions out loud. Pretend you're going to send this video to me to decode. That is to say, speak in full sentences, make sure the lighting is decent (we'll be looking at small signals on your face), and pretend you're really talking to someone. If you can't immediately think of an answer, that's okay—**don't pause the recording**. What you do while you *think* about your answer is just as important to code. Think of your answers as quickly as possible.

Answer the following questions into the camera:

QUESTION #1: What did you have for breakfast yesterday?

QUESTION #2: What is your most embarrassing moment? Please share the full story with as many details as possible.

QUESTION #3: Make up an embarrassing story that did not really happen to you. When you're ready, tell it to the camera in as convincing a manner as possible.

Done? Great job! Save the video and we'll review it at the end of the chapter.

The first question is a *recall* task. The goal is to see what you look like when you remember a truth that is not embarrassing or stressful but just factual.

The second question is an *embarrassing recall* question. The goal is to see what you look like when remembering a truth that's slightly embarrassing or anxiety provoking.

The third question is your lie.

At the end of the chapter, we'll code the nonverbal cues in each to see how you express yourself when recalling, embarrassed, and lying.

We've had hundreds of people play this on our website and send in their Lie to Me video. My amazing team and I have spent countless hours coding the videos looking for patterns. We've found that no one cue signals someone is lying—and the research backs this up. Unluckily for us, there's no Pinocchio's nose in real life.

However, some cues do signal anxiety, shame, and guilt. When you see these cues, it's important to note that they don't necessarily denote lies but rather are red flags that should be investigated further.

DANGER CUE #1: Distancing

"I am not a crook. I've earned everything I've got," said President Richard Nixon at a press conference on November 17, 1973.

Of course, as it turns out, that famous line was a lie. Nixon was very much involved in the Watergate criminal conspiracy.

I'd always heard this line but never seen it myself. But when you watch the original footage of Nixon delivering this line, you'll notice an interesting nonverbal cue.* Immediately after saying it, he takes a large step back from the podium.

This is a **distancing cue**. When we don't like something, we have the urge to physically distance ourselves from it. When we think something is threatening or dangerous, we want to get as far away from it as possible.

And you know what's really dangerous? Telling lies. Deception gets us into trouble. It makes us feel guilt and shame and fear—emotions physically distressing to our body.

One of the first cues my team and I noticed in the Lie to Me videos was that on question 3, the lying question, people tended to lean back away from the camera, scoot their chair back, or turn their head away while they lied (or prepared to lie).

---

* See your digital toolbox at scienceofpeople.com/bonus for the clip.

Always be on the lookout for sudden distancing behaviors, like:

- Stepping back
- Leaning back in a chair
- Turning your head or body away
- Scooting back
- Turning away to check your phone
- Angling backward

Distancing is a subtle signal that someone has said, seen, or heard something that didn't sit right with them.

Of course we also need to make sure *you* are not accidentally distancing. Others won't respond well when they sense that you are pulling or turning away. **Physical distancing can trigger emotional distance.** The most charismatic people are stable, present, and engaged. They front, they lean in, they get closer. Distancing is the opposite of those positive cues.

Not only does distancing make you less charismatic, it can also negatively impact the people you are with. In one study, physical therapists were videotaped while they were working with clients. They found that the physical therapists who exhibited negative nonverbal cues—specifically looking away and not smiling directly at their patients—had a negative effect on their patient's *health* outcomes. The more distancing the physical therapists demonstrated, the worse their clients' physical and cognitive functioning was at discharge *and* three months later! The physical therapists who nodded, smiled, and leaned in had better client outcomes.

I've noticed people tend to distance accidentally. This happens in two ways.

First, **phubbing**. Phubbing (a word that combines *phone* and *snubbing*) is when you ignore the person you are with by turning away to check your phone. Not only is this *super* rude, research finds it also makes you appear less trustworthy. It lands you squarely in the Danger Zone.

The second way we accidentally distance can occur while you are presenting, giving a toast, or standing in front of a room. In our Powerful Presentations course, I asked students to send in videos of presentations that didn't go well—you know, those moments you wish you could've done over? A frequent pattern we encountered was that nervous presenters often got in front of the room, delivered their first line, then took a step back or leaned on their back foot. This forced them to deliver their first few points while they were rocking back and forth from their back foot to their front foot, making them look unsure.

This was a double hit for their charisma. That backward distancing signaled a lack of connection with the audience and made them look unstable. It was also distracting.

Another accidental flub? We noticed presenters making excellent points . . . while their back was facing the audience. Presenters would turn to draw things on the board or gesture to slides behind them by turning their back on the audience, so they ended up fronting with their slides instead of their people.

Here's how to avoid these negative cues:

- Before you start, pick one spot on the floor to deliver your opener. Walk to it and plant.
- Avoid nervous feet—the step back, the hop side to side, the shuffle— or standing on the edge of your feet.
- Always use a remote to change slides so you can click without having to turn around or hunch over a computer.
- Try to memorize the order of your slides and notes so you don't have to keep checking behind you or turning toward your monitor to see what's up next.
- When you need audience members to look at your slides or a board behind you, move to one side and practice the open palm gesture.
- If you're drawing on a whiteboard or screen, try to save your important points for when you're done or take a break from drawing to make the point while facing the audience.
- If you're sitting while talking to people, try to use a chair that swivels to make it easy to turn. If you do choose a swivel chair, be sure not to accidentally swivel away (or wiggle in your chair).
- Do you have a tendency to step backward while presenting? I've seen

nervous presenters end up with their back practically to the wall after presentations! To avoid this, put water, your notes, or your computer on a table in the area you want to present from. That will keep you anchored toward the front.

Have you ever blanked out in a presentation? Or lost your place? While taking a step back can be damaging for interpersonal relationships, it can be helpful for *you* when you are trying to figure something out. A group of researchers found that when people take a literal step back from an overwhelming project, they feel more capable and in control.

When you have a blank-out moment, just take a step back to gather your thoughts. Move back, catch your breath, take a sip of water, and then step forward when you're ready to get back on track.

Can't figure something out? Can't think of that word? If you're alone at your desk, try scooting back or stepping back. The enhanced physical space can create more mental space.

PRINCIPLE

Physical distance can create emotional distance. Don't turn away, turn toward. Don't step back, move in.

WHEN YOU MIGHT SEE DISTANCING

- You said or did something that made someone nervous or uncomfortable.
- Someone just lied and they want to get as far away from that trouble as possible.
- When someone is distracted by their phone, screen, computer, or slides behind them.

WHAT TO DO IF YOU SEE DISTANCING

- **Research:** What was the trigger that caused someone to distance? What's the reason *you* distanced?

- **Resolve:** Add clarification, clear up confusion, and get back on the same page.
- **Rapport:** Find something you can both lean in to. Find a reason to bond, connect, and turn toward.

DANGER CUE #2: Self-Comfort

Britney Spears is on *Dateline* and is getting grilled about her second husband, Kevin Federline. It's 2006 and they already have a nine-month-old son. Spears is pregnant again.

The interviewer asks Spears about how their relationship began. Immediately Spears sits back in a distancing gesture.

She proceeds to pull both hands up to her forehead and pull her hair out of her face. This is a ventilating gesture. **Ventilation** is an attempt to draw airflow to the skin to prevent nervous sweat. People "ventilate" by lifting their hair, pulling their collar away from their neck, or fanning themselves.

One second later, Spears begins to rhythmically rub the side of her calf with her hand. This is a **comfort gesture**.

Research finds that we self-touch more when we are talking about anxiety-producing topics. Think of parents with small children—moms rub a baby's back and dads pat heads to calm kids down. Even after we reach adulthood, this desire for soothing remains, and we self-touch by rubbing our neck, wringing our hands, or stroking our legs to calm ourselves. Touch produces oxytocin, which makes us feel calm and connected.

Comfort gestures like biting nails and sucking on pens are called **pacification** gestures because, like a pacifier, they can be used to soothe anxiety. We also pacify by biting our lips or sucking on the inside of our cheeks. All of this reminds us of having a pacifier or a bottle in our mouth—which felt very comforting indeed.

We can also comfort ourselves by **preening**. This is when we use self-touch to make ourselves look better—either purposefully or out of habit. We touch our hair, fix our makeup, or fidget with our clothes. Spears's attempt to push her hair out of her face might also have been a preening cue.

Flirty Preen

Preening is not always a Danger Zone cue. It can also signal flirtation. One study found that women preen more than men and typically do it in new or developing relationships. Women do not preen as much when they're already paired with someone. This could be because preening is a way to boost self-esteem, improve physical appearance (straighten clothes, comb hair, or fix makeup), or even call attention to physical features by touching lips or hair. If you don't see any other Danger Zone cues, you might be the target of someone's romantic interest!

Here are some common comfort gestures you'll see:

- Rubbing arms or wringing hands
- Rubbing the back of the neck
- Stroking thighs or calves
- Cracking knuckles
- Biting nails or pens
- Sucking on cheek or biting lips

Another type of comfort gesture is a comfort movement. This is when people sway back and forth, rock onto their toes, jiggle their feet, or pace. Again, parents rocked us to sleep, bounced us when our tummies hurt, and paced our bedrooms to get us to calm down. As adults, we try to do it for ourselves as well. It's why a rocking chair is so relaxing. You might notice presenters swaying back and forth as they deliver their points—this is an unconscious way of keeping themselves calm.

The nose touch is another unique self-touch gesture. Something happens to your nose when you lie. Your nose won't grow like Pinocchio's, but it might itch. Psychiatrists used thermographic cameras and found that when people lie, their nose actually heats up! This can cause nerve endings to tingle, which is why people may have the instinct to touch or scratch their nose while lying.

Researchers Alan Hirsch and Charles Wolf dissected Bill Clinton's testimony in the Monica Lewinsky trial and found that when he lied, he touched his nose twenty-six times.

Self-touch gestures negatively impact your charisma on two levels. First, comfort gestures make you look anxious. **Study after study finds that comfort gestures, fidgets, and extraneous movements make you look less charismatic.**

Powerful people don't waste energy on purposeless movements. They gesture to explain, they lean in to emphasize, they're still unless they have a reason to move.

And this brings me to the second reason comfort gestures are so damaging: Self-touch or comfort movements are distracting to others. Our eye is drawn to motion. If you're talking but also cracking your knuckles or stroking your leg, people find it hard to give full attention to your words. If you're pacing back and forth, people find it difficult to focus on your words and not your body. Comfort cues detract from the quality of your message.

Self-soothing gestures also make your *audience* nervous. One team of researchers found that when speakers were fidgety onstage, it raised the cortisol levels of the audience members watching them! Remember the Cue Cycle? Our nonverbal cues are contagious. **Your nervous gestures inspire nervousness.**

Okay, so you know comfort gestures are damaging to your charisma, but how do you stop them? If you're a fidgeter, pacer, or nail biter, you'll find it hard to stop. I know this because pacing is one of my nonverbal vices. Instead of trying to quit cold turkey, I encourage you to use what I call **displacement tactics.**

When we're anxious, we pace to give our legs something to do. We fidget because we don't know what to do with our hands and need a way to work out the anxiousness. Displacement tactics help you focus on something mentally and give your body something to do physically. Here are some ideas:

- Hold a pen or pencil.
- Use a clicker—this has helped me so much as a presenter! It allows me to front more with my audience and limits my extraneous gestures.
- Carry a mug of tea or coffee. I do this at networking events. I leave the hand I use for shaking free but carry a drink in the other. This helps me fidget less.
- Lean against a podium to stop from swaying.
- Make your hairstyle fluff proof. I had bangs for a month but had to grow them out because I was constantly pushing them out of my face.
- Don't wear jewelry or clothes that require adjustments.

FUN TIP

Thumb Hold

I once was interviewed by a news anchor while we were standing in a big open pavilion. This was my first standing interview and I kept swaying back and forth. The reporter gave me a trick to stop myself from swaying on-camera. She told me to put my hands by my sides and press my thumb and index finger together and to hold it during the interview. I was shocked that this trick actually worked! It also prevented me from using jazz hands (I tend to be an over-gesturer). It's invisible to others and really works!

PRINCIPLE

Comfort gestures distract and detract from your charisma.

WHEN YOU MIGHT SEE SELF-COMFORTING
- If someone is anxious, doubtful, or uncomfortable.
- If someone is a habitual fidgeter or preener.
- In hands—wringing hands or cracking knuckles. Near the mouth— biting lips, sucking cheeks, or biting pens. On the neck—rubbing or playing with jewelry.

- **Research:** What did you say to make someone nervous? Are they fidgeting from anxiety or is it just a nervous habit? Some people's comfort gestures are merely habitual. If someone continually displays the same nonverbal tic, try to ignore it (or tell them how to stop by giving them this book).
- **Resolve:** Do you notice someone stops fidgeting when you do, say, or address something? I was once talking to a colleague who was playing with her earring. I didn't think much of it until she stopped the moment I mentioned our New Year launch. Her *stopping* the cue made me aware that I had hit something important. After some digging, I realized she had been very nervous about the end-of-the-year rush and was hoping to ask for some extra help.
- **Rapport:** Do you make someone nervous? Get to know them more. Find commonalities. Help them feel heard with warmth cues— mirror them, smile encouragingly, use the eyebrow raise.

DANGER CUE #3: Block It Out

Michelle Poler conquered a hundred fears . . . and filmed every single one. She skydived, got a bikini wax, and ate spicy food.

When she posted her fear-conquering videos to YouTube, they went viral. Her courage started a movement, inspiring others to conquer their own fears. I took part in one of her episodes—helping Michelle conquer her fear of talking to strangers. We filmed a video of us together walking through the streets of New York handing out flowers.

I love watching Michelle's videos because they're inspiring and a great nonverbal snapshot of what someone looks like right *before* they're about to do something that makes them feel afraid.

In one hilarious episode, Michelle got her first bikini wax. You see her enter the room and touch her **suprasternal notch**. This is the indent right between your two collarbones. She does it again when she lies down on the table.

People often touch this spot or fiddle with something *near* the notch—a necklace, tie, or scarf—when they want to calm themselves down. It makes us feel safe to have our hand over our heart, chest, and neck, the most vulnerable parts of our body.

Michelle also displays what I call a **fear smile.** She is smiling and showing the whites of her eyes. This is a Danger Zone cue because it is incongruent and often happens when someone is trying to smile to hide their nerves. Sometimes people accidentally do this in their profile photos (especially if they hate having their photo taken). Check your profile photos to make sure you're not showing the upper whites of your eyes. It will only distract from your smile.

FUN TIP

Notch to Calm

Be careful not to touch your suprasternal notch absentmindedly. It's distracting and signals anxiety. However, it can be used if you need to calm down quickly. I teach my students in my speaking class that if they have anxiety before speaking, one way they can calm down quickly is to stroke this notch. Weird, but it works.

Touching the suprasternal notch is also a **blocking gesture.** We learned about anti-blocking in chapter 3. Blocking our body with our arms, our hands, or a prop like a computer or notebook makes us feel protected but signals close-mindedness. We block when threatened or uncomfortable to protect our most vulnerable areas.

There are three types of blocking gestures, and Michelle exhibits all of them:

- **Body blocking** protects our heart, lungs, and abdomen. In Michelle's videos, she gives herself self-hugs, puts an arm in front of her chest, touches her suprasternal notch, and clutches items in front of her body.
- **Mouth blocking** protects our only mechanism for consuming nutrition and water (and our best way to communicate). When people are

afraid, they often bring their hands up to their mouth or clap their hand over their mouth. This is a mouth block. Biting nails is both a mouth block and a comfort gesture. This is why people have such a hard time breaking that habit!

- **Eye blocking** shields our eyes from harm. Receivers of bad news will often cover their face or eyes with their hands or pull their glasses off to rub at their eyes in exasperation. Subconsciously they're trying to block out what they just received *and* give themselves a moment to process. It's like shutting everything out to give yourself time to think. Rubbing the eyelids stimulates a special nerve in the eyelids called the vagus nerve, which helps slow down heart and breathing rates when it's massaged. A quick eye touch is one of the fastest ways to calm down.

Michelle actually has an entire playlist of fears related to pain. Unsurprisingly, these have the most eye and mouth blocking. When we are experiencing pain, it's all we can focus on, so we want to literally block out the rest of the world. And we mouth block when we are in pain—biting on our knuckles, covering our mouth, sucking on our lips because we're trying to stifle the urge to scream. Yikes!

FUN TIP

Let Me See You

When you want to bond, try purposefully taking off your glasses. You're subtly saying, "I want to see you clearly and have no barriers between us." Of course, if you need glasses to actually see the other person, be sure to keep them on! But if you use them for reading, make a point of removing them at the start of an interaction as if to show, "I want to see you."

An increased **blink rate** is another kind of eye block. Research finds that our blink rate speeds up when we're nervous. This shields out potential threats but also gives us time to think.

One researcher coded President Nixon's blink rate during the Watergate hearings and found that his blink rate increased significantly when he was asked a question he was not prepared to answer.

To see this in action, watch Britney Spears in her *Dateline* interview. When Spears was asked if she was concerned about her husband cheating, she fluttered her eyes in a rapid series of blinks and took a deep breath before answering. That question made her very nervous indeed.

Be sure to decode sudden blocks and put people at ease when you think something has made them nervous or uncomfortable.

Most important, **don't encode your own anxiety with accidental blocks**. These cues will immediately drop you into the Danger Zone.

PRINCIPLE

We block our bodies, eyes, and mouths to protect ourselves.

WHEN YOU MIGHT SEE BLOCKING

- If someone's feeling anxious, upset, or uncomfortable.
- If someone needs time to think and block everything else out.
- If someone just heard something surprising, negative, or threatening.

WHAT TO DO IF YOU SEE BLOCKING

- **Research:** Be on the lookout for sudden blocks. This is usually a signal that someone needs a little extra reassurance. You just need to find out why and how you can help.
- **Resolve:** Once you know the cause of someone's anxiety, you have a choice: soothe or solve. Can you help quell their anxiety? Can you solve their problem?
- **Rapport:** Can't solve or soothe? Give them space. Sometimes people like to process anxiety on their own.

DANGER CUE #4: The Signal of Shame

On July 3, 2005, comedian and actor George Lopez pulled up to his home in Los Angeles, California. A city official, eight workmen, and two tractors were waiting for him.

According to the city official, Lopez had missed five letters from the city claiming his property was breaking code and they would need to tear down an entire room in his home. Lopez protested and argued. He questioned and begged, but the work crew was ready. There was no solution. The tractor began knocking down a wall in the front yard.

Moments before the tractor reached the house, actor Ashton Kutcher came running down the street with cameras. The city official and workmen were all actors in an elaborate ruse to fool Lopez for the TV prank show *Punk'd*.

Upon seeing Kutcher and hearing about the joke, Lopez immediately put both hands on his forehead and looked down. This is the quintessential **shame cue**. When we feel ashamed, we lightly touch our forehead with our fingers or hands. It is often accompanied by a look down or a tilt of the head down.

Watch any prank show and you'll see it the moment the joke is revealed. It's a combination eye block and self-soothing gesture. When we feel shame, we try to block it out. We do this by averting our gaze, looking down, and touching our fingers to our forehead in order to shield our face from the offending information or person. This is also a way to cover our embarrassed facial reaction.

Once I learned the shame cue, I was shocked at how often I saw it in everyday interactions. Here are the most common scenarios in which you might spot shame:

- **Talking about money.** I often see the shame gesture when people are discussing financial matters. Talking about money embarrasses us. If you see this cue, take special note! You now possess an incredible piece of insider information—money is sensitive or emotionally charged for this person. Keep it simple, put it in writing, and try to give them advance warning of any money discussions.

- **Lack of knowledge or confusion.** People often show shame when confused. Ask a colleague about their timeline on a new project and see the shame gesture? They might be confused or embarrassed about the project, the timeline, or an aspect of the work.
- **Too much information, too soon.** I really love deep, long, intimate conversations (and walks on the beach), but not everyone does. Sometimes I find that I ask introverts personal questions too soon. If I overstep and ask too many questions, I often see the shame gesture. Then I know to slow down and verbally back up.
- **Someone made a mistake.** When people make a mistake, they often use the shame touch. This might happen when you call them out on their mistake OR when they realize they've made one, which might be before you realize it! I've caught mistakes early by noticing someone's shame touch at their own internal realization.

Shame is one of the most powerful cues to spot because it's an indication that you're close to the Danger Zone. Shame, in itself, is not a bad cue, but it is a leading indicator that you might be stumbling into a topic, an idea, or a scenario that is making someone nervous. **Shame means you're entering the Danger Zone!** If you see it, tread lightly.

> **PRINCIPLE**
>
> **The shame touch is a signal flare of nervousness.**

WHEN YOU MIGHT SEE SHAME
- When you've embarrassed someone.
- When you've stumbled onto a topic that's too personal or too much. This happens more frequently with introverts.
- When someone is confused or worried and doesn't know how to talk about it.

WHAT TO DO IF YOU SEE SHAME
- **Research:** Did you say or do something that made someone feel embarrassed, ashamed, or confused? Find out what!

- **Resolve:** Welcome shame with open arms. Don't shame shame! If you don't honor shame, it can force someone to close up, withdraw, and lose trust in *you*. Work out shame by offering reassurance and acceptance.
- **Rapport:** One of the best ways to soothe shame is to share a mutual vulnerability. I once spotted shame on a new team member when we were reviewing our highly technical email software. I immediately went into reassurance mode. "You know what? This took me *months* to learn. You've gotten so far in the last few days. You got this! And we'll be here to help as you learn." It turned a shame moment into a bonding moment.

DANGER CUE #5: Are You Okay?

I have a problem. I have what's called RBF, or resting bothered face. My face looks downright perturbed when I feel completely neutral.

Ever had someone ask you if you're mad when you're perfectly fine?

Or tell you that you look tired even when you had a long night's sleep?

I feel you!

RESTING BOTHERED FACE

Looking a little irritated, down, or mad even
when you're completely fine.

What does your face look like when you are thinking? Listening? Working? This matters more than you think. As humans, we're very attuned to others' faces, constantly scanning them for cues. Faces give us a wealth of information—not only does someone's facial expression tell us what *they* are thinking, it can also tell us what *to* think.

If you don't like something, maybe we won't like it either.

If you're afraid, maybe we should be afraid too.

We constantly scan the faces of people around us to look for hidden clues for what to think and feel. This behavior starts at a very early age.

One researcher had parents hold their one-year-old baby on their laps. He then put two boxes on the table in front of them so the baby could see both him and the boxes.

First, the researcher opened one of the boxes and reacted with an expression of happiness. He made sure the baby saw his reaction but not what was in the box. Then he opened the second box and showed a negative expression. Again, the baby could see only the researcher's face.

Then the researcher put both boxes in front of the baby. He found that *all* the babies immediately reached into the happiness-provoking box but avoided the disgust-provoking box. **We learn what we want to engage with by observing people's facial expressions.**

Three negative facial expressions contribute the most to resting bothered face.*

1. **Anger:** When angry, we pull our eyebrows down into a furrow. This creates two vertical lines in between the eyebrows.

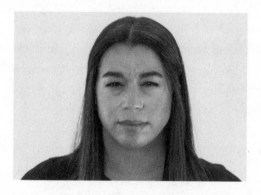

The muscle that pulls your eyebrows down and together is called the corrugator supercilii. It's used to express a variety of negative emotions from anger to worry to confusion, so we recognize the furrowed brow as something negative. If your resting face includes a furrowed brow—and many people do activate the corrugator supercilii in concentration—others might think you're bothered.

---

* Dr. Paul Ekman has discovered seven universal facial expressions: happiness, contempt, fear, sadness, disgust, surprise, and anger. I have an entire chapter dedicated to them in my book *Captivate.*

Here's where this gets more interesting: A furrowed brow doesn't just look negative, it *feels* negative.

Researchers find that when they force people to furrow their brow, this act actually generates more negative emotions. **A furrowed brow makes us less happy, less agreeable, and less engaged overall.**

Talk about motivation to relax those brows!

FUN TIP

Botox

Incredibly, research found that people who use Botox to numb their furrow muscles feel less angry and irritable. When your muscles physically can't make the face of anger, you actually feel less angry. However, if people Botox their smile lines, they also feel less joy.

- **Encoding anger:** Look in a mirror while concentrating. Do you see two vertical lines in between your eyebrows? To avoid resting bothered face, try keeping your brows relaxed.

FUN TIP

The Sun!

Do a quick check of your profile photos. Are you furrowing your brow? Sometimes taking pictures in the sun can accidentally cause you to furrow your brow, making you look angry to anyone viewing your profile. **Researchers actually studied this and found that sun-induced frowning uses the same facial muscles as anger.** When participants walked in the sun without sunglasses, they felt angrier and more aggressive compared to those who wore sunglasses. That furrow is powerful!

- **Decoding anger:** Always be on the lookout for a furrowed brow. Is it their concentration face? Great, let them be. Are they a little angry? It's a red flag! Research and try to resolve it.

The Lip Purse

Sometimes when we are angry we tense our lips and press them into a hard line called a **lip purse**. Remember how Lance Armstrong pursed his lips after his lie? When angry, we often try to suppress a yell or contain an outburst. Emotionally we're trying to "keep it together," and physically this looks like tension—pursing the lips, tightening our hands into fists, or clenching our jaw. If you see someone exhibit the lip purse, they might be hiding something or on their way to full-blown anger.

2. **Sadness:** When sad, we pull the corners of our mouth down into a frown. We also droop our eyelids and pinch the corners of our eyebrows together.

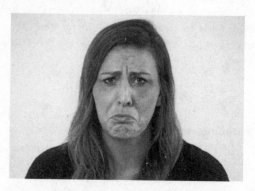

Sadly, my face looks dangerously close to sad while at rest. This is because I have a naturally downturned mouth—at rest, the corners of my mouth point down (like a frown). I also have extra-large eyelids—yup, weird facial trait! So I tend to look droopy even when I'm quite awake.

Now that I know this, I can correct for it. When I'm in an important meeting or recording a video, I open my eyes a little wider than normal and hold my mouth in a more up position.

I can also manage this with makeup. I use liner to pull the corners of my lids up and shadow my lids, so they look more open.* These small changes have a dramatic effect on my engagement.

Similarly, if you're challenged with RBF, try positioning your camera slightly higher than your eyeline. This makes you look up, which widens your eyes and makes you look more awake. When you are in an important meeting, angle the corners of your mouth up or raise your eyebrows during the first impression or during important points. This is a subtle way to show people you're engaged and not, in fact, bothered at all.

FUN TIP

The Mouth Shrug

A mouth shrug, also known as a deep frown, is an expression of doubt or disbelief. It's on its way to sadness—as in, it would make us sad if what we're seeing or hearing wasn't true. If you see it, pause and take note. Do you need to explain your point further? Get clarification? Check in that everyone is on the same page? Don't let the mouth shrug go unchecked.

- **Encoding sadness:** Which way does your mouth turn? Do your facial features encode a certain emotion? This is information you can use to be more purposeful when you need it.
- **Decoding sadness:** See someone pull their mouth into a frown? Spot a mouth shrug? With sadness you have two choices: address it to make someone feel better

---

* See me transform my RBF in a video in your digital bonuses.

or give them space. Sometimes, especially in professional settings, people need space to deal with their sadness.

3. **Contempt:** The smirk, also known as contempt, happens when we lift up one side of our mouth.

George W. Bush was running for president of the United States. And he had a problem. He smirked. A lot. And it rubbed people wrong. "The infamous smirk was creating 'the wrong impression,'" said political author Dr. Drew Westen.

The Republican Party took action and rapidly coached Bush on how to reflect "gravitas instead of hubris."

"The smirk is causing much justifiable worry in Republican circles," reported *Slate* in a 1999 article called "George W.'s Smirk."

It's the simplest of the facial expressions but also the most confusing. Contempt—scorn, disdain, or superiority—is most often confused with boredom, apathy, and apprehension. When researchers asked participants to identify facial expressions, only 43 percent correctly identified contempt—the lowest score of any expression!

I see this contempt confusion all the time when people mistakenly use the smirk emoji 😏 when trying to convey happiness 🙂. That asymmetrical smile shows scorn, not soft happiness!

Research shows contempt is the most common form of resting bothered face. And this matters for our professional, social, and even romantic relationships.

Dr. John Gottman is a marriage counselor and researcher in Seattle. He ran a thirty-year-long experiment to find out why certain couples get divorced while others stay together. He wanted to know if he could spot patterns among couples that could predict the future of their relationship.

Gottman found one single cue to predict the fate of these couples: contempt. If one or both people in the marriage flashed contempt about their partner in the intake interview, there was a 93 percent likelihood that couple would divorce!

SPECIAL NOTE

Punctuators

Researchers discovered that most people have an expression or gesture they use to punctuate or emphasize their words. These are called **punctuators**.

Punctuators are cues, gestures, or facial expressions humans use to emphasize their words without the corresponding emotional meaning.

For example, actor and podcast host Dax Shepard is often teased by his *Armchair Expert* cohost, Monica Padman, about his nonverbal punctuator—**the nose flare**. Also known as a nostril flare or nasal wing dilation, it's a Danger Zone cue and a nonverbal signal of aggression.

When we need to quickly take in air, our nostrils flare and expand. We also tense and expand our nostrils when we're angry.

But Padman noticed that Shepard does this when he isn't actually angry (so it's merely a punctuator). She has advised him to keep his nostrils in check because it signals aggression to their guests.

If *you* encode a punctuator that happens to be a negative cue, try to switch it to a more positive or neutral cue.

If you see colleagues, friends, or family members show the same cue over and over again, seemingly at random times, it's likely just their punctuator.

Contempt is a very powerful emotion. If it's not addressed, it festers. Unchecked contempt can grow into disrespect and hatred if it's not quelled.

- **Encoding contempt:** Be sure you're not accidentally smirking—at rest, in your profile pictures, or when listening.
- **Decoding contempt:** If you see contempt, immediately identify the source. What was said, what was felt, what happened to trigger it? Then see if you can reassure, reaffirm, or resolve the cause of the negativity.

PRINCIPLE

Be aware of what cues your face is sending at rest—avoid accidental anger, contempt, and sadness.

How to Negotiate for a Car . . . or Anything You Want

Up to this point we've been talking about avoiding the Danger Zone cues. However, there are rare times when Danger Zones cues can help enhance your communication. **You can use Danger Zone cues to subtly signal disapproval, dislike, or disengagement.**

Is someone making you uncomfortable? Cover your mouth and step back.

Did someone bring up something you disagree with in a meeting? Lean away and cross your arms.

My favorite way to expertly use Danger Zone cues is when negotiating. As a people pleaser, I find it a little challenging to say no. And sometimes a verbal back-and-forth can be exhausting and filled with tension. I much prefer letting my nonverbal cues speak for themselves.

My negotiation strategy is to let your nonverbal communication speak *for* you. This has the effect of making your counterpart negotiate with themselves.

Here's how it works: When the person you're negotiating with says something positive or something you agree with, reciprocate with positive nonverbal signs and give verbal encouragement.

Let's take the example of negotiating for a new car. This might sound like:

"Wow!" [Smile.] "I'm thrilled that your financing rate is so low."

[Lean in.] "It includes heated seats. Love that."

[Nod and make eye contact.] "Really? You give 100 free car washes if I buy today?"

Most people make the mistake of not looking too excited when negotiating for something they want. This actually works against you! Using nonverbal warmth and competence both builds rapport with your negotiator and helps them respect you—which might get you a better deal.

Researchers even found that nonverbal ambivalence (trying to be neutral) hurts your ability to negotiate. **They found that showing nonverbal signs of disappointment when you hear a bad offer can actually cause the person you're negotiating with to make larger concessions.**

This is a more authentic way to negotiate—why hide your excitement or stifle your upset? Show it all! Highlight your true feelings. When you hear something that you don't like or don't agree with, switch to your Danger Zone cues. This is a nonconfrontational yet clear way to show disappointment and get the other person to make concessions without having to say a word.

They offer you a bad price: you lip purse.

They offer an unworkable timeline: you furrow your brow and cross your arms.

They don't give you what you need: you shake your head no and turn away.

These are subtle nonverbal ways of saying, *No thanks. Can you do any better?*

What's important to remember when negotiating is that being ambivalent or hiding your feelings can actually hurt your chances and authenticity. It also makes your negotiator trust you less. Show your real feelings to foster real rapport.

Congruence Breeds Authenticity

Ambivalence doesn't just hurt you in negotiations. It can also be damaging professionally.

Ever heard someone start a meeting with "I'm so happy to be here," but they say it with an unhappy face, a bored voice, and a very tired-looking posture? This is called an **incongruity**. The words don't match the cues.

CONGRUENCE

When our nonverbal cues and verbal content align.

When our words and body language cues are incongruent, it's as if there's a misfire. We sense something is not right. Not only does it come across as inauthentic, but it also confuses us. Which should we believe? The verbal message or nonverbal cues?

Here's what is important to remember about Danger Zone cues: When they're accompanied by the congruent verbal message, they can be reliably seen as negative. If someone *says* they're angry and *displays* anger, then that's congruent. **It's negative, but you know nothing is being hidden from you.**

For example, Michelle Poler shows all kinds of Danger Zone cues in her videos and people still love them! Why? They're congruent. She says she's afraid, anxious, and nervous, and her nonverbal cues match.

When a Danger Zone cue is *not* accompanied by the matching verbal cue, then you have a red flag. That needs to be investigated further.

My rule of thumb is to look for a **cluster** of three red flags in a row. One red flag might be an accident, context related, or a fluke—someone touches their neck because they have a mosquito bite you can't see, someone crosses their arms because they're cold, someone shows contempt because they had a random internal criticism that had nothing to do with you. But three incongruent nonverbal cues around the same topic should raise your concern.

Research confirms that looking for a cluster of cues in context is the safest way to accurately assess someone's true feelings.* For example, one researcher found that when participants withheld information, they showed a specific nonverbal cluster: a trunk swivel (distancing), rocking back and forth, and shaking their head.

CHAPTER CHALLENGE

We have made it to the end of the nonverbal section! Here are all the warmth and competence nonverbal cues you should know:

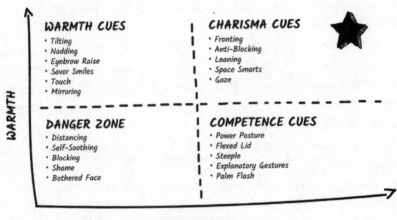

WARMTH CUES
- Tilting
- Nodding
- Eyebrow Raise
- Savor Smiles
- Touch
- Mirroring

CHARISMA CUES
- Fronting
- Anti-Blocking
- Leaning
- Space Smarts
- Gaze

DANGER ZONE
- Distancing
- Self-Soothing
- Blocking
- Shame
- Bothered Face

COMPETENCE CUES
- Power Posture
- Flexed Lid
- Steeple
- Explanatory Gestures
- Palm Flash

WARMTH

COMPETENCE

Now it's time to analyze your Lie to Me video! Pull it up and use the chart below to mark every time you see yourself show one of the Danger Zone cues.

This will help you identify what you encode when you're recalling (question 1), when you're embarrassed (question 2), and when you're

---

* Lie detection is a complex science. I teach a five-step model for lie detection in one of my courses. Clusters are just one of the steps to ensure that you don't falsely accuse someone.

lying (question 3)—and even when you're just thinking (in between answers).

	QUESTION 1	QUESTION 2	QUESTION 3
Lip Purse			
Distancing			
Ventilating			
Comfort Gesture			
Preen			
Suprasternal Notch Touch			
Body Block			
Mouth Block			
Eye Block			
Shame			
Anger			
Nose Flare			
Sadness			
Mouth Shrug			
Contempt			
Punctuator			
Other			

BONUS CHALLENGE: Ask five people in your life to play the Lie to Me game with you. I have five blank Lie to Me tables in your digital bonuses. See if they would be willing to record *their* Lie to Me video. Then you can uncover and record one another's tells together.

Vocal, Verbal, and Imagery Cues

Vocal Cues

CHAPTER 7

Sound Powerful

W here are you from, Cameron?" asks Lauren.
"I'm from the state of Maine," answers Cameron.
"I don't think I've met anyone from Maine before."
"I'm the only one you'll ever need to meet."
Lauren laughs. "I like that, I like that."
Lauren Speed and Cameron Hamilton are on a blind date. Like, literally, a blind date. They're participants on Netflix's *Love Is Blind*, where thirty men and women speed-date each other in different "pods." They can talk to each other but not see each other. By the end of the show, they have a chance to get *engaged*. Crazy? I thought so too, but then something amazing happened.

Lauren and Cameron bond immediately and quickly get to know each other. By the end of their first date, they're already building a strong connection.

"Gosh, I really want to get to know you more," said Cameron.
"I know, I like you," said Lauren.
"I like you too."
"I like your voice too, you *sound* cute."
They both laugh flirtatiously.
Over the next few days, Cameron and Lauren go on multiple blind

dates, getting to know each other more through the wall, simply by hearing each other's voices and answering questions. No body language, no nonverbal cues, no touch, no eye contact, just voice.

On the fourth day of their knowing each other, Lauren and Cameron say they love each other.

On the fifth day of knowing each other, Cameron says, "I know she's the one. I'm ready to propose to Lauren."

And then later that day, he does.

Lauren says yes! You read that right. They got engaged without ever seeing each other . . . **after only five days of hearing each other's voices**.

As of this writing, over two years later, they're still happily married.

What cues can we learn from voices? Why do we like some voices more than others? What does your voice say about you? Let's find out.

Your Vocal Power

How we say our words—our tone, volume, pace, syntax, and cadence—is just as important as *what* we say. We can tell a lot about a person, their emotional state, their intentions, and their personality from their voice.

Our voice is so indicative of our internal state that companies now use voice analysis software on earnings conference calls to predict a firm's financial future. When a manager uses more positive, confident vocal cues, analysts become more bullish on the future prospects of the stock price.

Vocal power translates into earning power.

Understanding vocal cues is incredibly important for uncovering others' feelings toward you, your work, and your projects.

FUN TIP

Fighting Voice

An analysis of the vocalizations of Mixed Martial Arts (MMA) fighters found the intensity of their roars predicted their perceived fighting ability.

One study completely blew me away. Researchers recorded surgeons talking to patients during consultations, then edited them into ten-second clips. They took these clips and "garbled" the words so you could hear only the vocal cues, like pitch, volume, and cadence, but not any actual words. They were trying to test the impact of vocal cues alone without attaching any meaning to the words being said.

The researchers then asked participants to rate the surgeons on warmth, hostility, dominance, and anxiety. Imagine this for a second—you must decide how competent or warm someone is based on a clip of gobbledygook. Study participants had to rate each surgeon based on the audio track alone.

Here's what's astounding: Doctors who received poor ratings on their vocal power experienced higher rates of malpractice lawsuits. In other words, we don't just sue doctors based on their skill level, we sue them based on our *perceptions* of their skills—and this judgment is made within just a few seconds of *hearing* them.

So what makes a doctor—someone already elevated in terms of perceived competence—sound incompetent, unbelievable, or dangerous? What made some doctors sound confident, powerful, and trustworthy?

Cultivating your most charismatic voice is an essential part of effective presence. If you want to project an image of confidence and professionalism, you must leverage your vocal power. Let's start with the vocal power cues of competence and confidence. In the next chapter we'll review the cues that make someone sound warm and trustworthy.

VOCAL POWER CUE #1: How to Sound Confident

"Were you scared to face an audience in the beginning?" asked six-time Emmy award–winning actor Alan Alda of Betty White, the legendary comedian and actress.

"I still get stage fright," said White.

Alda wonders what happens when she's nervous. "Your heart beats faster, does something happen to your voice?" asked Alda.

"Yes . . ." and then Betty White forces her voice up a few octaves into a high pitch. "Hellooooo?" she squeaks, "Hello, everybody? I'm so . . . I'm so . . . happy to be here."

Both Alda and White laugh in recognition.

When we're nervous or stressed, our voice tends to pitch higher. I call this cue **nervous pitch**.

Remember our **postural expansion** cue? When we're anxious, our body contracts—we tuck our chin in, tense our neck, clench our jaw, cross our arms, slump down, or roll our shoulders in. All this contracting allows less space in our lungs, making it hard to take in air and therefore difficult to project our voice. This is why our voice cracks or gets higher when we're nervous.

But when we're confident, we pull our shoulders down and back, puff out our chest, look up and around, and use our arms. This relaxes and expands the muscles we use to speak—our lungs, diaphragm, vocal cords, neck, throat, mouth, and tongue.

Let's try our own experiment. First, try saying, "I'm happy to be here," in whatever posture you're currently in. This is your neutral expression.

Now contract your body and get as small as possible. Cross your arms, tuck your chin in, and clench all your muscles, including your jaw and lips.

Now try saying, "I'm happy to be here." Does your voice sound small? Try saying it as loud as you can. (Hopefully no one else is around. If someone is, have them join in.)

It's hard to speak loudly in this coiled, defeated posture, right?

Next open your body up as broadly as possible. Roll your shoulders back, take in a deep breath to expand your lungs, and relax your jaw, lips, shoulders, and neck.

Now say, "I'm happy to be here." Sound better?

Try to say it as loud as you can. You can go much louder, right?

The more space your body takes up, the more vocal freedom you have to project.

The less space you occupy, the more restricted and limited your vocal confidence, the more nervous you sound, and the harder it is for people to be confident in what you're saying.

We instinctually mistrust people using nervous pitch. We wonder if we should also be nervous or worry that we can't trust what's being said. Nervous pitch can also be a signal of lying. One research team found that participants unknowingly raised the pitch of their voice when they weren't telling the truth.

FUN TIP

Babies

There's one very cute exception to high-pitch preference. Babies prefer interacting with adults with a higher-pitched voice, which may be why adults instinctively raise their voices into that higher pitch when talking to babies.

While we're uncomfortable listening to a nervous pitch, we *love* hearing a **confident pitch**. When we use our lowest comfortable pitch, we project confidence. It's important to draw a distinction here. Confident pitch is not as deep as you can possibly go in your vocal range, but is the lowest pitch you can employ *comfortably.*

Researchers find that lowering the pitch of your voice makes other people perceive you as more powerful. They also showed that when participants speak in their lowest comfortable pitch, they also *felt* more powerful and thought more abstractly. What an easy way to think more broadly.

Now, I love a low pitch, but don't go too low! Elizabeth Holmes, the now-infamous founder of defunct health technology company Theranos, stood out for her low baritone voice. Many of her former coworkers claimed it was fake. *The Cut* reported that she often "fell out of character" and exposed her real, higher voice while intoxicated.

If it feels unnatural using a deep pitch, it's too low! There are two ways to keep it natural: space and breath.

ACTION STEPS
- **Step #1: Use the posture fixes.**
  You can instantly improve your vocal confidence and physical confidence at the exact same time! Use the same posture quick fixes we

learned earlier. As a reminder, maximize the distance between the tops of your shoulders and earlobes. Plant your feet three inches wider than you normally would. Relax your hands and rotate them to parallel from the shoulder.

- **Step #2: Speak on the out breath.**
Taking a deep breath is one of the fastest ways to feel and sound more confident. Try not to speak at the top of your inhale. Rather, take a deep breath in and speak as you release the breath.

PRINCIPLE

Use space and breath to engage the lowest end of your natural tone.

VOCAL POWER CUE #2: Be Taken Seriously

A few years ago, I consulted with a large business software company to improve their sales funnel. We workshopped everything from behavior cues in their emails to vocal cues on the phone to nonverbal cues they used at trade shows.

My favorite part of this process was helping an inside sales rep who unfortunately had the lowest conversion rate on the team. Let's call him Elliott.

Elliott is a great guy, but he had one big problem: He couldn't close.

He was charismatic and knowledgeable about the product, so it had to be a cues issue. Clients and colleagues respected and liked him. Elliott and his managers were baffled as to why he couldn't reliably make his quota. And when he did close deals, he had to offer all kinds of discounts to get the yes.

I listened to a few of his recorded sales calls and immediately identified the issue.

His entire pitch was great—low tone, lots of vocal charisma. Yet when it came time to discuss the all-important price of his offering, he gave away all his vocal power. Each and every time Elliott mentioned the price, he used the **question inflection**. This is when our voice pitch rises at the end of our sentence.*

Elliott would say, "We'd love to have your business." And then ask what should have been a statement: "The price of our service is $500?" *Ooof.*

We'd love to have your business. The price of our service is $500.

Elliott wasn't *stating* his price, he was *asking* it. And this cued his prospects to question it too. They pushed him for discounts. They haggled and negotiated with him. Elliott was unknowingly cueing them to question his price because he was using the question inflection.

When Elliott asked his price, it changed the way customers were listening. Researchers find using the question inflection on a statement cues our brains to switch from just listening to scrutinizing. And when the question inflection is mistakenly used on a statement, it signals conversational weakness and insecurity.

Liars often accidentally use the question inflection incorrectly because they're subconsciously asking the listener, "Do you believe me?" When we hear a misplaced question inflection, it reminds us of dishonesty.

The question inflection was killing Elliott's deals at the worst possible moment. All the rapport and credibility he built up in the first part of his pitch was lost the moment he used the wrong inflection.

Fortunately, this is an incredibly easy cue to change. Elliott noticed a huge shift the moment he switched to a neutral inflection on price. Not only did he get less pushback, less haggling, and close more deals (yay!), but he also *felt* more confident in his price. The virtuous Cue Cycle at work.

---

* To see a funny version of uptalk in action, watch the *Saturday Night Live* skit "The Californians" in your digital bonuses at scienceofpeople.com/bonus.

When you incorrectly use the question inflection, you invite people to doubt your competence. I hear this most often when people talk about themselves and their ideas.

I hear it on voicemails. "Hi, this is Sarah? So glad you called? I'll get back to you soon?"

Hi, this is Sarah? So glad you called? I'll get back to you soon?

I hear it in introductions. "Let's get started? Let's talk about the new project? I'll kick us off?"

Let's get started? Today we are going to be talking about the new project? I'm going to kick us off?

I hear it when people share their ideas. "I have an idea? I worked on it a lot? I think it will be more effective?"

I have an idea. I was thinking we could do this part first? I think it will make us all more effective?

If you ask your statements, you're asking others to doubt you. **Even the most confident words said with the question inflection invite less confidence.** If you want people to take you seriously and believe in what you have to say, then *tell* people what you're thinking, don't *ask* them.

ACTION STEPS
- Listen to your voicemail greeting. Are you using the question inflection? Rerecord it!

- Listen to an old presentation or video call. Did you accidentally use the question inflection on statements or with certain people?
- If you have something important to say or an idea to pitch, practice saying it without the question inflection.

PRINCIPLE

If you want people to stop questioning you, then stop accidentally using the question inflection.

VOCAL POWER CUE #3: Eliminate Vocal Fry . . . Forever

Have you ever heard of vocal fry? It's when someone's voice cracks, creaks, and sounds raspy.* It's called *fry* because it sounds like bacon sizzling in a frying pan.

Vocal fry, or glottal fry as it's sometimes called, is used by both genders but it has become widespread among young women. Research finds that using vocal fry is one of the fastest ways to undermine professional success. This is because vocal fry signals *anxiety,* undermining you and your message. **Vocal fry kills competence.**

Why does this happen? When we're anxious, we have trouble taking deep breaths, and when there isn't enough breath being pushed through the vocal cords, vocal fry occurs. When we breathe, our vocal cords separate. Then when we speak, those cords rub together, and that vibration creates sound. If you speak without enough breath throughout, your vocal cords cannot rub together effectively, and they create a creaky, hollow sound. With vocal fry, it's as if you're hearing someone's vocal cords rattling next to each other. Gross, right?

Listening to vocal fry can be like nails on a chalkboard. It's grating on the ears and triggers anxiety in listeners. And this makes sense. It's a Dan-

---

* Watch me demo this in a video in your digital bonuses.

ger Zone cue that signals low confidence and low competence. Confident, competent people have enough breath and space to avoid vocal fry.

It's incredibly hard for people to take you seriously, listen to you, and believe you when you speak with vocal fry. And it often happens by accident! Vocal fry most often occurs at the end of a run-on sentence. By the end of a run-on sentence, you're more likely to run out of breath. When we get nervous, we have the tendency to rush our words, smushing all of our thoughts into one big exhale.

Here's the worst one of all: I've noticed people mistakenly use vocal fry when trying to sound casual, ambivalent, or easygoing. It's as if less vocal intensity signals less energetic intensity. Don't be fooled! **Vocal fry is not an indication that you are laid-back, it's a signal of self-consciousness.**

Fortunately, there's an easy vocal fry fix. **If you hear yourself using vocal fry, take a breath and speak a tiny bit louder.**

Upping your volume, even just slightly, is the fastest way to get out of vocal fry. It's an easy way to push your vocal cords together to produce a more natural sound.

What if someone you're with is speaking with vocal fry? Simply ask them to speak up. It eliminates vocal fry instantly.

ACTION STEPS
- Speak in shorter sentences.
- Don't speak too fast.
- Speak louder or use more breath.

PRINCIPLE

Vocal fry undermines your vocal confidence.

VOCAL POWER CUE #4: Volume Control Shows Emotional Control

When my team and I asked readers to submit Lie to Me videos, we noticed that along with raising their pitch, many liars also dropped their volume. Go back and listen to your own video—do you drop your volume?

Liars accidentally drop their volume because they're nervous, lack confidence in their words, and instinctively don't want people to hear their lie—in case they get caught.

This is one reason we show increased confidence in those who speak with higher volumes. Surprised by this? Research has backed it up—we tend to like people who speak on the louder side. In one study called "How the Voice Persuades," researchers examined how persuasive people attempt to influence others using paralanguage—volume, pitch, and inflection. They found that a strong, confident vocal demeanor persuades others because it signals that speakers strongly endorse their own message.

The best communicators speak louder and vary their volume. Volume is a critical aspect of power—it takes breath and expansiveness to be loud.

Speaking louder also has all kinds of nonverbal benefits for you *and others*. Ask someone to speak up and they will:

- Sit up straighter (expansive cue).
- Take a deep breath, which helps with nerves.
- Plant their feet (expansive cue).
- Tilt their head up or bring their chin up (nodding cue and expansive cue).
- Clear their throat and get rid of vocal fry.

Does this mean we should try to be as loud as possible? No! True vocal power comes from showing mastery of **volume dynamism**. Controlling your volume shows you have control of your message. It takes deep competence to be able to match your volume to your content. When master communicators want to show excitement, they speak up. When they want to share secrets or insider information, they speak quietly, forcing listeners to lean in.

ACTION STEPS
- When passionate or excited about something, speak louder. Charge your words with volume.
- When letting people know insider information or sharing a secret tip, lower your voice and lean in.
- When emphasizing agreement or encouraging someone, say, "Yes!" or "I agree," a bit louder than normal.

PRINCIPLE

Vary your volume to highlight what's important.

VOCAL POWER CUE #5: Pause for Power

For the first twenty-seven years of my life, I was addicted to verbal fillers. Specifically, I used *um, so, like, well,* and *you know* when I was nervous, thinking, waiting, or stalling, and sometimes simply out of habit.

Verbal fillers *destroy* your credibility. One study found speakers who use fillers are seen as less prepared and less competent.

Another study asked participants to listen to and review speeches about Brexit. One speech had no fillers but was filled with fake facts. The other speech was factually accurate but had lots of verbal fillers. When speakers didn't use fillers, even though they had their facts wrong, they were rated as more competent, better with people skills, and more attractive than those who gave the speech with fillers. A staggering **57 percent** of participants thought the speech with no fillers was given by a well-educated person despite their having their facts wrong! Only **36 percent** thought those giving the factually accurate speech with fillers were well educated.

FUN TIP

Ummo App

I highly recommend an app called Ummo. Ummo helps you count your verbal fillers when speaking. Use it when you're practicing speeches, having important conversations, or trying to identify when you use fillers and why.

We use verbal fillers for two main reasons. First, to stall for time while we are thinking of our next point. Second, because we're afraid of being interrupted. Ever worry if you stop talking, someone might think you are done and interrupt you? I call that **conversational scarcity**. We believe there isn't enough time or attention, so we fill our points with fluff words. This is also the reason people speak too quickly and then stumble over their words.

Here's the catch: You may find the *more* you use verbal fillers, the *more* you're interrupted. It's as if people can pick up on your lack of confidence and don't want to waste their time listening.

Is there a cure for verbal fillers? Yes! The power of the pause.

Pausing shows both competence and confidence. People confident in their delivery don't need to fill with fluff. And they know listeners will wait for them to finish their points.

The best kind of pause is a cue I call the **breathing pause**. This is when you pause *and* take in a breath. This is important because it gives you something to do *in* the pause.

Taking a deep breath has many benefits:

- It helps keep your vocal pitch nice and low.
- It prevents vocal fry.
- It allows you to increase your volume if you want.
- It gives you a moment to think if you need it.
- It makes you sound and feel more confident.
- And, of course, it prevents you from using verbal fillers.

Every time you feel yourself wanting to use a filler, simly take a breath.

If you do accidentally use a verbal filler, don't worry! Don't react. Definitely don't apologize. Just take the breath *after* the filler. This is a slow way to retrain your brain that it should pause instead of filling.

Below are a few guidelines for practicing pauses:

1. **Shorter is better.**

    Short pauses are best. One researcher found that long pauses in conversation can hurt comprehension, but short pauses are highly beneficial. Short pauses are essential for processing information.

    What's too long? Four seconds.

    What's the right amount of time? At the shortest, about a quarter to half a second.

    And luckily, a quarter to half a second is just enough time to take a breath.

    Here's where it gets even more interesting. The same researcher found that we tend to adapt our pauses to our conversation partner in a kind of pause mirroring. If the other person uses longer pauses, so do we, and vice versa.

When in doubt, take pause cues from your conversational partner.

2. In between pauses, speak slowly.

Is speaking quickly the best way to get all of your points across? Studies find that this doesn't actually work.

Researchers at Brown University determined that fast and slow speech convey information at the *same rate.* How can this be? Because faster speech communicates less information in each burst.

Verbal fillers are harmful to competence because they enable you to speak faster but not necessarily *better.* A slower speaking pace is best for increasing comprehension and signals higher competence to others.

Bottom line: Speak slowly to convey competence. Breathing pauses are one of the best ways to slow yourself down.

FUN TIP

Rhetorical Questions

Another powerful place to use a breathing pause is right after asking a rhetorical question. Researchers found that waiting five to seven seconds after asking a rhetorical question encourages listeners to reflect, generate answers themselves, and then be more engaged in later discussion. When I give presentations, I like to ask a rhetorical question, pause, and then use that opportunity to take a sip of water. This helps me and my listeners process.

3. Power pause, don't end pause.

I used to pause at the end of an idea or at the end of a sentence. This often made people think I was done talking, so they'd "interrupt" me. They didn't mean to be rude—they were just responding to my cues. The **end pause** indicates you have completed a point.

The best way to pause is to create intrigue. Pause right before you give an answer, reveal an idea, or deliver a punch line. I call this a **power pause**. It creates intrigue and interest and ensures people don't accidentally think you're finished.

Check out the difference between power pausing and end pausing.

"I discovered something fascinating that changed the way I see the world. [pause] It started in my childhood." This pause is likely to invite more interruptions at the end of *world*, even though I'm not done.

Here's a power pause: "I discovered something fascinating [pause] that changed the way I see the world. It started in my childhood."

Both pauses work, but the power pause invites less interruption and *creates* intrigue.

FUN TIP

Bad Behavior

There's one more great way to use the power pause—as a way to highlight bad behavior. When someone snaps at you or says something inappropriate, don't snap back or react reflexively. Take a breathing pause. Let it hang in the air. I've found this makes the snapper reflect for a moment. They will often take it back, apologize, or think twice before doing it again.

The bad news: It's hard to permanently scrub your language of *um*s. But it's possible to reduce them by a lot. Here's how:

ACTION STEPS

- Identify *why* you use verbal fillers. Pull up a recent recording of a presentation or meeting (or record a voice memo of just your end of your next phone conversation) and pay attention to when you use verbal fillers.
- Are you using them to stall for transitions? This tells you to work on alternative transitional phrases or stories.

- Are you using them because you're afraid of being interrupted? This tells you to work on more power pauses and to speak more slowly overall.
- Are you using them when you don't know something? This tells you that you need to practice more and get more familiar with your content.
- Are you using them out of habit? This is the hardest usage to break! Again, try a breathing pause *after* a verbal filler. It might take a while to retrain your brain, but it will work. You might also try putting a Post-it on your computer whenever you're on a call. When you see it as you're speaking, it will remind you to slow down and pause when needed.

PRINCIPLE

Powerful people pause purposefully.

Your Voice Gives You Power

When you want to ask someone a question, are you more likely to:

Call or text?

Hop on a video call or an email?

Send them an instant message or walk over to their office?

These days more and more of our communication happens over text, email, and chat. And most of the time, that's great—it's efficient and easy.

But when it matters, it's always better to leverage your vocal power. Psychological researchers Nick Epley and Juliana Schroeder found that our voice conveys secret cues about our personality.

They asked two groups of participants to grade job candidates on their competence, thoughtfulness, and intelligence. One group read a candidate's job qualifications. The other group listened to the candidate read the exact same job qualifications out loud.

When asked beforehand, the candidates did not believe there would be any difference between their spoken or written word. But there was a difference—a big one! The participants who heard the candidate's recordings rated them as more competent, thoughtful, and intelligent—even though the words being read were exactly the same. Merely hearing the candidate made them like the candidate more overall and be more interested in hiring them.

Epley and Schroeder were able to repeat these findings with professional recruiters from Fortune 500 companies.

Your voice gives you power. It showcases your confidence, competence, and talents. When it matters, use it.

CHAPTER CHALLENGE

If you want to sound more competent, have people take you seriously, and get interrupted less, use these five vocal cues more often. Let's add them to our Cues Chart.

CUE	DECODE	ENCODE	INTERNALIZE
Low Tone	Do you have anyone in your life who speaks too high? How does it feel when you listen to them?	Try standing in a power posture for your next few phone calls. Is it easier to speak deeper?	Do you like the sound of your voice? Try different notes to find the one that is most comfortable.
Question Inflection	Who uses the question inflection on statements? Are they secretly nervous or is it just a habit?	Practice delivering hard news, prices, timelines, or commands with a neutral or downward inflection.	When do you use the question inflection incorrectly? Are you nervous or is it just a habit?
Vocal Fry	Do you know anyone who speaks with vocal fry? How could you help them fix it?	Every time you hear yourself going into vocal fry, try slowing down and taking a breathing pause.	Do you talk too fast when you're nervous? Do you take shallow breaths when you're nervous? Try to identify your nervous vocal tell.

CUE	DECODE	ENCODE	INTERNALIZE
Volume	Do you have someone in your life you are constantly asking to speak up? Talk softer? What does it say about their personality?	Try to vary your volume with different people in your life and when talking about different topics. Does it help you articulate your ideas?	Are you comfortable speaking with a louder volume? If not, don't do it!
Breathing Pauses	Who speaks too fast? Too slow? How does it affect your impressions of them?	Try a few power pauses and see how they feel. Do they slow you down? Increase your confidence?	Do you speak too fast? Too slow? Why?

BONUS CHALLENGE: Rewatch your Lie to Me video. Do you use any vocal cues of deception? Do you ask your lie? Drop volume? You might have a vocal tell!

CHAPTER 8

Vocal Likability

She was called the Iron Lady for her strong and uncompromising leadership style. She was the first female and longest-serving British prime minister of the twentieth century. And through all that Margaret Thatcher struggled with her voice.

"Physically she had a problem in that she spoke from the top of her chest. . . . She had a schoolmarmish, slightly bossy, slightly hectoring voice," recalled Tim Bell, one of Thatcher's chief advisers.

Before she ran for prime minister, her advisers had her work with famed actor Laurence Olivier to transform her voice. Olivier taught her how to lower her vocal pitch naturally with breath. It helped but didn't fix the problem.

Thatcher was consistently interrupted and ignored in the House of Commons. She particularly struggled during Question Time, which is a long-standing opportunity in the British Parliament for MPs to question government ministers. It can get very heated and very loud. This is what caused Thatcher the most trouble. When she was trying to project her voice, it became higher pitched and more strained.

This is a common struggle. To be heard or sound confident, we turn up our volume. But speaking louder takes more breath. So quickly we either become raspy or shrill, set our pitch too high, or hit vocal fry (neither loud nor powerful).

Women are faced with an even greater challenge: a strong "prejudice against women's voices and their supposed shrillness, emotionalism, and lack of authority," according to sociologist Dr. Anne Karpf.

What can be done? Playwright Ronald Millar taught Thatcher to lower her voice and speak slower so she could be heard *through* the noise.

This was the start of one of the greatest vocal transformations in political history. In 1975, Thatcher was elected prime minister. She continued to work on her vocal charisma. During broadcasts to the nation, Thatcher also employed a unique vocal technique. If she was giving a broadcast that required a sympathetic and sensitive voice, she drank a cup of honey tea to relax her vocal cords. When she wanted to add oomph, she drank ice water. (Fun fact: This actually works. Try it yourself!)

This made Thatcher a truly exceptional communicator—she worked to project *both* competence and warmth with her voice.

Remember, the best communicators use the Charisma Scale like a dial. They always stay in the Charisma Zone but flex between competence and warmth depending on their goals.

In chapter 7 we learned to use vocal competence cues—employing a lower tone, using varied volume, correctly timing the question inflection, adding more breathing pauses, and avoiding vocal fry.

How about warmth? How do you add personality to your voice? How can you sound more dynamic? Let's learn the warm vocal cues. It all starts with your hello.

VOCAL WARMTH CUE #1: Make a Memorable Vocal First Impression

Researchers find that people determine how confident you are within the first 200 *milliseconds* of hearing you speak. That means your vocal first impression happens with your first spoken word. This is most often "Hello?," "Hey!," or "Hi."

Here's the problem: When we prepare for an interview, presentation, or meeting, we think about our credentials, accomplishments, and stories, but we rarely practice our opener. That's a missed opportunity you can capture.

A few years ago, I wanted to know how emotion changes our voice—in particular, how emotion affects our *hello*s. We conducted an experiment in two parts.

First, participants recorded six different versions of their typical hello. Try each of them yourself:

1. **Normal Hello:** Say hello as you would when you normally answer the phone. This was our control hello.
2. **Happy Hello:** Say hello while thinking of something that makes you happy and wearing an authentic smile.
3. **Sad Hello:** Say hello while thinking of something that makes you sad and holding a sadness expression.
4. **Angry Hello:** Say hello while thinking of something that makes you angry and looking angry.
5. **Power Pose Hello:** Say hello while adopting an expansive posture—hands on hips like Superman.
6. **Normal Hello:** Say hello one more time as a secondary control hello—after you've been warmed up.

Clearly each hello sounded different, even though it was the same person speaking.* We wanted to know: Can you decide how much you like a person based on their hello? We asked thousands of new participants to rate each recording on likability.

Turns out, you can and you do.

When we tallied up the rankings, a clear pattern emerged. Can you guess which hellos got the highest likability rating? The lowest?

Sad hellos were scored as the least likable. Anger was a close second.

What does this mean? Don't answer the phone when you're in a bad mood! **Your irritability changes the sound of your voice.** (I keep a

---

* You can hear me play the hellos for you in my TEDx London Talk!

picture of my daughter as the background on my phone, so if I *must* answer the phone when I'm feeling a little off, I look at her to spark some love.)

The control hellos and the happy hellos both ranked equally in likability. This is great news! It means you do *not* have to maniacally smile (especially not fake smile) every time you answer the phone. Neutral or positive both work.

FUN TIP

Do You Like the Sound of Your Voice?

Do you cringe when you hear the sound of your own voice? Do you ever think, *Is that what I really sound like!?* There's a scientific reason we sound different than we think we should. We normally hear our own voice while we are talking, and because it is conducted through bone, our voice sounds lower in our heads and higher in recordings. Our voice also gives away our anxiety levels, irritation, and personality traits we might like to hide.

There was one big surprise in this experiment. The power pose hello didn't achieve high likability ratings. It ranked only slightly better than anger, coming in third place behind smiling and neutral.

Why do we think this happened? We like confidence, but power posing can sometimes come across as a little aggressive. Pride can be a powerful and even intimidating force.

This is more good news: You do not need to stand like Superman or Rocky on your phone calls. As long as you have enough breath, you're good.

Speaking of breath, there's one more mistake people make when saying hello. They hold their breath.

What do you do when you hear your phone ring? I noticed I take in a quick inhale and then hold it until I can answer. Sometimes this can last for a few seconds as I search for my phone. This causes me to answer the phone in a small, tight voice and with very little breath. In fact, when I recorded my phone calls, I noticed my "Hello?" was the highest-pitched word in the entire phone call!

When I work with sales professionals, I find this same pattern can happen when you call someone else and wait for them to answer. This is especially true if you're nervous.

Don't hold your breath while saying hello.

Instead, practice saying your hello on the out breath. This packs a double punch—it relaxes your body and gives you more breath, which makes you both sound and feel more confident.

And don't forget to do this in person, in video calls, and on the phone. A confident hello works in every medium.

PRINCIPLE

Never answer the phone in a bad mood—or while holding your breath.

HOW TO SAY HELLO

- Take a deep breath or two.
- Self-check: Are you in an okay mood to answer? If so, pick up. If not, consider a callback in a few.
- Smile if you're happy to talk to the person. Maintain a neutral expression if you aren't.
- Speak your first line on the out breath.

VOCAL WARMTH CUE #2: Sound Friendly

Here's everyone's secret worry in an interaction: Do I belong here?

And next: Am I wanted?

Your voice is the single best way to welcome someone with reassurance and belonging.

Here's how: Use a **warm-up cue**. Warm-ups are phrases that signal delightedness to another person. It shows them that they triggered *your* warmth. Here are some of my favorites:

- Oh, it's so good to hear from you!
- I was hoping you would call.
- This is such a nice surprise.
- So glad you called!

These are simple phrases, but I guarantee they will comfort the person on the receiving end. You can also use a warm-up cue when you recognize the person calling by saying . . .

- Hello, friend! So happy you called.
- Hello, [insert name]! Good to hear from you.
- Well, hello you. Nice to see your name pop up.
- Hi, [insert name]! What's good in your world?
- Hi there! It's been way too long.

As we learned in the last cue, smiling helps you sound happier and be more likable. However, smiling can be a challenge in professional settings. How do you smile authentically on routine, even boring calls at work? Easy! Use warmth words.

When you utter phrases like "Wonderful to hear from you!" or "Happy Monday, team!" or "Good morning!" it's easier to authentically smile. Try adding these to your first few moments of conversation to harness vocal warmth right from the start. Here are some others to try:

- Happy Friday, everyone
- Thrilled to be here
- Lovely to see everyone
- Wonderful to hear from you
- What a lovely day it is outside
- Anything exciting in your neck of the woods?
- Good morning
- Good afternoon
- Good evening

Send Verbal Hugs

As more and more of our communication moves to video, I worry about losing some of the benefits of in-person rapport. Can you possibly replicate the warming effects of a handshake on a video or phone call? I partnered with Dr. Paul Zak to find out. We set up an experiment to find out if using verbal warmth cues would have similar effects as their nonverbal counterparts. Could *saying* warm words like *hug* or *high five* stimulate the same connection as an actual hug or high five?

In our experiment, we found that when I used verbal warmth cues, people felt more connected to me. Like:

- I'm sending a virtual hug!
- Here's a digital high five.
- I'm fist-bumping my camera.
- I'm sending a double cheek kiss your way.

By measuring skin conductance on smart watches, we found that people actually felt more engaged when they heard these verbal warmth cues as opposed to the standard neutral positive openers like "Thanks for coming" or "Great to see you."

This is an easy way to add in vocal warmth: **Use words that cue for nonverbal warmth.** If you wish you could hug them, say so. If you would have given them a handshake in person, let them know. I do this when I want to be warmer on the phone, in video calls, and even in texts and email.

FUN TIP

Flu Season

Don't want to touch? With social distancing amid the COVID-19 pandemic, I would see a colleague or friend and simply say something like "Sending a hug from here" or "Air high five!" It always produced a smile and a little bit more warmth.

Warm people up with permission, authentic
happiness, and a vocal hug.

VOCAL WARMTH CUE #3: How to Sound More Interesting

Do you ever feel like people tune you out? Or worse, find you boring? Ugh, I know that feeling! Here's the good news: It likely has less to do with your content and more to do with your *delivery*. And that's easy to fix!

When we listen to someone speak, we're listening for two things: **confidence and emotion**.

- **Confidence** is a power cue. It makes people take you seriously. A low tone and the right inflection signals to others: *I feel good about what I'm saying and so should you.*
- **Emotion**, as an aspect of warmth, makes people think you're interesting. Vocal variety and a lively vocal personality signal to others: *I have something really interesting to say, so you should listen to it.*

We signal emotion with a cue I call **vocal variety**. Researchers found it takes just a tenth of a second for our brains to recognize emotions conveyed by voice cues. It's one of the primary ways we communicate our emotions, moods, and attitudes to others.

Many professionals think emotion gets in the way of their message, but it actually enhances it.

Emotion is what captures people's attention and hooks them in to want to listen. Words imbued with emotion are more easily remembered.

Want people to listen to you? Add emotion. Vocal variety is the spice of speech.

When nurses used more vocal variety while talking to their patients, they were seen as both warmer *and* more competent. Professionals tend to hide emotion. They don't want to be seen as overeager or over-the-top.

Going emotionless doesn't sound casual or cool, it sounds careless.

If you sound bored, you cue boredom.

When you feel proud of an idea, don't act casual. Speak with gratitude and motivation.

When you care about something, don't act ambivalent. Share your thoughts with power and emphasis.

Vocal variety can make people feel self-conscious. It can feel safer to project that you aren't overly passionate about something. Showing emotion makes you vulnerable to others—but that's what hooks people in!

Introverts in particular struggle with vocal variety because it calls attention to yourself. Here's a reframe: You've worked hard to accumulate your knowledge, skills, and ideas. **You're not calling attention to yourself; you're calling attention to your ideas.** Vocal variety does more than just help you sound more interesting. It actually helps people be more interested in what you have to say. It's a hook that benefits them and you.

You know the biggest killer of vocal variety? Scripting. Scripting is a great way to ensure your *words* might be perfect but makes it hard to add *genuine* vocal variety and emotion.

Data scientists at Quantified Communications used software to analyze more than 100,000 presentations from executives, politicians, and speakers. They looked at word choice, vocal cues, facial expressions, and even gesture cues. **They found that just a 10 percent increase in vocal variety greatly increases your audience's attention!**

I often work with speakers crafting their TED Talks. I find they make two common mistakes: They overly script their talk, and then they rehearse all the emotion out of it.

In one practice session, a client started in the most bored, monotonous tone possible, saying: "Today I want to share the most exciting scientific development of the last decade. It's going to change your life. And I'm thrilled to share it with you."

"Wait, wait, wait," I said to him. "Are you actually thrilled? Is it really exciting? You don't sound very excited."

"Oh yes! It's amazing. I've been working on it for twenty years and it's a game changer. It could completely revolutionize the way we think about—"

"Okay, NOW you sound excited! Where's that emotion?"

"Hmmm, I've practiced this so many times to get the words right, I forgot all about my delivery."

We took his script and we *filled it* with emotion. I also *unscripted* a few of his stories so he could speak off the cuff. I highly recommend keeping your stories and emotional parts of your presentations unscripted. Write out a few key bullets you want to remember. This forces you to tap into the true emotion underlying your words instead of falling into the memorization trap.

FUN TIP

A Lesson from Reagan

Ronald Reagan was known as the great communicator. Well, that wasn't always the case. Early in his career, he was fired from a radio station for sounding boring and flat while reading ads. To improve, he practiced reading scripts of FDR's Fireside Chats. He knew Roosevelt was reading, yet he still sounded dynamic. Reagan realized if he read a short phrase from the script and then restated it while speaking in a conversational tone, it sounded much better. He memorized and then "conversationalized" the idea. If you must read a script, try taking this tip from Reagan. Read, and then look up. Memorize, and then conversationalize.*

Create a Nonverbal Script

Lord Tim Bell used an interesting technique with Margaret Thatcher. He added cues to her written speeches and reminders about when to sip the lemon tea or the ice water.

---

* Story told by former presidential speechwriter and author James C. Humes in his book *Speak Like Churchill, Stand Like Lincoln.*

"For public meetings we put pause lines in her speeches. We didn't put applause lines in—she'd get petrified if they didn't applaud," said Bell.

A surviving printed copy of one of Thatcher's speeches from January 13, 1976, is marked with a note to herself: **"Keep voice low & relaxed. Don't go too slow."**

At this point Thatcher had given many, many speeches. By 1976 she was already a member of Parliament, had been elected education secretary, and was leader of the opposition, yet she *still* added vocal reminders for herself. Even the most experienced speakers use cue reminders.

You can do this with a powerful tool I call a **nonverbal script**.

Nonverbal scripting is when you add cue reminders to your verbal script or notes. **The best way to use a nonverbal script is to help you remember where you need to add vocal variety, nonverbal emphasis, or helpful gestures.** If you've ever read a script for a movie or play, you'll know this is commonplace, but it's never used for presentations! Until now.

Here's a sample script I use when I first greet an audience.

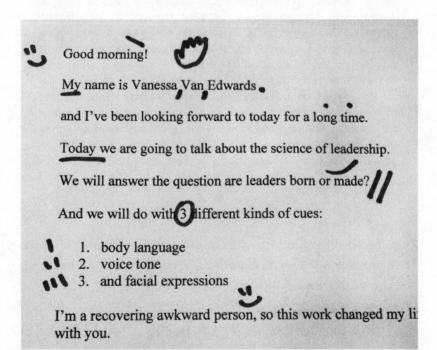

Good morning!

My name is Vanessa Van Edwards

and I've been looking forward to today for a long time.

Today we are going to talk about the science of leadership.

We will answer the question are leaders born or made?

And we will do with 3 different kinds of cues:

1. body language
2. voice tone
3. and facial expressions

I'm a recovering awkward person, so this work changed my li
with you.

When I say, "Good morning!" I smile and give a wave to the audience to enhance warmth. I also signal competence with a low voice tone. I've had to break a bad habit of accidentally using the question inflection on my opening statement. A nonverbal script has been key to breaking that habit. **Nonverbal scripting helps you overcome charisma traps.**

When I'm nervous, I tend to swallow my name. I've had to practice slowing myself down. When I say my name, I gesture toward my heart and enunciate my name clearly, instead of rushing through it. I've found many people rush through their name. After all, we've heard our own name a million times but your audience hasn't, so say it slowly.

When I say, "I've been looking forward to today for a long time," I like to give a small affirmative nod and make eye contact with as many audience members as possible.

I tend to speak fast, so I add breathing pause reminders for myself. Sometimes I can sound bored when telling stories, since I've told them a hundred times to a hundred audiences, so I always leave my stories as bullets, which helps me tap into real emotion and change them up when I tell them.

PRINCIPLE

Vocal variety makes you sound more interesting.

Here's how you can use nonverbal scripting: Imagine you're getting help from a famous director. What would they have you add or punctuate? How would they encourage you to add emotion and spice?

ACTION STEPS
- Struggle with pauses or speak too fast? Add pause lines.
- Speak too slow? Print slow sections in a different color. I like green for fast (as in a green light) and red for slow.
- Forget to smile? Type or draw a smiley face in your notes.
- Want to lean in, nod, or add emphasis to a certain section? Bold it or add the cue in the margins.

- Find it difficult to make eye contact with the audience? Add "LOOK UP →" cues to your script.

VOCAL WARMTH CUE #4:
Sound Encouraging and Inviting

I pulled up to the Starbucks drive-through window in desperate need of coffee. My toddler was screaming for a croissant (unfortunately for us, she knows that word). My husband was ready for his mocha.

A friendly voice came out of the speaker in front of me. "Good morning! What can I get you?"

"Let's see. We will have one Mocha Frappuccino."

"*Mmmm*, good choice," she said.

"And a croissant," I added.

"*Ooooo*, yum. Uh-huh. Uh-huh," she intoned, vocally encouraging me to keep going.

"And let's do one breakfast sandwich," I said.

"*Mmm-mmmm-mmmm*," she enthused, "delicious."

"You know what? Make that two," I said.

"Ahhh, excellent idea," she said.

I was beginning to feel like an *excellent* orderer indeed.

I tried to remember what else we needed. "Uhhhh," I said, stalling for time.

"Uh-huh, uh-huh, take your time," she said.

"*Mmmmm*. Oh, right! I'll have a tall coffee with a splash of almond milk," I added, remembering.

"Oh, great! *Mmm*," she said, "love that."

"That's it!" I said.

"That's it!" she mirrored. "Your delicious order will be ready shortly. Please go to the next window."

I pulled forward, feeling confident, encouraged, and cheerful.

This incredible Starbucks employee (wish I had gotten her name) used what I call **vocal invitations**. Vocal invitations are how we use our voice to include, invite, affirm, and welcome others. We use vocal invites to encourage someone to keep talking, to show agreement, to demonstrate interest, and to show we're listening.

There are three different types of vocal invitations:

First, **listening sounds** are nonword exclamations of joy, interest, and intrigue. Some typical ones are *ah, oh, uh, mmm, ooo, mmm-hmm, uh-huh,* and *aha*. These are the noises you make when you listen. You make these sounds to show someone you're engaged. These instantly improve your vocal warmth.

If you've ever been told you're cold and intimidating or make people nervous, here's an easy remedy: **Start using nonword vocal invitations with others.** If they say something interesting, say, "*Ooo.*" If they pause in thought, say, "*Mmm-hmm.*" If they look to you for acknowledgment, nod and say, "Uh-huh." And you can always add an eyebrow raise, a smile, or a lean if you feel comfortable. A vocal invitation is a great way to add warm rapport.

FUN TIP

Under-Expressers

This is especially helpful for overly stoic folks—people who are under-expressive with their face and gestures. If you know you're under-expressive nonverbally, try dialing up vocally—and this can be very, very subtle. Many of my under-expressive students feel more natural adding a quiet "aha" or *"mmm"* than using more hand gestures or smiles.

The second type of vocal invitation is using **encouraging words** with a warm and enthusiastic sound. Most commonly: "Yes," "Wow," "Go on," "Tell me more," "Interesting," "Really?," "Great," "Fascinating," "I see," and "Keep going," to name a few. You can think of these as **verbal nudges**. Typically, verbal nudges are under three words and are said to punctuate or encourage the other person to keep going. You're nudging them with a few choice words.

The last type of vocal invitation is called **vocal mirroring**. This is when you subtly mirror someone else's sounds, words, or vocal invitations. Whether she realized it or not, the Starbucks employee did this with me. I said, "*Oh*, right! I'll have a Tall coffee." And she replied, "*Oh*, great!" I said, "*Mmm*," while I was thinking, and she said, "*Mmm*," in response.

In a naturally great conversation participants mirror each other—in fact, this is what makes it great. Mirroring both amplifies our signals and syncs us up. The more we mirror each other's vocal invitations, the more we affirm each other. I say, "Aha," while listening to show I'm interested. Then when I'm talking, my partner says, "Aha," to show he's listening. And then we both know, "Great, we're on the same page!"—without ever saying it.

As we build a strong connection we sync up and start using similar words, vocal invitations, and voice pitch. Vocal mirroring happens naturally, but you can also use it purposefully to spark faster rapport.

One of my students works as an undercover police officer. As someone who meets new people who are under stress on a regular basis, he always vocally mirrors to quickly build rapport. He copies their verbal nudges, vocal invitations, and **even the types of words they use**. He told me if his contacts use the word *rig* instead of *truck* or *soda* instead of *pop*, he uses the words they do. In his experience, this is the key to building trust quickly. This isn't disingenuous, it's his way of showing respect and paying close attention to the people he is with.

I learned from him that I should research the professional vocabulary that my clients use. Before a presentation, I find out if they use the term *client* or *customer* or say *sales pitch* as opposed to *proposal*. Then I change the words in my presentation to match.

One study examined vocal mirroring at the start of salary negotiations. Researchers found that employees who used more vocal mirroring earned more money in their final salary agreement.

How can you vocally mirror authentically? The key here is **subtle and natural**. If you hear a word you like, use it! This is easy when someone is asking for confirmation:

They say, "Okay?"

You reply, "Okay!"

They say, "Got it?"

You say, "Got it!"

They say, "Aha!" while listening to you.

You say, "Aha!" while responding to them.

Of course, don't go crazy with this! Too much vocal mirroring can sound like a parrot. (Of course, no offense to parrots, especially the endangered kind.)

A few subtle vocal invitations can encourage an introvert, engage a new friend, or soothe someone important to you.

FUN TIP

Expectations vs. Reality

My childhood friend Elizabeth believes she's effusive and warm, but she comes across as stoic and distant—even when she's feeling happy. Every few months one of our mutual friends asks me, "Is Elizabeth mad at me?" And I have to explain, nope, she just under-signals.

We tend to overestimate how obvious our warmth, interest, and excitement is to others. Vocal invitations are one of the easiest low-barrier ways to signal.

A few years ago, I worked with a new manager who was struggling to build rapport with his team. I listened in on a few of his phone calls and immediately identified the problem. He was exhibiting a cue I call vocal denial.

The opposite of a vocal invitation cue is a **vocal denial**. A vocal denial shows dislike, disagreement, and disgust in a word or sound. They discourage people. They sound like "Ooof," "Eeek," "Oy," "Eeesh," or "Ay-ya-ya!" They can come in short words like "No," "Yuck," "Nope," "Yikes," or "Ouch."

They're often used accidentally! My student didn't even realize that as he listened to his team members, he would say, "Eeeeek." It was his natural listening cue, but it discouraged the people he was speaking with. Imagine their position. Why would they want to continue to share with him when they received what sounded like negative vocal feedback?

If you use vocal denial, use it purposefully. For instance, vocal denials can be used in place of or to preempt a harsh *verbal* denial.

Here's the thing: Verbal denials are intimidating. Vocal denials and vocal invitations can do the talking for you while entailing less social fear. A correctly placed vocal denial can subtly let someone know you don't agree without your also having to say the words "I don't agree." The level of effort and courage required to utter those words can be substantially more difficult to muster.

In 2018, we rented a huge studio to film our course People School in front of a small live audience. I was very, very nervous. I had over three days' worth of live content to teach in front of twenty new students, with a twelve-person crew on a multi-camera custom-designed set. It was expensive to put it all together, so the pressure was on to get it done on time.

One audience member, Bob, was my vocal lifeline. Bob is very vocally expressive and has this wonderful habit of murmuring "*Mmm*" to himself whenever he feels inspired or interested. Whether he realized it or not, every few minutes he would "*Mmm*" me with encouragement.

When I surprised him with a study or new fact, he would audibly say, "Aha!" in the otherwise silent soundstage. It gave me more confidence.

He's also an authentically loud laugher—cueing others to laugh heartily along with the awkward jokes that I like to share while teaching. From my spot onstage, I could hear his subtle vocal encouragement every time I shared a good point.

His vocal invitations were gifts to me as a teacher. It was as if he was tossing me little vocal snacks from the audience, giving me energy to keep going and keep at it. Most important, these vocal invitations were encouraging for other students! I noticed when he said, "Aha!" other students would look up from their notes and nod. When he laughed, they laughed. Vocal invitations create warmth for everyone.

VOCAL WARMTH CUE #5: Channel Your Charisma

Let's play a vocal game. Get ready to share an answer to the following questions out loud—if you're close to someone, ask them if they would be willing to listen and play along. Ready?

Version A: Describe your favorite meal in detail. What is it? Where do you get it? How good does it taste?

Pause. Take a deep breath. Now let's try Version B:

Version B: Now pretend you're Steve Jobs. Channel him for a moment. Stand or sit like you think he would stand or sit. Hold your hands like you think he would have held his hands. And now tell me about your favorite meal as you channel Steve Jobs. What is it? Where do you get it? How good does it taste?

Did you sound different when you pretended to be Steve Jobs? Did you speak louder? Emphasize more words?

This ridiculous exercise was an actual experiment. Researchers found that when they asked students to channel Steve Jobs, the students instantly became better speakers! Specifically, when students channeled Jobs, they used more purposeful eye contact, better vocal inflection, more volume, and clearer hand gestures.

This exercise improved their body language and vocal charisma so much that researchers now recommend channeling **speaking role models** as one of the fastest ways to improve public speaking.

Who's your speaking role model? Is there a TED Talker, podcaster, or presenter who you love listening to? Channel them! My speaking role models are Brené Brown, Tracee Ellis Ross, and Mel Robbins. I find them genuine, funny, and authentic.

This visualization process works best as a warm-up exercise. Before you hop on your next important phone call or while getting ready for your next presentation, pull up a video of your favorite speaker and do some breathing exercises while you watch. Practice delivering your opening line and key points like your speaking role model.

Here are some other ways to warm up your voice and your charisma before your next big thing.

What to Do Before Your Next Big Thing

To sound like your warmest and most charismatic self, I recommend warming up your voice before you go onstage. Use the techniques listed below whenever you need to dial up your charisma.

Find a private space if you're feeling shy—it's hard to do this one quietly.

1. **Take some deep belly breaths.** The trick here is not to breathe with your shoulders–keep them down as you breathe; good vocal breathing is all in the belly.
2. **Do your quick posture fixes.** Roll your shoulders down, widen your feet, and roll your hands out.
3. **Try a vocal exercise.*** Before every important call or speaking event, I hum my favorite songs to myself. It takes only two to three minutes and is a great way to get your vocal cords ready for vocal variety.

---

* To learn my go-to warm-up routine, check out the digital bonuses at scienceofpeople.com /bonus. Hint: It involves, shushes, hums, chants, and enunciation exercises.

4. **Got another few minutes?** Watch your favorite speaker on your phone to get you into flow. Practice your opening thirty seconds and your closing thirty seconds.

Take a screenshot of these two pages and save it for your next big thing. You got this!

BONUS: How to Record a Charismatic Voicemail Greeting

Listen to your voicemail greeting. Do you like the way you sound? Do you sound bored? **Rerecord it with emotion and confidence.** Here's how:

- Sit down in a nice quiet place. I recommend using headphones to make you sound less echoey and distant.
- Before hitting record, do some vocal warm-ups from above.
- Take a deep breath and say hello a few times in your lowest range. This way, you can speak and record in that same register.
- Think about someone you love talking to and imagine greeting them. Take that positive feeling and smile if it feels natural.
- Keep your language simple. I recommend saying a greeting, your name, and your request to callers. Then end with a nice goodbye or sign-off wish. Here's my template:

Hello!
This is _____.
Please leave a message for me after the tone.
I hope you have a great day!

Remember, your vocal charisma works like a dial. If you want to dial up warmth, use more warm vocal cues. If you want to dial up competence, use more competent cues. And if you want to sound like your best self, be sure to avoid the Danger Zone vocal cues: a misplaced question inflection, vocal fry, and vocal denials.

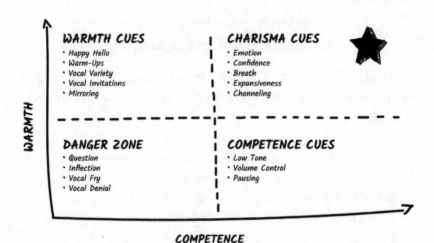

WARMTH

WARMTH CUES
* Happy Hello
* Warm-Ups
* Vocal Variety
* Vocal Invitations
* Mirroring

CHARISMA CUES
* Emotion
* Confidence
* Breath
* Expansiveness
* Channeling

DANGER ZONE
* Question
* Inflection
* Vocal Fry
* Vocal Denial

COMPETENCE CUES
* Low Tone
* Volume Control
* Pausing

COMPETENCE

Let's put your warm vocal cues into action. I've added these cues to your Cues Chart.

CUE	DECODE	ENCODE	INTERNALIZE
Charismatic Hellos	Who has the best hello?	Try a few different versions of your hello. Try a smiling hello or an out-breath hello and see which sounds best to you.	When you're happy to talk to someone, show it. When you aren't happy to talk to someone and want them to know it, show it! Sometimes I do use an angry hello if I have asked someone not to call me—especially telemarketers!

CUE	DECODE	ENCODE	INTERNALIZE
Friendly Warm-ups	Do you feel welcomed by the people you speak with? Does anyone make you feel unwelcome? Why?	Try out a few different vocal warm-ups and find one that works for you and your personality.	Feel the warm and fuzzies toward someone? Send them a virtual high five or digital hug.
Vocal Emotion	Do you know anyone who lacks emotion? Comes across as cold? Pay attention to their voice. It's likely a major part of the problem.	Every time you hear yourself getting bored or sounding bored, pull from your emotions. Use more stories. Share more awe.	Is it hard for you to show emotion? I know it can feel a little silly, so start slow. Pick one cue to start with until you feel confident!
Vocal Invitations	What's your favorite vocal invitation? I love when people say, "Aha!" What encourages you most? Share that with the people who matter.	What vocal invitation feels most natural to you? Try them all!	Do you accidentally use vocal declines? Listen to a recent speaking event or call to make sure.
Vocal Channeling	Who has great vocal charisma in your life? Try to learn from them.	Try on a few vocal role models. Speak like Steve Jobs, Oprah, or Mel Robbins and see what feels best to you.	Can you use yourself as a vocal role model? Have you ever delivered a great presentation or nailed it in a meeting? Pull up that recording whenever you need to be inspired!

Verbal Cues

CHAPTER 9

How to Communicate
with Charisma

I t was 1996 and Sabeer Bhatia and Jack Smith were hard at work pitching an idea for a new web product. After months of pitches and twenty meetings with venture capitalists, the duo finally landed a $300,000 seed investment. It was just enough money to quit their day jobs. They quickly built the first version of the site and on March 27, 1996, bought the domain Hotmail.com.

As they neared launch, their worries turned to growth: How would they get the word out and attract the millions of users they needed to become successful? They considered billboards and radio advertising but didn't have the money. Then they had an epiphany. What do you do with email? You send each message to *other people*. They decided to put a one-line message at the bottom of every email sent from Hotmail.

But what should it say? A straightforward advertisement? An appeal for help? They decided to try for both a heartwarming feel and a straight ask. They came up with this line and added it to the bottom of every email:

"PS: I Love You. Get Your Free Email at Hotmail.com."

In just the first few weeks, Hotmail exploded in popularity. Bhatia and Smith didn't realize the postscript is one of the most read parts of a message. In his research, communications consultant and author Dr. Frank Luntz found that **the postscript is the second most read part of a message after the opener**.

The founders credit that simple sentence as the single biggest driver of user growth. "Eighty percent of those who signed up said that they learned about it from a friend," reported *TechCrunch*. Just one year later, Hotmail went on to be acquired by Microsoft for $400 million.

Bhatia and Smith used the right words to cue the right people. Are you using words that send the right cues?

Power Words

Let's imagine I ask you to play a game with a stranger. I tell you the name of this game is the Community Game, but I tell your opponent it's called the Wall Street Game. Do you think the titles would influence how you both played?

Turns out the resounding answer is YES! A team of researchers introduced one group of participants to the Community Game (a warm title) and another group to the Wall Street Game (a competent title). The rules of the actual games were identical, but take a guess which group worked more collaboratively? In the Community Game, two-thirds of the participants collaborated, compared to just a third in the Wall Street Game. Simply changing one verbal cue changed how people acted in the group.

What do you call your meetings? Your calls? Your teammates? Yourself? The words you use change people's actions and their perceptions of you. This is an easy way to dial up your charisma. **If you want to project warmth, use more warm words. If competence is your goal, use more competent words.**

Warm words convey friendliness, trust, and optimism. These are words like *connect, collaborate, happy, both,* and *together.* Warm words have the same effect as a smile or a head tilt. They make us feel the warm and fuzzies—connected, encouraged, and heard. I also consider emojis and exclamation points warmth cues. One study found that customers who texted with customer service agents gave higher ratings to agents who used emojis and rated those agents as more personable.

FUN TIP

Emojis

Emojis are a great way to add nonverbal cues to your emails, texts, profiles, and chats. It's also essential to use the right emoji to convey an emotion. Look in your digital bonuses for my comprehensive guide to emojis.

On the other hand, competent words cue power, knowledge, and effectiveness. These are words like *brainstorm, effective, productive*, and *science*. Competent words are the equivalent of a steeple or a purposeful gesture. They make us feel motivated, capable, and like we're in the right hands. Data, charts, and research are all competence signals.

A few rare charismatic words are so inherently good, they hit the sweet spot of both warmth and competence all by themselves. For example, *confident, great*, and *creative* are both warm and competent because they trigger optimism and interest.

And of course the Danger Zone words are either negative or signal very little at all. We're fighting sterility in the Danger Zone. **Most people don't use overly negative words, just boring ones.**

Not sure which words are warm, competent, charismatic, or boring? This is more art than science. Think about what a word makes you think of. Is it a person, symbol, or thing that reminds you of warmth or competence? That's good enough! To help, I've put together an extensive glossary of warm and competent words in your digital bonuses. And here's a quick snapshot of the different types of charisma words:

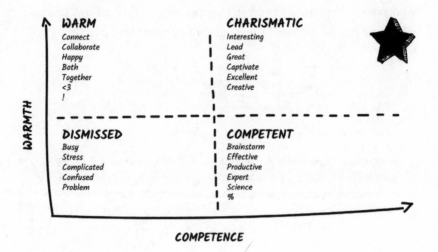

How to Send Better Emails

More and more of our professional communication has become sterile—lacking any charisma cues at all. What a waste! I used to send emails like this all the time. Can you see what's wrong with it?

Brian-

I'm all set for the meeting next week. I will prepare an overview and sample proposal for you. Then we'll review them all in the meeting. Let me know if you have any questions.

Keep me posted,
Vanessa

First, it's really boring. Second, there are no charisma cues at all. This email is basically asking the other person's brain to just shut off. Sterile words are so overused we don't even register them anymore.

This email gets the point across, but it could be doing *so much more.* Adding verbal cues can turn an okay message into a great one. This email has the exact same word count but feels completely different:

Good Morning, Brian,

I'm looking forward to collaborating next week. I'll prepare a goal worksheet and overview of desired outcomes for both of us. We can power through everything together. Happy to answer any questions.

All the best,
Vanessa

Each of the underlined words are charisma cues. The email has both warm words like *goal, together, happy,* and *desire* as well as competent words like *forward, outcome,* and *power through.* When people hear phrases like *together* and *happy,* they're more likely to *actually feel* happy together.

As we know, when we read words like *collaborate,* we're more likely to *be* collaborative. When we hear words like *together, we, our, us,* and *both,* we're more likely to feel connected. When someone tells us they're "happy to answer our questions," we're more likely to feel safe asking questions. **Many people assume there is warmth in their boring, sterile emails, but connection should never be assumed.**

Each verbal cue you choose can help set you and your team up for success. Here's how you can use verbal cues more purposefully:

Step #1: Email Audit

Do you communicate with charisma? Let's find out! The best way to see what kinds of cues you give others about your warmth and competence is with an **email audit**.

Here's how to perform your email audit:

- Open up your email sent folder.
- Pull up your five most recent important messages.
- Count how many warm words you use.
- Count how many competent words you use.
- Count how many charismatic words you use.

- Finally, do you use any negative words like *problem, mistake, bad,* or *stress?*

What patterns do you see? Thousands of students have performed this audit, and they typically find that they use a lot of one type of cue—overly warm or overly competent words. This is why they're stuck in one part of the Charisma Scale.

Or people find they have very few charisma cues at all. Most of their communication is dangerously close to the Danger Zone.

You might even notice you send different types of words to different types of people. Do you send lots of competent words to your boss and lots of warm words to your colleagues? This might be why people treat you differently—**you're cueing them to do so.**

Here's an example of a highly warm email:

Hi, Rod!

I absolutely <u>loved connecting</u> with you yesterday about the new proposal. As always, it is <u>great collaborating</u> with you! I think we're onto something <u>truly special</u>. I'll be able to finish my part today and then we can review <u>together</u>. =)

Best,
Andrea

Here's a competent version of the same email:

Dear Rod,

Thanks for the <u>powerful</u> <u>brainstorm session</u> yesterday. This new proposal is absolutely spot-on. I think we're really onto something <u>next level</u> with it. I'm <u>pushing through</u> my part by end of day today and then I'll <u>shoot</u> it over.

<u>Onward,</u>
Andrea

These emails are pretty much the same word count but send completely different cues. And notice neither of them is sterile. **When writing emails, imagine not just what you want your recipients to *know* but how you want them to *feel*.** This is *not* about just loading your communication with extra words. It *is* about being purposeful with how you choose your words, so they help you (and your team) achieve your goals.

Bhatia and Smith likely had no idea that the cheeky phrase "PS: I Love You. Get Your Free Email at Hotmail.com" also happens to have the perfect balance of warm and competent words. "I love you" is the warmest phrase there is and cues people to think of the folks they love. And an invitation to get anything free triggers our competence to get, achieve, and attain. This made them sound more charismatic and encouraged their people to share more. That last-minute add was a game changer.

I was particularly impressed by an email LinkedIn sent to me that struck the perfect blend of warmth and competence. They used the subject line "Your <u>expertise</u> is <u>requested</u>." This is a highly specific, high competence opener that also made me feel needed and wanted. Then they balanced out the high competence subject with a warm header right at the top of the email that said "LinkedIn would <u>like</u> to <u>hear</u> from you!"

Whether intentionally or accidentally, they used a nice balance of warm and competent cues in the body of the email, including signing off with a "We <u>appreciate</u> your <u>time</u>. <u>Best</u> <u>regards</u>"—a great blend of warmth and competence.

A few correctly placed cues can make all the difference.

> **PRINCIPLE**
>
> **Your written cues signal warmth, competence, and charisma just as much as nonverbal cues.**

Step #2: Stop Being Boring

There's a major crisis facing professionals today: really, really boring meetings. Do your meetings start on professional autopilot? It feels like most video calls and conference calls all start in the same tedious, sterile way:

> Hi, everyone. Today we're going to go over some weekly office updates. I'll review the docs I emailed earlier this week and leave some time at the end for questions. I'm going to wait a few minutes while people log on. We will get started in a few.

These words communicate very little—except that this meeting is going to be the same as all the others. This is a missed opportunity. Let's rescue this dreary opener and inspire charisma. This version has the exact same word count but uses both warmth and competence verbal cues:

> <u>Happy</u> Monday, <u>team</u>! So <u>great</u> to see all of you. Today we have some <u>interesting</u> updates to go over <u>together.</u> I'll <u>open up</u> the floor to <u>discussion</u> and make sure all your questions are <u>taken care of</u>. While we wait for folks, anyone do anything <u>fun</u> this weekend?

These small changes set up both the speaker and everyone in the meeting to be more successful.

Now you may be worried about becoming a corporate-speak robot zombie if using charismatic words feels fake. We don't want to use cues to cover up or gloss over broken practices on teams. But they can help nudge meetings or relationships in a positive direction.

Here are some easy ways to add more positive verbal cues to your communication. And it doesn't take a lot. Simple phrases can put you in the sweet spot on the Charisma Scale.

Let's start with **openers**. Make the first few words you say in an email, in conversations, or in an important chat match where you want to be on the Charisma Scale. This works in meetings, phone calls, video calls, and chats.

My rule of thumb: **Focus on the first ten words.** Don't just say "Hi," "Hey," or "Hello." Spice it up!

Start with language like "Hi, friend!," "Happy to be here," "What a pleasure," "Glad to connect," and "I'm thrilled to do this together"—all trigger warmth.

FUN TIP

Culture and Location

Let's take a cue from supermodel and *Project Runway* host Heidi Klum. She always says goodbye in her native language: "auf Wiedersehen!"

A really easy way to add warmth is to use culture- or location-based words. I love sending a beso—kiss in Spanish—to my friends.

I often start fun or check-in emails with a "Howdy!" My Hawaiian friend always starts with "Aloha." I love it when our international students start with their native language in greetings or sign-offs. "Ciao!" or "¡Hola!" or "Bonjour." These are great ways to add verbal personality.

Competent openers cue participants to feel productive and capable. Openers like "Let's do this," "This is going to be a productive day," "Hi, partner," "Let's solve this," and "Can't wait to power through" all juice our competence.

And words like *team, excited, welcome,* and *kickoff* hit the perfect balance of charisma. Try "Good morning team!," "Excited for today," "Welcome everyone," "Let's kick off this collaboration," or "Can't wait to get started together."

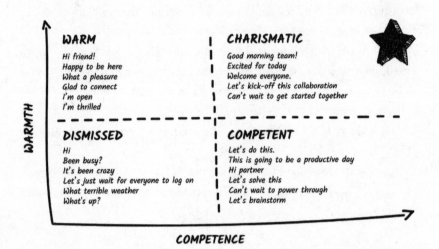

FUN TIP

Signature Sign-Off

I've written an email newsletter for over a decade. I send out my latest tips and tricks for communication and interpersonal skills. I used to agonize over my sign-off, but then I thought, *What do I want people to feel at the very end of every email?* The bottom line—the mission of my work, the reason I have an email newsletter in the first place—is to help people feel more successful. So I began to use the sign-off "To your success, Vanessa." Readers and students began to reference it and use it back with me. They would sign their emails using "To Your *Success*" and write to me saying, "Thank you for giving me all these *success* tips." It's an easy ritual for me and an on-brand reminder for my readers. Can you create a signature sign-off that sends the right message?

How about closers? Always end with charisma.

My favorite warm closers are "Cheers," "Best," "Can't wait!," "Warmest regards," "Yours truly," "Faithfully," "Warmly," and, of course, "Love."

My favorite competent closers are "Sincerely," "Regards," "Respectfully," "Appreciatively," and "Onward."

My favorite sweet spot closers hit the perfect balance. Try "Excited to work with you," "Looking forward to this," "Happy to answer any questions," "We got this!," "To your success," "Great work," or "Thank you for everything."

Avoid sterile or boring sign-offs like "Bye," "Talk soon," or, worse, no sign-offs at all.

Here's my cheat sheet:

If it fits your brand, you could even try "You can rely on us" as a high competence sign-off or tag line. Or use the warm version: "You can trust us."

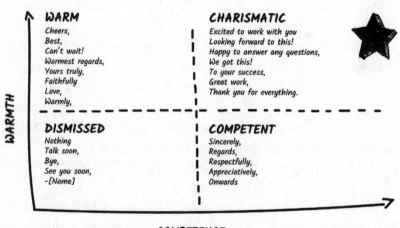

PRINCIPLE

When your communication matters, use verbal cues to make it memorable.

Step #3: Create Charisma

We wanted to see how the verbal cues you use can change people's perceptions of you in a résumé. So my team and I decided to run an experiment. First, we created two mock résumés. We used the same photo and name, but just slightly modified some of the written cues used in the very first line of the résumé—this looked just like your headline on LinkedIn or the overview section of a résumé. Both headlines had ten words total.

The warm version said, "I <u>help</u> <u>teams</u> <u>collaborate</u> and build <u>relationships</u> for <u>happier</u> customers."

The competent version said, "I <u>streamline</u> <u>corporate</u> <u>systems</u> to <u>increase</u> <u>productivity</u> and customer <u>outcomes</u>."

Over a thousand people rated this person on their warmth and competence. The change was small but worthwhile for only swapping out a few words. The warm words made people rate the person as 5 percent warmer. The competent words made the raters see the same person as 5 percent more competent. Is this a game changer for your perception? No, but it's an easy place to tweak the dial.

Next, we wanted to see if the effect would be different in video. We had a male and a female model record two short video introductions—one warm and one competent version. The warm version's script was: "Hi, I'm Alex. I <u>help</u> <u>teams</u> <u>collaborate</u> and build <u>relationships</u> for <u>happier</u> customers." The competent version script was: "Hi, I'm Alex. I <u>streamline</u> <u>corporate</u> <u>systems</u> to <u>increase</u> <u>productivity</u> and customer <u>outcomes</u>."

We instructed them to use nonverbal and vocal cues that were as similar as possible but to change the script.

Then we asked people to rate them on warmth and competence. This time we saw a bigger difference—and it changed for each gender!

The female who used more competent words was rated as 15 percent more competent than when using the warm version. This is a pretty incredible shift for swapping out only five words. When she used warm words, she was rated only 5 percent warmer than her competent script.

The male was rated as 11.5 percent warmer when he used warm words. Again, a pretty easy way to dial up warmth. But there was no difference in his competence when he used competent words.

This indicates two important takeaways. First, words do matter. Just changing your verbal cues can change people's perceptions of you. This works in résumés, online profiles, and the words you say in video or in person. Be sure to update your profile and résumé with the right verbal cues.

Second, it confirms how gender affects our perceptions. Research shows that women tend to be seen as higher in warmth and men tend to be seen as higher in competence. Using the right cues is critical to counter stereotypes.

Women have to be aware that society will perceive them as higher in warmth right off the bat. They have to do extra work to dial up competence purposefully by using more competent nonverbal, vocal, and verbal cues.

Men have to be aware that they're seen as higher in competence by default and need to use more warmth nonverbal, vocal, and verbal cues if they want to increase their warmth.

There are so many opportunities for you to trigger charisma in small but powerful ways. Get creative! Here are some ideas for inspiration:

- Some companies have *loyalty* programs (high in warmth). Others have *VIP* levels or *elite* status (high in competence). Others offer *reward* points (high in both warmth and competence).

- Before starting meetings or giving presentations, play peppy oldies (warm) or calming classical (competent) warm-up music.
- Whenever I fill out a name tag, I always add little extra verbal cues. If I want to dial up competence, I add a piece of trivia under my name or a unique personal fact. If I want to dial up warmth, I write a great conversation starter or something funny under my name.
- If I have extra time at the start of a meeting or presentation, I start with a purposeful warm-up. If I want to trigger competence, I might show a section of a powerful TED Talk or share an inspirational quote. If I want to create warmth, I might do an icebreaker or put some fun trivia in chat.

FUN TIP

Never Wait

"I'll wait to get started until everyone's here." That's probably one of my least favorite phrases at the start of a phone call or meeting. It's a cue for everyone to check their email or check out. (It also makes everyone wish they had shown up a little later.) This is the perfect time to ask a charismatic question, keep people engaged, and foster warmth. Want to start on a warm note? Ask people, "Do anything fun this past weekend?" or "Have any big plans for the holiday coming up?" If you want to start on a competent note, ask people, "Anyone listen to any good podcasts recently?" or "Anyone reading any good books?"

What do you wish for your interactions? Can you balance out warmth and competence in your brochures, business cards, invites, résumé, website, or tag lines? How about in your profiles, emails, canned responses, or chats? Never miss an opportunity to add purposeful verbal cues.

PRINCIPLE

Use warm cues to call out to warm people. Use competent cues to call out to competent people. When in doubt, use charisma cues to hit both.

Step #4: Inspirational or Informational

The time had come. We needed a new mattress. My husband is a researcher—high in competence. He set out to find the best-tested, highest-rated, latest research-backed mattress on the market. Meanwhile, I looked at pictures on various social profiles and texted two friends who recently bought mattresses and asked what they thought.

My husband was using competence to make a decision—data, numbers, and scientific proof. And I was using warmth—intuition, photos, and my friends' recommendations. We couldn't decide.

Then, sitting at a restaurant one day, we looked outside and saw an advertisement on a bus. It said: "Casper: Obsessively engineered. Outrageous comfort at polite prices."

We looked at each other and said, "That's the one!"

The ad's tag line appealed to both of us because it's a perfect blend of warmth and competence. "Obsessively engineered" is a signal to competent folks like my husband. On the website there are all kinds of competent callouts like "Awarded Best Overall Mattress by *U.S. News & World Report*," and "10-year limited warranty," and "100-night risk-free trial."

You know what hooked me in? "Comfort at polite prices" was a warmth cue that went straight to my heart. *Yay!* I thought. *I won't have to haggle over prices.* When I went to the website there was a picture of a kid giggling in bed and a funny testimonial from *Vogue*. There's even a charismatic video entitled "Meet the Brains Behind the Beds" that lets you meet the engineers and researchers inside Casper labs. That snagged both of our interests.

We bought one for every bed in the house.

Warmth and competence cues can signal the right people. People who respond to warmth want to be **inspired**. They like stories, jokes, metaphors, and social proof.

People who respond to competence want to be **informed**. They want data, research, case studies, and facts.

Not sure if your audience is high in warmth or competence? Think you have a mix of both? Great! Go for the balance. When I teach, and in my videos, I try to strike a perfect balance of warmth and competence.

Here are some guidelines for balancing high competence with high warmth (you might have even noticed these while reading this book):

- Whenever I mention the word *research* or *study*, I follow up with a story.
- Whenever I share a data point, I often add a case study or a metaphor.
- Whenever I mention something competent, I add a splash of warmth, humor, or vulnerability.

I give presentations to all different kinds of audiences—often to leadership teams and engineers, but also to human resources departments, sales reps, entrepreneurs, and doctors. I want to make sure my content cues both inspiration and information, so it resonates with everyone in the audience. I actually count the number of warm and competent cues in my slides to make sure they are balanced.

My warm slides use examples and have funny GIFs, videos, or stories. Competence slides use data, research, charts, and studies. Slides that hit the sweet spot combine both warm and competent elements—I might share a study in story form. Or show a video demo of research. Or animate my data to make it come to life.

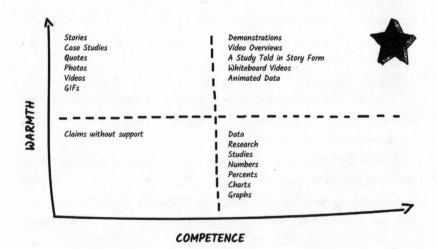

Can you balance inspiration and information?

When socializing with colleagues, can you appeal to their unique charisma characteristics? If you know someone on your team to be a highly warm person, you can *honor* their warmth by matching their charisma with warm topics. Start a meeting by asking about their family and personal life. Point out their family photos at their desk. Share a personal story. And, of course, use more warm words and warm nonverbal cues. Typically, a highly warm person loves chitchat and building rapport.

On the other hand, competent people typically prefer to get right to the action. If *you* want to chitchat, you're best sticking to competent topics—industry news, headlines, sharing professional wins. Use competent words and competent nonverbal cues. In your emails, use more competent language to get them to respond more quickly. They love questions like "Have any big projects coming up?," "Did you see the headlines?," or "Did you hear about [insert industry news]?"

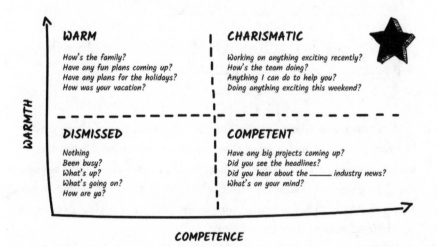

No matter what, steer clear of the Danger Zone by avoiding asking anything boring or negative. Never ask "Been busy?" and try to stay away from non-question questions. These are questions that are so socially scripted we don't even register them. "How are ya?," "What's up?," and "What's going on?" are boring, shmoring. No more, please!

My favorite highly charismatic questions tickle both warmth and competence. Try "Working on anything exciting recently?," "Anything I can do to help you?," or "Doing anything fun this weekend?" Or my personal favorite casual opener, "What's good?"

Want your ideas to resonate? Align your communication cues with the style your audience prefers.

PRINCIPLE

Warm people seek inspiration. Competent people seek information.

Step #5: Be a Verbal Chameleon

Think about the five people you spend the most time with—or the most time thinking about. Who are they? Write their names below:

1. _____
2. _____
3. _____
4. _____
5. _____

Do you know where they fall on the Charisma Scale? Open up the last five emails, chats, or texts they sent you and count the number of warm and competent words they use. You can also take a peek at their social profiles and count the number of warm versus competent words they use. Mark if they're warm, competent, or hit the perfect sweet spot of charisma next to their name above.

The greatest gift you can give these folks is honoring their charisma language. Compliments that highlight their unique blend of charisma are guaranteed to be appreciated. **Highly competent people love to get confirmation of how competent they are.** Tell your competent friends:

"You're so interesting!"

"You always give the best advice."
"I knew you would know what to do."
"I love working with you on projects."

Honor highly warm people with warm feedback and genuine compliments. Tell them:

"You're the best."
"You know how to get the party started!"
"You always make me feel so comfortable."
"I love opening up to you."
"I trust you."

If you aren't sure where they fall, try to hit both warmth and competence with:

"I love having you on the team."
"Thank you for your help and expertise on this."
"This _____ reminded me of you."

Or try my personal favorite: **"I was just thinking of you!"** *Everyone* likes being thought about, whether they're more warm or competent. The usual caveat applies—say these only if they are true. If you don't actually like working with someone, don't say it! If you don't really trust someone and feel uncomfortable saying it, that is a good signal *to you* that you need to work on rebuilding trust with them.

What if you can't think of anything nice to say? If you find yourself always giving negative feedback like "You're always late," "You're being difficult," or "I never know with you!" then it's time for a reboot and a reset. Make it your goal to find at least one genuine warm or competent trait you can highlight.

With difficult people in my life, sometimes all I can find are really small things: "Thanks for always taking notes in the meeting," or "We take our coffee the same way!" Small commonalities can be just as powerful as big ones. It's a great place to start.

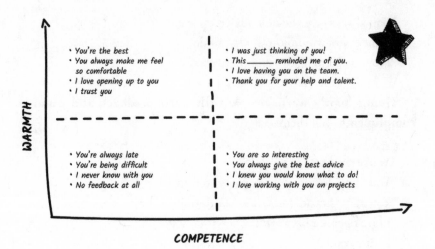

You have another choice when interacting with the important people in your life: Consider verbally matching the person you are with by mirroring subtly—the key here is *subtly*. This is using similar positive or neutral words to the person you're speaking with. I call this being a verbal chameleon.

VERBAL CHAMELEON

Subtly mimicking the kinds of words someone uses to match their charisma style.

Servers who repeat orders back to customers, using their *exact* words, earn 70 percent more in tips than servers who simply use polite and positive words.

In another study, researchers asked participants to negotiate via virtual chat. One group was told to mimic the words of their negotiator in the first ten minutes of the chat. Another group was told to mimic the words of their negotiator in the last ten minutes. And the control group wasn't told to mimic at all. The early mimickers achieved significantly better outcomes than the other groups. **Try verbally mimicking in the first few minutes of an interaction.**

What does this look like in action? Let's look at a talented verbal chameleon: Ellen DeGeneres. Here are just the first four seconds of an exchange between her and Jennifer Aniston.*

JENNIFER: Hello!
ELLEN: Hello!
JENNIFER: Honey. It's good to see you!
ELLEN: It's good to see you.

It was like verbal ping-pong! One of the reasons Ellen bonds so quickly with people who come on her show is that she almost always verbally mirrors during her interviews.

You can do the same in your interactions. If a potential speaking client says to me, "We need a little more proof before moving forward. Do you have any data? The team is a bit worried about having another boring training. We're really looking to inspire change."

I might say, "Absolutely. Like you, we always want proof. I've attached some great testimonials and data. And, of course, we're anti-boring. I have a number of engaging activities planned where the entire goal is inspiring change. Would you like to see a video demo?"

Advanced tip: Sometimes I even match the emoji they prefer. Do they use a :) or a =)? Out of verbal respect, I use their cue.

Just remember to never mimic in a way that doesn't feel like you. I can use one exclamation point, but three feels like overkill. Blogger and illustrator Tim Urban tilts strongly toward competence. He recently tweeted, "I spend a lot of time deciding which sentence in the email is gonna have to take one for the team with the exclamation point." He knows he has to add a little warmth, even if it's a little painful in the process.

A highly warm fan, Matt Popovich, replied to him on Twitter, "I always start with an exclamation point after every sentence, then realize 'wait, they can't ALL have exclamation points, I sound like a lunatic,'

---

* Watch the full video in your digital toolbox.

then pare them back one by one until only a single exclamation point remains."

That's a warm versus competent perspective in action.

I want to make a special note here: Upping your verbal charisma can feel a little unusual at first. It's like flexing a new muscle. One of our students, Allegra, wanted to send over twenty thank-you emails to fashion designers she had met with over Zoom. Allegra noticed that one specific designer used more warm words, so she thought adding charisma cues might make her simple thank-you emails more powerful . . . even if it was a little out of her comfort zone.

"Admittedly, I mostly wanted to get the task done, and copy and paste a formula. However, with this one designer, I went more personal and more WARM. Even a little more expressive than I usually would, using words such as 'Talking with you remains one of the highlights of these events' and 'You are inspiring.' I still slightly cringe but these words were actually true," she explained to me.

Almost immediately the designer emailed back with an offer to meet again.

One study discovered "that thanking a new acquaintance for their help makes them more likely to seek an ongoing social relationship with you."

This might seem obvious, but the *way* you say thanks matters. Allegra's copy-and-paste response didn't create any special replies. But her crafted response, employing more warmth with a warm person, worked. It put her a bit out of her comfort zone, but she made sure to stick to the truth. **Never verbally mirror or use words that feel fake.**

Verbal matching, as with all our cues, also happens unconsciously in your listener. One of our students, Seraphim, found that when he asks, "Would that bother you?" people are more likely to mirror him by saying, "Yes, that would bother me." He now asks, "Are you good with that?" With this small change, he found people look to agree and are more likely to say, "All good."

The more you meaningfully use verbal charisma cues, the more you will generate meaningful responses.

The words you use cue others.

How are you communicating your charisma? Let's do some charisma audits! Review the following assets and count the number of warm and competent words you use. Do they match your charisma goals?

	WARM WORDS	COMPETENT WORDS
LinkedIn profile		
Voicemail		
Email signature		
Your last ten social media posts		
Business card or marketing materials		

Imagery Cues

CHAPTER 10

Creating a Powerful Visual Presence

L et's play a game. Imagine gazing at the moon hanging over the ocean. Really picture it in your head. It's a clear night and the moon is floating in the sky above murky ocean waves.

Now quickly tell me the name of a laundry detergent brand. Go with the first name that pops into your head.

Did you say Tide?

When researchers asked participants about their preferred detergent after they'd been exposed to words like *ocean* and *moon*, they were more likely to mention Tide.

Why? Because the image of a moon over the ocean activates a **neural map** in your brain that includes other words and images related to moons and oceans like tides, water, gravity, and waves. When I asked you to imagine the moon, it brought to the front of your mind everything associated with moons and oceans. And this influenced your answer to the question about detergent.

Everyone's neural maps are slightly different, but most people have similar underlying themes to the emotional associations behind images and ideas. This is how visual cues work best. For example, you might see a picture of a fire engine and that might bring up a neural map of *fire engine* linked to *red* linked to *roses.*

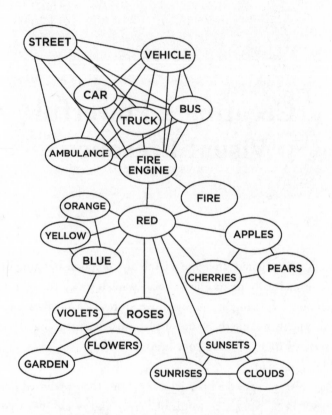

This happens all the time in daily life. Say, for example, you're skimming through photos on Facebook. One potential friend has a picture of her holding a snowboard. That activates your own neural map around snowboards. You think of adventure, ice, mountains, vacation, and family. That gets you excited and nostalgic for trips you took as a kid. You click accept.

Recently, I was walking by the store in my local gym and saw these bags for sale:

Notice anything funny about these gym bags? They have abs! Like rock-hard six-pack abs. If you're going to the gym to work on your six-pack (aren't we all?), these bags will appeal to you.

Visual cues are one of the best ways to attract, welcome, and retain the right people. We can also use visual cues to trigger warmth or competence based on our goals. Are you using visual cues? Let's find out.

VISUAL CUE #1: Elevate Your Prices, Your Look, and Your Brand

"That looks expensive," I said to my husband.

He had just placed a little blue box in front of me.

"Is it jewelry?" I asked.

"Better," he said.

I carefully opened the powder-blue box to reveal nine perfectly nestled cases of exquisite artisanal candy. I have a passionate sweet tooth, so

my husband had handpicked nine different types of Sugarfina candy tailored to my taste. I sampled pink champagne bears, lotus flower gummies, cold-brew cordials, and heart-shaped peach bellinis.

Everything about the experience felt expensive. As soon as I saw the box, I thought it was jewelry. Then it hit me: Tiffany's. The boxes were remarkably similar in size, shape, color, and weight to a Tiffany's jewelry box.

The candies were named after expensive things—bourbon bears, rosé all-day gummies, peach tea, and even single-malt-scotch cordials. Even their green juice gummy bears were in a miniature-sized green juice bottle—and anyone who's ever bought green juice knows how expensive those can be. They triggered my neural maps for other expensive things—making it easier, even enjoyable, to pay four times more than you should for candy gummy bears.

From the beginning, the founders of Sugarfina, Rosie O'Neill and Josh Resnick, wanted to create an elevated candy experience for adults. The made-up name Sugarfina combines *sugar* with the Italian word for fine (great verbal cues). Their stores are nothing like those big candy bin stores in the mall. They're luxurious and artisanal.

Instead of bins upon bins of candy, Sugarfina created an experience like fine dining in their stores. You get your own salesperson who walks around and handpicks one candy to sample at a time. You discuss the finer notes, flavors, and texture of the various gummy and chocolate creations. It's remarkably similar to shopping for fine cheese, wine, or jewelry. Which reminds you that each piece is expensive and should be savored.

Sugarfina uses verbal cues, color cues, and **visual metaphors**. A visual metaphor is a creative representation of an idea, person, place, or thing that creates an association, like designing a candy box after a jewelry box.

Another interesting way Sugarfina was able to get customers to swallow their high prices: visual placement. When Sugarfina started, it was available only at Nordstrom, a luxury retailer. Not in supermarkets or gas stations like other candy brands. Compared to $100 cashmere socks at the register, champagne bears seem cheap!

If you want to elevate your prices, your look, or your brand, try accessing people's neural maps for the finer things.

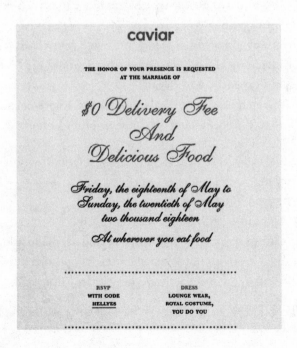

The previous page shows another example of a visual metaphor from the food delivery company Caviar. Does this email remind you of anything?

It looks a lot like a wedding invitation, right? This is a clever email for a few reasons. First, timing. Caviar sent this email on May 18, 2018—the day before Meghan Markle's royal wedding to Prince Harry. This timing (and the $0 delivery fee) makes it a no-brainer to order in food for royal watch parties.

Second, the font, style, and colors were all an immediate visual metaphor for a wedding invitation. And for most people, that's a positive association. There's nothing better than spending a Saturday celebrating love, bopping around the dance floor, and getting free steak. Plus: cake.

Third, it gets you excited! No delivery fee! Delicious food! Yes, please. The visual cues also encourage you to splurge and order wedding-like food. Salmon fillet, anyone?

And last, the invite makes you laugh. The location is adorable: "At wherever you eat food." The dress code was spot-on: "Lounge wear, royal costume, YOU DO YOU." And did you notice the RSVP code? "Hellyes" is a great verbal cue for excitement.

With a few visual cues, Caviar elevates our curiosity, need for their service, and price point.

One great way to use visual metaphor is with fonts. This is critical to the Caviar invitation above. They used what I would call "fancy font." To me, it looks expensive and elegant.

In fact, research has found that people ascribe emotional and personality qualities to typefaces. Here are some helpful findings:*

- People find satirical content as funnier and angrier if written in Times New Roman.
- In comparison, Arial is not funny.
- ALL CAPS LOWERS COMPREHENSION.
- If you want to spark creativity for your readers, make it look pretty. Yes, really. Creativity improves when text is optimized for aesthetic appeal because it reduces activation in our frowning muscles.

---

* Some font associations are cultural. For example, the Japanese find serif fonts elegant, classical, and sleek, compared to narrow fonts, which they see as modern and positive.

- Comic Sans is good for memory. Researchers asked participants to read a story about a fictional alien creature. They remembered more when the story was printed in Comic Sans compared to Arial or Bodoni fonts.

Keep in mind people are surprisingly sensitive to font and have lots of personal preferences. If you're interested in font science, you can find more general rules of thumb in your digital bonuses!

Colors, fonts, and visual metaphors aren't the only things that help us decide someone or something's quality. We take cues from *everything* in our environment. In one study, participants had to assemble puzzle pieces that were either rough (like sandpaper) or smooth. The participants were then asked to rate ambiguous social interactions. Subjects who handled the rough pieces said the interactions were less coordinated, more difficult, and more awkward than those who had the smooth pieces. The rough pieces somehow primed the subjects to see the interactions themselves as rougher.

This was repeated in a number of different experiments. Subjects who sat in hard chairs were more likely to rate others as less flexible and harsh. When a candidate's résumé is read on a heavy clipboard, it's judged as more serious than when it is on a lightweight clipboard. And the most important part: Subjects had no idea that the puzzle pieces, the chairs, or the clipboards were affecting their opinions. We don't realize how much cues affect us.

What does this mean for you? Think about all the cues you're sending to others. Not just your words, vocal power, and body language but also the cues in your environment. How can you elevate them? I was recently looking for a new dermatologist. One dermatologist's office felt like a spa. Plush couches, fresh flowers, cucumber water. Soft music was playing and aromatherapy candles were burning. It was all very warm.

Another dermatologist's office felt like a hospital. It was minimal, clean, and sterile. Everyone was in scrubs. There was no music and no cucumber water. It screamed *competence.*

Can you guess which one I chose? My family has a history of skin cancer, so I take my annual visits extremely seriously. I chose the hospital-like environment.

Neither of these offices are better or worse. Some people resonate more with the warm, cushy environment and want their trip to the dermatologist to resemble a spa visit. Others, like me, resonate more with a medical environment.

Here are some ideas:

- **What words and visual metaphors do you use to describe yourself, your work, or your service?** This is in your tag line, social profiles, marketing materials, and even the posters in your office! I once walked into an office that offered small mandarin oranges in a bowl instead of candy. That felt fresh and fun to me and immediately got me more excited for the visit.
- **What music do you play before a meeting starts, in your waiting room, in your living room, or while customers are on hold?** I noticed that every company I call has different waiting music. The best match their brand. I called Apple support and they were playing "Don't Worry, Be Happy" by Bobby McFerrin. I called my financial services firm, and they were playing calm classical music. How can you use music?
- **What's your go-to font?** My friend Judi Holler, an author and improviser, has a distinct font (Northwell) that she uses in all her posts, on her book cover, and even inside the description of her Instagram

posts—I didn't even know you could change the font in your feed! In her video studio she has a neon sign in her signature font and pink color. Now whenever I see Northwell, I think of *her*!

VISUAL CUE #2: Images That Inspire

Quick question: What do you think of when I say the word *plumber*?

Did you think about water? Toilets? Pipes? Or . . . cracks?

Did you say the word Einstein? Probably not.

I recently witnessed a service truck with the words *Einstein Plumbing* emblazoned on the side, with a huge cartoon depiction of Einstein himself. Their tag line was "The smart choice." I thought this was a clever use of a neural map to differentiate themselves from competitors. They used a visual cue (and verbal cues in their name choice and tag line) that activates common neural maps of intelligence, complicated problem solving, and genius. If you have tough plumbing issues—a stubbornly clogged toilet, old pipes—would you be more apt to try Einstein Plumbing or Wezee's Plumbing (a competitor nearby)?

I shared this story at a recent speaking event and was approached afterward by Jim, the owner of a different plumbing franchise. His company uses *pink* trucks and sports a large picture of a woman (the owner's sister) in an elegant white blouse on their vehicles, website, and marketing materials. Jim said his goal is to appeal to women who want a polite, clean plumber. They take extra care to wear disposable booties over their work boots, they vacuum under the sink after they fix something, and they wear impeccably clean uniforms. He told me the company had always focused on being clean and polite, but when he added the picture of his sister and used the pink branding, the company took off.

Einstein Plumbing uses visual cues to call out to people who value competence. Jim wants to appeal to people who value warmth. Visual cues, especially images, can be used to inspire the right feelings in the right people. Images can even spur physical changes in your body. If you imagine yourself sunbathing on the beach, you'll become more relaxed and warm.

Our brain can identify images we see for as little as thirteen milliseconds, meaning that all the images we see on websites, advertisements, and profiles and in our offices affect our behavior and even our performance. In one study, some phone operators read scripts printed on plain paper, while other operators used scripts with a photo of a runner winning a race on top. Both groups of operators spent three hours dialing for dollars to raise money for a charitable cause. By the end of the three-hour shift, **the group with the image had raised 60 percent more money.** The image of the runner likely triggered neural maps of perseverance, speed, and winning.

The best way to leverage the power of visual cues is to use them as emphasizers. The words *Einstein Plumbing* on the side of a truck is a great verbal cue. But the giant picture of Albert Einstein is more powerful.

One company very familiar with the power of images is Netflix. In one fascinating dive into Netflix's user experience, data scientists found that 82 percent of users' viewing choices are based on images rather than text descriptions. Better images directly translated to increased hours of streaming.

Curious which image cues performed better? Images with three people or fewer did better (even when the show or movie had a large cast). Images of villains performed better than heroes. And this one is really surprising: **Complex facial expressions elicited more views than smiling ones.**

Here are some ideas for how you can cue with images:

- **Your background on video calls.** In a YouTube video of a virtual interview of comedian Kevin Hart, he had a collage of other Black comedians behind him showing positive nonverbal cues. The positive cues on display gives Hart a nice halo effect. Chris Rock is pictured with an eyebrow raise, Bernie Mac is showing a surprised expression, and Richard Pryor is depicted talking into the microphone with one hand raised in a wave. Second, seeing other famous funny comedians makes you associate Hart with their positive legacies. What does your background say about you? Make it count.
- **Images to support your presentations.** Research finds students learn best when presented with images *and* words rather than just words alone. Never-ending bullet points are the worst! Can you add visual

cues to help your audience remember what you have to say? I used to teach nonverbal cues with boring stock images of each cue. Then during a presentation for the Producers Guild of America (my audience were producers and actors), I decided to swap a few stock images for ones with celebrities and athletes showing the body language gestures. Engagement with those slides shot up dramatically. The audience asked more questions and even laughed at some of the images.

- **Use image cues to support your brand or message.** Someone once sent me a picture of the outside of a lawyer's office. There was a giant shark's head bursting out of the top of the door. It was a great cue: "This lawyer is a shark!"

- **Use cues to put people in the right mood.** Last year I arrived in Cabo prepared for a torturous customs experience. And then . . . I was surprised. I arrived to a redone terminal. The walls were lined with wall-sized screens showing lapping waves and swaying palm trees. Soothing music was playing. There were plants and palms placed around the room. Curiously, the line did not move faster, but it felt more relaxing. It actually got me even more excited to be in Mexico and jump on the beach. A few visual cues made all the difference.

- **Don't forget about hidden visual cue opportunities.** What image do you use as your desktop background or the lock screen on your phone? Those images cue you and the people who see your phone or computer. Or what about the images on the back of your business card? Try adding some warmth cues, such as images of people, to humanize yourself or your products and increase sales. Or add competence cues like certification stamps, pictures of your signature at the bottom of an email, or seals of approval to your branding.

Special Note: Beware of confusing visual cues. A few years back, a pizza restaurant in our old neighborhood devised a terrible marketing campaign. They printed up yellow envelopes containing pizza vouchers that looked *exactly* like parking tickets and put them on people's cars. This cue certainly got me to open the envelope and look inside, but I wasn't relieved, I was angry. And I was definitely not in the mood for pizza.

VISUAL CUE #3: Your Nonverbal Brand

Benjamin Franklin was sent to Versailles as the American minister to France. He wanted to stand out among the other members of Louis XVI's court. The fashion of the time included powdered wigs, velvet coats, and silk pants. Stylish!

But Franklin decided to be different.

"I want to look more like a pioneer than a prince," he told his daughter as he prepared for the trip.

He decided to go wigless and sported plain American cotton. It was a hit! He looked different, he acted different, and court members were delighted and intrigued at this strange specimen from the new world. Franklin wanted to be a walking representation of American values and pioneering spirit. He created a **nonverbal brand**.

NONVERBAL BRAND

Using visual cues to signal values, culture, and personality.

My friend David Nihill, an author and a comedian, created a nonverbal brand by accident. Before Nihill's comedic and speechwriting career took off, he was looking for a job. He landed a promising role at one of the world's largest private education companies in London. The day before his job started, he washed all his clothes and laid out his outfit. Then he realized he had one big problem: He had somehow shrunk all of his shirts in the dryer.

He didn't have time to buy new shirts on such short notice. So he devised a clever way to hide most of the shrinkage. "I rolled up my shirt sleeves so you couldn't tell the sleeves were waaaay shorter than my arms," Nihill explained.

Every day for the first week he wore a different shirt with rolled-up sleeves. He prayed no one noticed. But they did, and in a different way than Nihill expected. "People started to call me a roll-the-sleeves-up kind of guy and started calling me a problem solver. It was amazing, it was as if the rolled-up sleeves made me look ready to work. Ready to dig my hands in. Ready to get to it," explained Nihill.

Nihill became the designated problem solver for the company—even though that was not what he was hired to do. "I began to bypass people. I became the director of special projects, where my entire job was to fix stuff. My salary multiplied by three, and in a company of over fifty thousand people I was suddenly reporting to the CEO. And everyone just knew me as David, the Irish roll-the-sleeves-up kind of guy, all because I couldn't solve the original problem of drying my own shirts," said Nihill.

This visual cue changed people's perceptions of Nihill *and* changed Nihill's perceptions of himself. "I started to think of myself as a problem solver and doer. I made decisions faster and asked forgiveness rather than permission, I experimented, I even took the whole staff bungee jumping, even though I had never done it before myself. I got braver. I grew into the assumption that I was a go-getter," said Nihill.

Without realizing it, Nihill created a nonverbal brand with a simple visual cue. A great nonverbal brand is interesting enough to attract attention while also signaling values. Nihill's rolled-up shirt sleeves cued others to think of him as a doer.

The best nonverbal brand cues also embody personality characteristics of the owner. Think Lucille Ball's fiery red hair or Prince's outrageous suits. Nonverbal brands also help people become instantly recognizable: Sinatra had his signature fedora, Coco Chanel wore pearls, and Mr. T donned gold chains. And there are many, many other famous examples: Charlie Chaplin's mustache and bowler, Bill Nye the Science Guy's bow tie and lab coat, Elton John's quirky glasses, Paris Hilton's Chihuahuas and little purses, or Sherlock's deerstalker hat, pipe, and trench coat.

Visual cues can instantly tell people what you're all about—what you do and what's important to you. For example, the late U.S. senator Robert Byrd reportedly carried a copy of the U.S. Constitution in his jacket pocket just so he could wave it around and remind everyone who controlled the checkbook. Another favorite symbol for politicians? A flag pin. A flag pin in itself seems to symbolize political aspirations.

Visual cues are one of the fastest ways to sway people's opinions and behavior. Researchers found that the mere presence of a backpack or briefcase in the research lab changed behavior. The backpack inspired more cooperation (a warmth cue); a briefcase, more competitive behavior (a competence cue).

Crafting a nonverbal brand is a great way to use visual cues to help you achieve your personal goals. For example, award-winning television producer and movie studio executive Lee Tomlinson wears a hospital gown onstage during his presentations—even during his TED Talk. When Tomlinson beat stage 3 throat cancer, he dedicated the rest of his life to inspiring healthcare professionals. He found that when he took the stage in a hospital gown (rather than a suit), it immediately triggered the audience's compassion and put them in a warm state of mind. They didn't have to visualize him as a patient, they could *see* him as a patient. Visual cues bring ideas to life.

FUN TIP

Glasses or Contacts?

Glasses are an instant symbol of competence. In our internal study, we asked people to rate the same person on warmth and competence with and without glasses. Warmth scores did not change at all, but when the same person wore glasses, they were rated as 8 percent more competent. A small but important boost. If you want to dial up your competence, consider ditching the contacts.

My favorite way to build a nonverbal brand is with **teaching aids**. I've been filming YouTube videos for the last fourteen years. Since I use YouTube for teaching, I've now had to get creative to make my videos stand out from all the makeup tutorials and unboxing videos. **The key is to create a consistent cue language across your brand assets.**

I use visual cues to help my viewers make decisions. I discovered I could immediately orient people in a video by using certain props. When sharing a highly competent concept, where I'm demoing or explaining a complicated idea, I pull out my whiteboard.

In my videos on presentation skills, I record from behind a podium, so my public speaking students know exactly which videos are for them.

When I give virtual webinars, I hang framed pictures of my favorite chemicals—oxytocin, serotonin, and dopamine—so they appear in the background on the wall behind me. This cues competence right from the first frame of the webinar. I also use them as teaching aids during the presentation. I've noticed when I don't have these behind me, it's hard for people to grasp the importance of these chemicals. Visual cues can help enhance understanding and reinforce your message.

FUN TIP

Post-it Power

I've found Post-its are one of the easiest visual ways to encourage someone to remember something. In my presentations, I show pictures of Post-it notes on slides with the takeaways written on them. This visually cues for memory and subtly reminds people to write down the takeaway in their notes.

We can also use a nonverbal brand to **symbolize a change**. In her memoir, *You're Never Weird on the Internet (Almost)*, Felicia Day tells a story of how no one attended her violin performances. She decided to hook people in with a **nonverbal rebrand**. Instead of putting up boring posters with her name and photo, she mocked up a new flyer showing her in a *Xena: Warrior Princess* outfit with the title "Felicia: Warrior Violinist." You can bet more people started to attend her violin performances.

When I lead all-day workshops, I've found one great visual cue helps me mark a change of pace: a wrapped gift. I often put a wrapped present onstage toward the end of a long day to get people excited for the last section. When people see the wrapped present, it literally triggers dopamine, gets people excited, and beats the afternoon slump. And then I gift it to a stellar audience member.

FUN TIP

Don't Hold a Cat!

If you are single, male, and heterosexual and on a dating app, you might want to put down the cat. Research finds women rate men holding a cat as less masculine and less dateable. I'm sorry to cat lovers everywhere.

Think about the cues in your office, in the background of your video calls, or on the walls of your home. Degrees, awards, and certificates all signal for competence. Family photos, funny quotes, and mementos all cue for warmth. Our friend Judi Holler of Northwell font fame has a piñata in the background of her videos—it's an immediate representation of her fun spirit.

How can you playfully use more visual cues? Can you put pins on your backpack? Stickers on your laptop or bumper? Can you get props that represent your ideas in presentations or pitches? Every visual cue helps shape people's perceptions of you.

VISUAL CUE #4: Color Me Confident

In 1967, a secret club opened in Disneyland. It was invite only. It was the only spot in the Magic Kingdom you could purchase alcohol. And, boy oh boy, was it exclusive. To get in, you had to join a waiting list and pay thousands of dollars. And Disney Imagineers worked hard to conceal it.

In fact, many visitors walk right by Club 33's door nestled in the heart of New Orleans Square. The door isn't concealed or blocked, but it's still relatively invisible. Why? It's painted with two colors Disney created to hide things.

They call these colors "go away green" and "no seeum grey."

Administration buildings, staff entrances, and utility boxes are all painted in these two colors. Compared to the bright and opulent colors of the park, the chosen colors make things blend into the background. Color is one of the best tools we have for calling attention to important elements (or hiding ones we want out of sight). Color is also one of the fastest ways to activate neural maps.

One study found people make up their minds within 90 seconds of their initial interactions with either people or products. And **62 to 90 percent of that assessment is based on color alone**.

Color psychology is mostly pseudoscience. We know color matters but we aren't able to understand with 100 percent certainty how. No one has yet produced a reliable map of all colors and their associations. However, there are some promising visual cues we can use from color research. The most important cue is that color activates neural maps in the brain.

For example, in one fascinating study, researchers gave participants placebo pills in warm (orange, red, yellow) and cool (blue, green, purple) colors. Think the Matrix but less cool. They found that warm-colored placebo pills were reported as more effective than cool-colored placebo pills! Whoa. Why?

The scientists believe warm colors are associated "with a stimulant effect, while blue and green are related to a tranquilizing effect."

The best way to use color is to think about *common* neural maps. What does a color remind you of? What are some universal objects that use this color? What international brands use a certain color combo? Does your culture associate certain colors to certain things?

For example, in China, the color yellow is associated with royalty. The first emperor of China was known as the Yellow Emperor.

In the United States, Democrats are the blue party, Republicans are the red party. During the 2020 U.S. presidential election, Fox News, a known conservative news network, colored the word *presidential* in the phrase *presidential debate* red on all of their banners.

MSNBC, a liberal network, used blue for the word *presidential* in *presidential debate* on all of their news banners during election coverage. This subtle color change indicated preference—Fox wanted a red president and MSNBC wanted a blue one.

While there aren't universal color associations, colors can cue us in certain circumstances.* Let's look at some of the patterns:

Red

When we flush with anger or blush with pleasure, we turn red. This happens across cultures, genders, and races. Researchers found that red has the greatest effect on our emotions, spurring feelings of dominance and arousal. It is a testosterone-based cue that connotes power, strength, threat, and dominance.

One research team found that competitors randomly assigned to wear red (compared to blue) were more likely to win in competitions. This was particularly the case with male competitors.

How does this help us? Red is an action-oriented color. It makes people take notice. If you wear red, it triggers attention. If you use red in your promotional materials, your office, or your profiles, it will stand out more than if you used more muted colors.

And this makes sense—when our cave-dwelling ancestors were foraging for berries, they were looking for brightly colored ripe fruit, often red strawberries or red apples. Red makes us want to take action—pick the berry or calm down an angry friend.

Below are a few tips for employing red strategically:

• Have an important note or callout in a presentation? Consider making it red.

---

* One research group is doing an international Colour-Emotion Survey and has collected thousands of responses on how each country interprets color. If you are curious what colors mean in your country, be sure to check out the link in your digital bonuses at scienceofpeople.com/bonus.

- Don't use red on unimportant items or notes in slides or graphics.
- Want someone to relax? Feel calm? Don't put them in a red room or a red chair.
- Want to blend in? Don't wear red. Want to stand out? Red might work for you.

Bottom Line: Red inspires action. Use it wisely.

Blue

No matter where you are in the world, a clear sky is the color blue. Universally, deep water looks blue. So for most people, blue triggers a neural map relating to calm. Anecdotal evidence also suggests that blue causes the body to feel more relaxed—perhaps activating the neural map when you see a clear blue sky or clean blue water. Some have even suggested that installing blue-colored streetlights can lead to reduced crime. In the business world, market research finds that when companies use blue in stores or in logos, it increases perceptions of quality and trust.

Other research finds that blue light increases alertness and performance in attention-based tasks. This has been reported in a number of studies—one even found that people are more productive when working in a blue room!

So how can you best use blue?

- Want to look calm and collected? Consider wearing blue. I wear it onstage to keep myself calm!
- Want to add some color to your office or desk? Add some sparks of blue.
- Want to make your presentations more interesting? Consider using blue instead of black and white in your handouts, materials, and slides.

Bottom Line: Blue is a great color for triggering calm, productivity, and trust.

Green

Over the last few decades, green has evolved and created new neural maps. Researchers found that using the color green in branding is highly associated with environmentalism.

Green is often used to portray eco-friendly, environmentally safe, chemical-free, "clean," and even socially responsible products and companies. We even say things like "Going green" or "Is it a green product?"

Other researchers have found that green is seen as a color associated with well-being and enjoyment. This resonated with me and reminded me that as a kid I played Red Light, Green Light. When someone shouted "Green!" it meant go, go, go, sprint as fast as you can, let loose, run wild. When you heard "Red!" you froze. To this day I still use green flash cards in an exercise to show a beginning and red flash cards to indicate an end.

Researchers also find that athletes who performed physical trials reported slightly higher levels of enjoyment when they were in a green environment than when they were in a red environment.

This makes sense from an instinctive point of view—when we're surrounded by green, it reminds us of a lush, fertile environment with plenty of water and nutrients.

How can you use green?

- Make it easy for people to follow rules by reminding them with color. During the COVID-19 pandemic, some companies issued red, yellow, and green armbands to employees who had to go back to work. Green armbands said, "Okay with hugs & high fives," yellow said, "Okay with talking but not touching," and red said, "Hi! I'm keeping my distance." People could quickly identify others' needs based on the color they were wearing.
- If you have an eco-friendly idea, product, or factoid, consider putting it in green. If you want to make someone feel refreshed and energized, green might be for you.
- Surround yourself with green whenever you can. Put a little succulent garden next to your desk. Make your desktop a background of

green trees. The green colors will activate positive associations of nature and relaxation.

Bottom Line: Green means go . . . and eco-friendly depending on your associations.

Yellow

In a comprehensive study of the color yellow, researchers found that across more than fifty countries, yellow is strongly associated with joy. And this makes sense, right? Think of all the happy days you spent playing in the sunshine as a kid. The warm feeling of the sun on your back, the endless possibilities of a cloudless day—this is why most people feel that yellow signals happiness.

This is why I chose yellow as the pop of color in Science of People's logo. We use a lot of white and black on our website, but we chose yellow to brighten everything up. However, we didn't know this would create an unforeseen problem for us: Yellow is a fatiguing color to the eye due to the high amount of light that it reflects. It's one of the most difficult colors to read, and using yellow as a background on a slide, handout, or computer can lead to serious eyestrain. Oops.

Yellow is great but don't overdo it.

How can you use yellow?

- Yellow is great for a pop of color but try not to have too much yellow in your presentations, documents, or marketing materials, as it will make them hard to look at.
- Want something to look joyful or happy? Yellow is your color!

Bottom Line: Yellow is like sunshine—it makes us feel warm and lovely, but too much and you get a sunburn.

Pair this color research with your own neural maps to cue the right color for your goals. Here are some ideas:

- **Colorize all of your assets.** When designing presentations or slides, pick colors that match your intention. Be purposeful when you choose a color to wear in your profile photos or headshot. Pick colors in your office or home that make you and the people in them feel welcome. What color is your business card? Can you do something more exciting than white and black?
- **Use colors that appeal to your team.** Back in 2016, my company was looking to hire a marketing agency. We received several proposals but one stood out. Why? The pitch used *our* brand colors, fonts, and images from our website. Instead of having their brand all over the presentation, they matched ours. It made the company's ideas look like *our* ideas because they were already using our brand visual cues.
- **Do you have a personal brand color?** I use A LOT of one kind of blue. It was the color I used on the American cover of my last book, *Captivate.* So everyone on my team calls it "Captivate blue." We have Sharpies, Post-its, notepads, and even candles in this color in the office. When we send out thank-you notes or gifts, they're always wrapped in Captivate blue paper. Many of the dresses I wear in presentations are the same color as my book cover and slides, which are in Captivate blue. Can you pick a personal brand color?

VISUAL CUE #5: Cues That Bias

So far in our journey together we've talked about cues that empower. We've talked about leveraging cues to connect with others and share our ideas. But some cues are a little harder to swallow. Cues that we need to know but aren't super comfortable to talk about. Gender, class, race, and attractiveness are all cues over which we have no control but are used to make decisions about people nonetheless. And many of these cues are unconscious.

An **unconscious bias** is a social stereotype we carry about certain groups of people. A single cue might activate a neural map we aren't consciously aware of. Sadly, researchers found that fictitious résumés with

"White-sounding names" received 50 percent more callbacks for interviews compared to résumés with "African American–sounding" names.

In another study, science faculty rated male applicants for a manager position as significantly more competent and hirable than female applicants. They also offered a higher starting salary to the male applicant.

One study found that people with stereotypically "gay-sounding" voices face more discrimination and stigma regardless of their sexual orientation.

Attractive people are viewed as more competent and earn higher salaries. It's called the beauty premium. This premium exists with both men and women.

Research also finds that women who wear makeup are seen as more trustworthy and receive larger money transfers in an economic game— and this is from both female and male transferers. Interestingly, the less attractive a woman was considered to be, the more the makeup increased her perceived trustworthiness.

Makeup isn't the only visual cue we notice. How you wear your hair sends cues as well. Black women with natural hairstyles were perceived to be less professional, less competent, and less likely to be recommended for a job interview compared to Black women with straightened hairstyles and White women with either curly or straight hairstyles.

While these cues may be difficult to grapple with and try to change, grapple we must. Here's the good news: Research finds unconscious biases are malleable. We *can* take steps to minimize their impact. We have to fight our unconscious bias cues on two fronts.

First, being more aware of your own unconscious biases is a first important step to fighting them. Harvard University championed an initiative called Project Implicit. They offer free tests to the public where you can gauge your true unconscious bias on disabilities, race, age, sexuality, gender, weight, religion, skin tone, and more. If you want to see where your implicit biases lie, I highly recommend taking some of the tests so you can begin to address your negative neural associations head-on.

Second, how do you fight *other people's* unconscious biases toward you? Even small visual cues can help. Researchers tested whether clothing could change people's unconscious bias toward Black men. The research team photographed five Black men in three different outfits—a championship soccer uniform, a sweatshirt and sweatpants, or a button-down shirt and trousers. They then asked participants to look at randomly assigned photos and rate the men on several characteristics.

First, participants who scored high on the Symbolic Racism Scale (which tests for unconscious racist biases) judged all the models more harshly.

However, Black men in the button-down shirt and trousers (the most formal of the outfits) got the most positive evaluations. They were rated as more trustworthy, intelligent, and warm than the men in soccer uniforms. They were also rated as more intelligent and hardworking than the men in sweat outfits.

I mentioned in a previous chapter that women tend to be seen as higher in warmth and men tend to be seen as higher in competence. As unfair as these biases are, knowing they exist is imperative. Women need to work purposefully to dial up competence if they want to be taken seriously. Men must consciously dial up warmth if they want to increase trust.

Here's what's key: **Know the biases that are working for you and against you, and counteract them slowly, consciously, and purposefully.**

I know that as a female speaker and an author on the younger side of the age scale, I have to work hard to dial up my competence cues, especially onstage. I do this in a few ways using all the tips I shared in this book:

- I use more competent words—especially in my introduction. I also add more competence cues to my bio, LinkedIn profile, and intro slide.
- I warm up my vocal cords longer so I can speak in my lowest natural register for longer periods of time. I practice my answers to the questions that make me nervous during Q&As so I don't accidentally use the question inflection or tip into vocal fry.
- I dress more formally than other people in the room.
- I dial up my competent nonverbal cues during my first and last impressions.

- I add competent visual cues to my slides, branding and teaching. The chemicals behind me in my videos, Science of People, the name of my company, and even the mini-experiments we do in our lab are all purposefully counteractive competence cues.

It would be a fairer world if we didn't need to change the way we acted based on the perceptions of others. **And it's especially unjust that you are the one who has to counteract someone else's biases**. I hope one day these biases will change. Meanwhile, let's work together to change our shared biases. What cues can you counteract?

CHAPTER CHALLENGE

Let's put everything we learned about visual cues into action. Look at the following nonverbal brand assets and take stock of the visual cues you use. Then brainstorm what visual cues and nonverbal branding you might like to create.

	CURRENT VISUAL CUES	IDEAL NONVERBAL BRAND
What does your profile photo say about you? Do you send any visual cues in your photos?		
What visual cues do you send in your business card, website, résumé, or other marketing materials?		
What props are in your office, home, or video background?		
Do you have a signature font or color you use?		

Cues Best Practices

Physicist Heinrich Hertz spent years studying electromagnetic waves. Finally, in 1889 he made an incredible discovery. He first conclusively demonstrated the existence of electromagnetic waves—which would turn out to change the way the world communicated forever.

Yet Hertz didn't see value in his ideas. When asked about the importance of his discovery, he said, "It's of no use whatsoever." When asked about the applications of radio waves he stated, "Nothing, I guess."

Nothing? Little did he know his groundbreaking discovery would go on to fuel innovation in communication, entertainment, and even warfare for *decades*. In 1930, his peers honored him by attaching his name to the unit of frequency.

Hertz grossly underestimated himself and his work. He didn't see the potential in his idea. He downplayed his experiments.

I meet people like Heinrich Hertz all the time. Brilliant, creative, innovative thinkers who underestimate themselves, doubt their talents, and downplay their work.

No more!

You have ideas worth sharing.

You deserve to be respected, taken seriously, and recognized for your hard work.

Heck, you finished this book, so I know you're smart as a whip (and amazing).

Every cue in this book has helped me in more ways than I can count. The cues I have shared with you are *exactly* the cues I use before every meeting, video call, or important conversation. My hope is that these charisma cues will help you and others feel more confident in your ideas. Competent cues will help people take you seriously, respect your ideas, and improve your credibility. Warmth cues will help people put more trust in you, want to work with you, and get excited by your ideas. **But cues are powerful only if you use them.**

Here are some best practices to keep in mind as you activate your cues.

RULE #1: Expect the Best

Learning to read cues is not about scrutinizing everyone you meet. It's not about creating "gotcha moments." It's not about catching people in lies or constantly being on the hunt for dishonesty. In fact, this approach actually makes you *less* effective.

Researchers found that the more trusting you are of others, the more accurate you are at spotting hidden emotions. True masters of cue reading expect the best and know how to spot the worst when it arises.

And remember: Cues should never be taken out of context. This is especially true for negative cues. Before jumping to *any* conclusions about a negative cue, ask yourself: What else might be happening? What has someone experienced *before* being with you? Did they have a fight with a partner? Did they just step off an airplane? Are they slammed at work? If you see a negative cue, look for context and background first.

RULE #2: Don't Fake It

Learning cues is not about pretending to be smarter or more likable than you are. It's not about using cues as a cover-up. Even the most powerful cues cannot fake expertise . . . at least not in the long run.

If you don't actually feel competent, please don't try to pretend. Competence cues will get you only so far, and eventually you will be found out. If you need to buff up your expertise or pump up your skills, make that a priority.

Can you fake warmth? Yes, it's possible. But it's also exhausting. If you don't actually feel warm toward a person, don't be phony. Work on building true rapport. Find something you actually like about them. Search for common interests. Highlight mutual goals you can agree on even a little bit. It's way more effort to cover up dislike and inauthenticity. Work on finding real reasons to like someone first so it's easier to send the right cues.

RULE #3: Use the Rule of Three

In this book we learned more than forty powerful cues from business leaders, politicians, and world-class communicators. Now you possess the same menu of cues to be charismatic in every interaction.

Challenge yourself to try every cue in this book at least three times. The first time it might feel a little uncomfortable. That's good! This means you're learning. The second time, hopefully it will feel a little more empowering. By the third time you'll be able to consciously decide if it's a cue you want to add to your toolbox.

The Cues Chart is the best way to track each cue and note how you use them. I recommend trying to

- Decode each cue at least three times in different scenarios.
- Encode each cue at least three times in different scenarios.
- Take notes on how each one could help with your charisma goals.

Here's a sample row of the Cues Chart to see how our students typically fill it out:

CUE	DECODE	ENCODE	INTERNALIZE
Leaning: Tilt your body forward to show interest, curiosity, and engagement.	1. Dan did this when he agreed in our meeting. 2. Local news when both anchors leaned into each other during a joke. 3. Kids leaned in while waiting for us to serve ice cream.	1. Mirrored Dan when he leaned into me! 2. Leaned in and down when talking to Sam about bad grades—worked! 3. Leaned in on video call to show interest.	*Need to add this to my next presentation!

Now it's your turn. Track your cue decoding and encoding and see how it makes you feel.

CHARISMA CUES

Use these cues any time you want to be seen as charismatic.

CUE	DECODE	ENCODE	INTERNALIZE
Leaning: Tilt your body forward to show interest, curiosity, and engagement.			
Anti-Blocking: An open body signals an open mind. Keep your body free of any blocks—arms, computers, notebooks, purses, or clipboards.			
Fronting: Align your toes, torso, and top toward the person you are speaking with to show nonverbal respect.			

CUE	DECODE	ENCODE	INTERNALIZE
Space: Observe all four space zones—intimacy, personal, social, and public—to match your goals.			
Confident Pitch: Use the lowest natural end of your voice tone to signal confidence.			
Breathing Pause: Pause in between your words to get breath, slow down, and create intrigue.			
Charismatic Words: Use words that match your charisma goals.			

WARM CUES

Use these cues to stimulate warmth, likability, and trust.

CUE	DECODE	ENCODE	INTERNALIZE
Nodding: Nod to show agreement and engagement.			
Tilting: Head tilt to show someone you're listening and interested.			

CUE	DECODE	ENCODE	INTERNALIZE
Eyebrow Raise: Raise your eyebrows to show intrigue and delight.			
Smiling: A genuine smile increases and encourages happiness.			
Touch: Appropriate touch increases the chemical that helps us bond.			
Mirroring: Subtly match someone's nonverbal gestures or posture to show respect.			
Permission Warmth: Start your calls, conversations, and emails by cueing for warmth.			

CUE	DECODE	ENCODE	INTERNALIZE
Vocal Variety: Avoid vocal funks or sounding too rehearsed. Add vocal emphasis and personality to your voice.			
Vocal Invitations: Make listening sounds, use verbal nudges, and vocally mirror people to increase warmth.			
Warm Words: Warm words trigger trust, compassion, and empathy.			

COMPETENT CUES

Use these cues to trigger competence, capability, and effectiveness.

CUE	DECODE	ENCODE	INTERNALIZE
Power Posture: Take up space to show confidence.			
Lower Lid Flex: Flex your lower lid to show you're intently listening and engaged.			

CUE	DECODE	ENCODE	INTERNALIZE
Steepling: Steeple to show you're relaxed and grounded and have it all together.			
Explanatory Gestures: Use clear hand gestures to demonstrate points.			
Volume Dynamism: Use volume to support your points—speak up when it matters, speak softer when you want people to lean in.			
Power Pause: Pause to create intrigue right before an important point.			
Competent Words: Competent words trigger intelligence, power, and credibility.			

DANGER ZONE CUES

Don't try these unless you want to be purposefully negative. But do make a note if you decode one of these cues or accidentally encode one.

CUE	DECODE	ENCODE	INTERNALIZE
Lip Purse: Pressed lips shows withholding or closing up.			
Distancing: When we don't like something or we want someone to move away, step away or lean back to create distance.			
Ventilating: When we get nervous, we try to get air on our skin to cool ourselves off or give ourselves space.			
Comfort Gesture: We self-touch to calm ourselves down or comfort ourselves.			
Preen: When we adjust our hair, makeup, clothing, or accessories to enhance our appearance.			
Suprasternal Notch Touch: When we're nervous or want to self-comfort, we touch the notch between our two collarbones (or the tie, necklace, or shirt near it).			

CUE	DECODE	ENCODE	INTERNALIZE
Body Block: When we want to protect ourselves or self-comfort, we put a barrier in front of our body, mouth, or eyes.			
Shame: When we feel ashamed, we might touch the sides of our foreheads with our fingertips.			
Anger: When we feel angry, we pull our eyebrows down into a furrow, harden our lower lids, and tense our lips.			
Nose Flare: We might flare our nostrils in anger.			
Sadness: When we feel sad, we pull the corners of our eyebrows down and together, move our lips into a frown, and droop our upper eyelids.			
Mouth Shrug: Pulling the corners of our mouth down into a frown signals disbelief or doubt.			
Contempt: When we feel scorn, we pull up one side of our mouth into a smirk.			

CUE	DECODE	ENCODE	INTERNALIZE
Question Inflection: When we're asking a question, we go up in vocal pitch at the end of our sentences. Don't accidentally use it on a statement.			
Vocal Fry: When we lose breath or feel anxious, our vocal cords rattle together to produce a grating vocal fry.			
Verbal Fillers: Fluff words and sounds like *um*, *so*, *you know*, and *like* all signal a lack of confidence or knowledge.			
Vocal Denials: When we don't like something, we make negative listening sounds like *ooph*, *yikes*, or *ugh*. These signal disagreement.			

Be sure to practice decoding and encoding each cue in a few scenarios with a few different people—at work, at home, with friends. Dial up your warmth and competence to always be in the sweet spot of the Charisma Zone.

Make every cue work for you. Modify them, adapt them, and add your own twists and flairs—although not a nose flare, which can be seen as aggressive.

I'm cheering you on and can't wait to see how cues change your communication, your interactions, and your confidence as they have changed mine. Even one cue can make all the difference.

To your success,
Vanessa Van Edwards

P.S. Thank you. Thank you for taking the time to read this book. Thank you for learning with me. Thank you for trusting me with your time. If you enjoyed it, please share this knowledge with someone else. Gift this book to a friend, loan it to a colleague, give it to someone who needs it. I'm grateful for you.

Corporate Workshops

Want to bring the power of cues to your organization? Science of People regularly hosts formal trainings for teams, organizations, and events.

For more information or to watch videos from my previous workshops, visit **scienceofpeople.com/speaking**.

I would love to meet you!

Digital Bonuses

We have so many bonuses for you along with this book, like:

- Lie to Me templates for your friends and family
- Video demos of advanced cues
- Discussion questions for your book club or reading partner
- Videos of the cues from the celebrities, politicians, and folks in this book

To get your extra reader goodies, visit:

scienceofpeople.com/bonus

Want even more learning? We have so many ways for you to advance your skills!

People School

Learn the twelve advanced people skills every professional should know. People School is a science-based interpersonal communication training program. It's designed to help you advance your career, stand out from your peers, and give you the communication foundation you need to develop purposeful, powerful, and authentic people skills. It took more than ten years to develop, and has taught 50,000-plus students in over fifty countries.

Powerful Presentations

Want to become a better public speaker? Learn to captivate any audience onstage, on video, and in meetings. You will learn the essential presentation skills for your professional toolbox, including the best way to start and end a speech, how to work a stage, expert tips for video calls, and how to keep an audience's attention. This virtual training will help you level up your stage presence whether you're in person or on video.

Decode Software

Want to practice reading facial expressions? Try our new Decode Software to test your skills. Learn how to read emotion and speed-read faces. Our software lets you practice your decoding abilities with full expressions, subtle expressions, and even expressions under face masks!

Check out all of our courses at:

scienceofpeople.com/products

Acknowledgments

I'm so grateful to many people for this book!

First, thank YOU for reading it. I want to send a heartfelt thanks to all of our readers, students, and YouTube viewers. Without you, I would not have been able to write this book. Your likes, support, comments, and shares over the last decade have fueled this incredible business and my ability to write. Thank you for supporting me.

Thank you to the stupendous Science of People Team, especially Rob Hwang, Vanessa Mae Rameer, Josh White, Haley Van Petten, and Courtney Van Petten—thank you for all the support you have given me while writing this book. Thank you so much to Maggie and Lacy Kirkland for the amazing photos and loving support.

Thank you to my amazing publishing team! David Fugate, Niki Papadopoulos, Kimberly Meilun, Leah Trouwborst, and of course Adrian Zackheim for helping me to share my ideas with the world.

I want to give a huge thank-you to the entire team at Impact Theory, especially Tom and Lisa Bilyeu and Chase Caprio. Thank you to Joe Gebbia. I feel lucky to know you. Also big thanks to Noah Zandan and the team at Quantified Communications.

Thank you to everyone who has helped me on this amazing journey. A special thanks to everyone who has given me sage business advice and support: Dr. Paul Zak, Chris Guillebeau, Jayson Gaignard, Lewis Howes, Jordan Harbinger, Zach Suchin, Charlie Gilkey, Nir Eyal, Shane Snow, Noah Kagan, Paige Hendrix Buckner, José Piña, Chase Jarvis, and the Creative Live Team.

Thank you to those of you who helped me with quotes, stories, and inspiration for this book, in particular, David Nihill, Brian Dean, David Moldawer, Michelle Poler, Judi Holler, Nicholas Hutchison, and Michelle Jones. Thank you to Dax Shepard and Alan Alda—your amazing podcasts were the source of many of these stories.

Thank you to my entire family, especially my parents, Anita First and Vance and Stacy Van Petten. To my friends and support system— thank you for all the pep talks and love.

Scott Edwards, you are the best business and life partner a person could have.

And, last, I know you can't read yet but one day you will: thank you, Sienna Edwards, for making me giggle, giving me inspiration, and being the joy of my life.

Notes

Introduction: The Signals That Are Secretly Shaping You

1   **when Jamie went on the show:** *Shark Tank*, season 5, episode 9, aired November 15, 2013, on ABC, http://www.imdb.com/title/tt3263264.

2   **Research has found that when the question inflection:** "The Unstoppable March of the Upward Inflection?," *BBC News*, August 11, 2014, https://www.bbc.com/news/magazine-28708526.

2   **When the question inflection is used:** Michel Belyk and Steven Brown, "Perception of Affective and Linguistic Prosody: An ALE Meta-Analysis of Neuroimaging Studies," *Social Cognitive and Affective Neuroscience* 9, no. 9 (September 2014): 1395–403, https://doi.org/10.1093/scan/nst124.

2   **the position of the mouth makes it impossible to speak:** Belyk and Brown, "Perception of Affective and Linguistic Prosody"; Maria del Mar Vanrell et al., "Intonation as an Encoder of Speaker Certainty: Information and Confirmation Yes-No Questions in Catalan," *Language and Speech* 56, no. 2 (2013): 163–90, https://doi.org/10.1177/0023830912443942.

4   **Liars halt. So do:** Desmond Morris, *Bodytalk: A World Guide to Gestures* (London: Jonathan Cape, 1994).

4   **Hundreds of subtle signals:** Aldert Vrij, *Detecting Lies and Deceit: Pitfalls and Opportunities*, 2nd ed. (West Sussex, England: John Wiley & Sons, 2008).

5   **We can predict a leader's:** Konstantin O. Tskhay, Rebecca Zhu, and Nicholas O. Rule, "Perceptions of Charisma from Thin Slices of Behavior Predict Leadership Prototypicality Judgments," *Leadership Quarterly* 28, no. 4 (March 2017): 555–62, https://doi.org/10.1016/j.leaqua.2017.03.003.

5   **When jurors exhibit:** Jolene Simpson, "Does Nodding Cause Contagious Agreement? The Influence of Juror Nodding on Perceptions of Expert Witness Testimony," (PhD diss., University of Alabama, 2009), https://www.semanticscholar.org/paper/Does-nodding-cause-contagious-agreement%3Athe-of-on-Simpson/f11758 10c56ddf6cf798cec9cf2c2935c9549fa9.

5   **Researchers found that voters:** Zijian Harrison Gong and Erik P. Bucy, "When Style Obscures Substance: Visual Attention to Display Appropriateness in the 2012 Presidential Debates," *Communication Monographs* 83, no. 3 (July 2016): 349–72, https://doi.org/10.1080/03637751.2015.1119868.

5   **If cues can be:** Alex Pentland, *Honest Signals: How They Shape Our World* (Cambridge, MA: MIT Press, 2008).

6   **Researchers find that nonverbal signals:** Jacquelyn Crane and Frederick G. Crane, "Optimal Nonverbal Communications Strategies Physicians Should Engage in to Promote Positive Clinical Outcomes," *Health Marketing Quarterly* 27, no. 3 (August 2010): 262–74, https://doi.org/10.1080/07359683.2010.495300.

Chapter 1: Cue for Charisma

9   **In a groundbreaking study from Princeton:** Susan T. Fiske, Amy J. Cuddy, Peter Glick, and Jun Xu, " 'A Model of (Often Mixed) Stereotype Content: Competence and Warmth Respectively Follow from Perceived Status and Competition': Correction to Fiske et al. (2002)," *Journal of Personality and Social Psychology* (April 25, 2019), https://doi.org/10.1037/pspa0000163.

10 **82 percent of our impressions:** Chris Malone and Susan T. Fiske, *The Human Brand: How We Relate to People, Products, and Companies* (San Francisco, CA: Jossey-Bass, 2013).

10 **managing these two traits:** Malone and Fiske, *The Human Brand.*

13 **"competence without warmth":** Malone and Fiske, *The Human Brand.*

14 **When he walked into the tank:** *Shark Tank* (@ABCSharkTank), "Remember Jamie Siminoff? Well, he's back, but this time it's a little different! #SharkTank," Twitter, October 4, 2018,

15 **In her own words:** Alan Alda and Goldie Hawn, "Goldie Hawn: She's Got Your Brain on Her Mind," September 29, 2020, *Clear+Vivid with Alan Alda*, podcast, 43:00, https://podcasts.apple.com/us/podcast/goldie-hawn-shes-got-your-brain-on-her-mind /id1400082430?i=1000492899514.

15 **And it worked:** "Our Mission," MindUp, accessed September 15, 2021, https://mind up.org/our-mission.

15 **A famous study:** Wendy Levinson et al., "Physician-Patient Communication. The Relationship with Malpractice Claims Among Primary Care Physicians and Surgeons," *JAMA* 277, no. 7 (February 19, 1997): 553–59, https://doi.org/10.1001/jama.277 .7.553.

15 **If you can't showcase:** Gordon T. Kraft-Todd et al., "Empathic Nonverbal Behavior Increases Ratings of Both Warmth and Competence in a Medical Context," *PLoS ONE* 12, no. 5 (May 15, 2017): e0177758, https://doi.org/10.1371/journal .pone.0177758.

16 **One study examined Winfrey's and Thatcher's:** Dana R. Carney, "The Nonverbal Expression of Power, Status, and Dominance," *Current Opinion in Psychology* 33 (June 2020): 256–64, https://doi.org/10.1016/j.copsyc.2019.12.004.

18 **In one early interview with *60 Minutes*:** "Jeff Bezos Takes Reporter on Exclusive Tour of Early Amazon HQ," *60 Minutes Australia*, 2000, video, 11:46, https://www .youtube.com/watch?v=44XbHVRxnMA.

18 **In a later interview with *Business Insider*:** "Jeff Bezos Talks Amazon, Blue Origin, Family, and Wealth," *Business Insider,* May 5, 2018, video, 48:30, https://www .youtube.com/watch?v=SCpgKvZB_VQ.

Chapter 2: How Cues Work

24 **A fist is a unique nonverbal cue:** Michael H. Morgan and David R. Carrier, "Protective Buttressing of the Human Fist and the Evolution of Hominin Hands," *Journal of Experimental Biology* 216, no. 2 (January 15, 2013): 236–44, https://doi .org/10.1242/jeb.075713.

25 **Our brains have dedicated:** Massachusetts General Hospital, "Study Identifies Neurons That Help Predict What Another Individual Will Do," *PsyPost*, March 1, 2015, https://www.psypost.org/2015/03/study-identifies-neurons-that-help-predict -what-another-individual-will-do-32117.

25 **One part of the brain:** Daniel Goleman, *Social Intelligence: The New Science of Human Relationships* (New York: Random House, 2011).

25 **Though our brain is incredibly skilled:** Srinivasan S. Pillay, MD, *Your Brain and Business: The Neuroscience of Great Leaders* (Upper Saddle River, NJ: FT Press, 2010), 30.

26 **Antoni Porowski even asks her:** *Queer Eye*, "The Anxious Activist," season 5, episode 5, aired June 5, 2020, https://www.imdb.com/title/tt12455268.

26 **When one person's emotions:** Elaine Hatfield, John T. Cacioppo, and Richard L. Rapson, "Emotional Contagion." *Current Directions in Psychological Science* 2, no. 3 (1993): 96–100, https://doi.org/10.1111/1467-8721.ep10770953.

26 **This is why we:** Madeleine L. Van Hecke, Lisa P. Callahan, Brad Kolar, and Ken A. Paller, *The Brain Advantage: Become a More Effective Business Leader Using the Latest Brain Research* (Amherst, NY: Prometheus Books, 2010).

26 **In one experiment:** Sigal G. Barsade, "The Ripple Effect: Emotional Contagion and Its Influence on Group Behavior," *Administrative Science Quarterly* 47, no. 4 (2002): 644–75, https://doi.org/10.2307/3094912.

27 **as soon as we see another person's:** Matthew D. Lieberman, *Social: Why Our Brains Are Wired to Connect* (Oxford, UK: Oxford University Press, 2013).

27 **people caught moods within:** Ron Friedman et al., "Motivational Synchronicity: Priming Motivational Orientations with Observations of Others' Behaviors," *Motivation and Emotion* 34, no. 1 (March 2009): 34–38, https://doi.org/10.1007 /s11031-009-9151-3.

27 **Simply moving our facial:** Alex Pentland, *Honest Signals: How They Shape Our World* (Cambridge, MA: MIT Press, 2008).

27 **Another person's nonverbal:** Daniel Goleman, Richard E. Boyatzis, and Annie McKee, *The New Leaders: Transforming the Art of Leadership into the Science of Results* (New York: Little, Brown, 2002).

28 **Decoding is how we:** Mary Seburn, "Encoding and Decoding of Meaning in Social Behavior," *McNair Scholars Journal* 1, no. 1 (January 1, 1997), https://scholarworks .gvsu.edu/mcnair/vol1/iss1/8.

28 **Social signals help us decipher:** Laura P. Naumann et al., "Personality Judgments Based on Physical Appearance," *Personality and Social Psychology Bulletin* 35, no. 12 (September 2009): 1661–71, https://doi.org/10.1177/0146167209346309.

29 **when we decode a cue of social rejection:** Pessi Lyyra, James H. Wirth, and Jari K. Hietanen, "Are You Looking My Way? Ostracism Widens the Cone of Gaze," *Quarterly Journal of Experimental Psychology* 70, no. 8 (August 2017): 1713–21, https://doi.org /10.1080/17470218.2016.1204327.

30 **employees who receive positive cues:** Mary P. Rowe, "Barriers to Equality: The Power of Subtle Discrimination to Maintain Unequal Opportunity," *Employee Responsibilities and Rights Journal* 3, no. 2 (1990): 153–63, https://doi.org/10.1007 /BF01388340.

30 **MIT researchers studied bluffing:** Pentland, *Honest Signals*.

35   **Growing up in Little Rock:** "Meet Kofi Essel," Rise and Shine by Children's National Hospital, September 21, 2017, https://riseandshine.childrensnational.org/meet-kofi -essel-md-mph.

37   **Nonverbal prowess is a:** Eddie Harmon-Jones, Philip A. Gable, and Tom F. Price, "Leaning Embodies Desire: Evidence That Leaning Forward Increases Relative Left Frontal Cortical Activation to Appetitive Stimuli," *Biological Psychology* 87, no. 2 (March 2011): 311–13, https://doi.org/10.1016/j.biopsycho.2011.03.009.

37   **One study found that:** Albert Mehrabian, "Inference of Attitudes from the Posture, Orientation, and Distance of a Communicator," *Journal of Consulting and Clinical Psychology* 32, no. 3 (June 1968): 296–308, https://doi.org/10.1037/h0025906.

37   **Researchers at the University of Victoria:** Robert Gifford, Cheuk Fan Ng, and Margaret Wilkinson, "Nonverbal Cues in the Employment Interview: Links Between Applicant Qualities and Interviewer Judgments," *Journal of Applied Psychology* 70, no. 4 (November 1985): 729–36, https://doi.org/10.1037/0021-9010.70.4.729.

39   **Researchers conducted a meta-analysis:** Hillary Anger Elfenbein and Nalini Ambady, "On the Universality and Cultural Specificity of Emotion Recognition: A Meta-Analysis," *Psychological Bulletin* 128, no. 2 (April 2002): 203–35, https://doi .org/10.1037/0033-2909.128.2.203.

39   **In a fascinating experiment:** Harmon-Jones, Gable, and Price, "Leaning Embodies Desire."

40   **researchers asked participants to look at photographs:** Mehrabian, "Inference of Attitudes from the Posture, Orientation, and Distance of a Communicator."

41   **Zoologist Desmond Morris:** Desmond Morris, *Peoplewatching: The Desmond Morris Guide to Body Language* (New York: Random House, 2012).

43   **Researchers asked professionals to rate:** Mehrabian, "Inference of Attitudes from the Posture, Orientation, and Distance of a Communicator."

44   **Evy Poumpouras is a former Secret Service agent:** Evy Poumpouras, "About," https://www.evypoumpouras.com/about.

45   **Physicist Neil deGrasse Tyson:** "Science and Communication: Alan Alda in Conversation with Neil deGrasse Tyson," 92nd Street Y, June 8, 2017, video, 36:54, https://www.youtube.com/watch?v=syIb73RQqVU.

45   **Researchers have even found that a podium:** Andrew J. Hale et al., "Twelve Tips for Effective Body Language for Medical Educators," *Medical Teacher* 39, no. 9 (September 2017): 914–19, https://doi.org/10.1080/0142159X.2017.1324140.

45   **In a mind-blowing study:** Valentina Rita Andolfi, Chiara Di Nuzzo, and Alessandro Antonietti, "Opening the Mind through the Body: The Effects of Posture on Creative Processes," *Thinking Skills and Creativity* 24 (June 2017): 20–28, https://doi .org/10.1016/j.tsc.2017.02.012.

47   **Then, in June 1984:** Dave Blackwell, "Jazz Surprise by Taking Stockton," *Deseret News*, June 19, 1984, https://news.google.com/newspapers?id=U _VSAAAAIBAJ&pg=5125%2C1607899; "John Stockton Stats," Basketball Reference, accessed September 15, 2021, https://www.basketball-reference.com/players/s /stockjo01.html.

47   **Despite retiring in:** "NBA All-Time Assists Leaders," ESPN, accessed September 15, 2021, http://www.espn.com/nba/history/leaders/_/stat/assists.

48   **Fronting is when you:** Marion K. Underwood, "III. Glares of Contempt, Eye Rolls of Disgust and Turning Away to Exclude: Non-Verbal Forms of Social Aggression Among Girls," *Feminism & Psychology* 14, no. 3 (August 2004): 371–75, https://doi .org/10.1177/0959353504044637; Rebecca P. Lawson, Colin W. G. Clifford, and

Andrew J. Calder, "About Turn: The Visual Representation of Human Body Orientation Revealed by Adaptation," *Psychological Science* 20, no. 3 (March 2009): 363–71, https://doi.org/10.1111/j.1467-9280.2009.02301.x; Jeffrey David Robinson, "Getting Down to Business: Talk, Gaze, and Body Orientation During Openings of Doctor-Patient Consultations," *Human Communication Research* 25, no. 1 (September 1998): 97–123. https://doi.org/10.1111/j.1468-2958.1998.tb00438.x.

48   **When someone is about:** Virginia M. Gunderson and Joan S. Lockard, "Human Postural Signals as Intention Movements to Depart: African Data," *Animal Behaviour* 28, no. 3 (1980): 966–67, https://doi.org/10.1016/S0003-3472(80) 80159-X.

49   **"People say, 'Wow'":** "John Stockton and Karl Malone," NBA, August 9, 2009, video, 3:21, https://www.youtube.com/watch?v=cYOf4hYa5A0&list=PLqaqx66q9hd_H4 -7NTabVEyK-wffKdzZp&index=44.

49   **And today Stockton:** "Top 10 All-Time Point Guards," SI.com photo gallery, March 11, 2009, https://web.archive.org/web/20090311053817/http://sportsillustrated.cnn .com/multimedia/photo_gallery/2005/11/22/gallery.alltimepointguards/content.6 .html.

53   **"He's nice. Bit of a close talker":** *Seinfeld*, season 5, episode 18, "The Raincoats," aired April 28, 1994, on NBC, https://www.youtube.com/watch?v=sRZ5RpsytRA.

53   **Hall identified four space:** Leslie A. Hayduk, "Personal Space: Understanding the Simplex Model," *Journal of Nonverbal Behavior* 18, no. 3 (1994): 245–60, https://doi .org/10.1007/BF02170028; Edward T. Hall, *The Hidden Dimension: An Anthropologist Examines Man's Use of Space in Public and Private* (New York: Anchor Books, 1969); Carlos E. Sluzki, "Proxemics in Couple Interactions: Rekindling an Old Optic," *Family Process* 55, no. 1 (2016): 7–15, https://doi.org/10.1111/famp.12196; Jorge Rios-Martinez, Anne Spalanzani, and Christian Laugier, "From Proxemics Theory to Socially-Aware Navigation: A Survey," *International Journal of Social Robotics* 7, no. 2 (2015): 137–53, https://doi.org/10.1007/s12369-014-0251-1.

55   **researchers directed a negative comment:** Edgar C. O'Neal et al., "Effect of Insult upon Personal Space Preferences," *Journal of Nonverbal Behavior* 5, no. 1 (1980): 56–62, https://doi.org/10.1007/BF00987055.

55   **Religious scholars argue:** Brant Pitre, *Jesus and the Last Supper* (Grand Rapids, MI: William B. Eerdmans Publishing Company, 2017).

56   **typically the boss or leader:** Vanessa Van Edwards, "How to Pick the Right Seat in a Meeting EVERY Time," Science of People, March 5, 2020, https://www .scienceofpeople.com/seating-arrangement.

57   **Research from Cornell University:** Karlton Lattimore, "The Effect of Seating Orientation and a Spatial Boundary on Students' Experience of Person-Centered Counseling" (master's thesis, Cornell University, August 19, 2013), https://www .semanticscholar.org/paper/The-Effect-Of-Seating-Orientation-And-A-Spatial -On-Lattimore/2643c3d0a4e54e88e08d3cc91fde3625e2f2ead5.

58   **the shape of your table can affect:** Juliet Zhu and Jennifer Argo, "Exploring the Impact of Various Shaped Seating Arrangements on Persuasion," *Journal of Consumer Research* 40, no. 2 (August 2013): 336–49, https://doi.org/10.1086/670392.

58   **When someone violates our space needs:** Mark L. Knapp, Judith A. Hall, and Terrence G. Horgan, *Nonverbal Communication in Human Interaction*, 8th ed. (Boston: Wadsworth, Cengage Learning, 2014).

65   **This quiz is based on:** Aeon, "How We Learn to Read Another's Mind by Looking into Their Eyes," PsyPost, July 17, 2017, https://www.psypost.org/2017/07/learn -read-anothers-mind-looking-eyes-49330.

65   **Turns out the old:** Tobias Grossmann, "The Eyes as Windows into Other Minds: An Integrative Perspective," *Perspectives on Psychological Science* 12, no. 1 (2017): 107–21, https://doi.org/10.1177/1745691616654457.

65   **Infants as young as:** Sarah Jessen and Tobias Grossmann, "Unconscious Discrimination of Social Cues from Eye Whites in Infants," *PNAS* 111, no. 45 (November 11, 2014): 16208–13, https://doi.org/10.1073/pnas.1411333111.

65   **Eyes provide more information:** P. J. Whalen et al., "Human Amygdala Responsivity to Masked Fearful Eye Whites," *Science* 306, no. 5704 (December 17, 2004): 2061, https://doi.org/10.1126/science.1103617.

65   **Study after study:** Kai MacDonald, "Patient-Clinician Eye Contact: Social Neuroscience and Art of Clinical Engagement," *Postgraduate Medicine* 121, no. 4 (July 2009): 136–44, https://doi.org/10.3810/pgm.2009.07.2039.

65   **Most of us don't:** Universitaet Tübingen, "Tiny Eye Movements Highlight the World Around Us," PsyPost, July 16, 2015, https://www.psypost.org/2015/07/tiny-eye-movements-highlight-the-world-around-us-35907.

67   **Eye contact is not:** Gregor Domes et al., "Oxytocin Improves 'Mind-Reading' in Humans," *Biological Psychiatry* 61, no. 6 (March 15, 2007): 731–33, https://doi.org/10.1016/j.biopsych.2006.07.015; Aeon, "How We Learn to Read Another's Mind by Looking into Their Eyes."

67   **Researchers used brain:** Takahiko Koike et al., "Neural Substrates of Shared Attention as Social Memory: A Hyperscanning Functional Magnetic Resonance Imaging Study," *NeuroImage* 125 (January 15, 2016): 401–12, https://doi.org/10.1016/j.neuroimage.2015.09.076.

67   **Gaze can literally:** Steven Pace, "Gazing Up and to the Right of the Audience Gives a Heroic Impression," PsyPost, April 18, 2016, https://www.psypost.org/2016/04/gazing-right-audience-gives-heroic-impression-42400.

67   **four months old:** University of Cambridge, "Eye Contact with Your Baby Helps Synchronize Your Brainwaves, Study Finds," PsyPost, November 29, 2017, https://www.psypost.org/2017/11/eye-contact-baby-helps-synchronize-brainwaves-study-finds-50285; Teresa Farroni, Gergely Csibra, Francesca Simion, and Mark H. Johnson, "Eye Contact Detection in Humans from Birth," *PNAS* 99, no. 14 (July 9, 2002): 9602–5, https://doi.org/10.1073/pnas.152159999; Mary Jane Maguire-Fong, *Teaching and Learning with Infants and Toddlers: Where Meaning-Making Begins* (New York: Teachers College Press, 2015).

67   **looking up and to the right:** Hironori Akechi et al., "Attention to Eye Contact in the West and East: Autonomic Responses and Evaluative Ratings," *PLoS ONE* 8, no. 3 (March 13, 2013): e59312, https://doi.org/10.1371/journal.pone.0059312.

69   **There are cultural differences:** Emily Shemanski, "Cultures Perceive Direct Eye Contact Differently," PsyPost, June 22, 2015, https://www.psypost.org/2015/06/cultures-perceive-direct-eye-contact-differently-35291; Academy of Finland, "Personality Shapes the Way Our Brains React to Eye Contact," PsyPost, June 6, 2015, https://www.psypost.org/2015/06/personality-shapes-the-way-our-brains-react-to-eye-contact-34929.

Chapter 4: The Wow Factor

73   **In September 1953:** Brooks Barnes, "Disneyland Map Is Headed to Auction," *New York Times,* May 11, 2017, https://www.nytimes.com/2017/05/11/movies/walt-disney-hand-drawn-map-of-disneyland-is-headed-to-auction.html.

73   **Almost seven decades:** Brady MacDonald, "How Many People Will Disneyland Admit with Reduced Capacity?," *Orange County Register,* July 14, 2020, https://www

.ocregister.com/2020/07/14/how-many-people-will-disneyland-admit-with-reduced
-capacity.

73   **Disney University teaches:** Disney Institute, *Be Our Guest: Perfecting the Art of Customer Service*, rev. ed. (New York: Disney Editions, 2011).

74   **Researchers asked two groups:** Richard E. Nisbett and Timothy D. Wilson, "The Halo Effect: Evidence for Unconscious Alteration of Judgments," *Journal of Personality and Social Psychology* 35, no. 4 (1977): 250–56, https://doi.org/10.1037/0022-3514.35.4.250.

75   **Researchers from the University of Amsterdam:** Camiel J. Beukeboom, "When Words Feel Right: How Affective Expressions of Listeners Change a Speaker's Language Use," *European Journal of Social Psychology* 39, no. 5 (August 2009): 747–56, https://doi:10.1002/ejsp.572.

76   **We like our potential:** Emma Otta et al., "The Effect of Smiling and of Head Tilting on Person Perception," *Journal of Psychology* 128, no. 3 (1994): 323–31, https://doi.org /10.1080/00223980.1994.9712736.

76   **When researchers asked people to pose:** Otta et al., "The Effect of Smiling and of Head Tilting on Person Perception."

76   **Experts found that:** Kimberly Schneiderman, "Using LinkedIn to Connect," *Career Planning and Adult Development Journal* 32, no. 3 (2016): 32–37, https://www .careerthoughtleaders.com/resources/Documents/Papers%20and%20Journals /Journal%20Volume%2032,%20Number%203,%20FALL%202016%20Job%20 Search%206.0%20(1).pdf.

76   **One group of ambitious:** Marco Costa, Marzia Menzani, and Pio Enrico Ricci Bitti, "Head Canting in Paintings: An Historical Study," *Journal of Nonverbal Behavior* 25, no. 1 (March 2001): 63–73, https://doi.org/10.1023/A:1006737224617.

77   **While a head tilt:** Otta et al., "The Effect of Smiling and of Head Tilting on Person Perception."

77   **This artery runs up:** Erving Goffman, "Gender Advertisements," *Studies in the Anthropology of Visual Communication* 3, no. 2 (Philadelphia, PA: Society for the Anthropology of Visual Communication, 1976).

78   **Major League Baseball player Alex Rodriguez:** Barry M. Bloom, "A-Rod Signals Support for Salary Cap Along with Mets Bid," *Sportico* (blog), July 17, 2020, https://www.sportico.com/leagues/baseball/2020/a-rod-signals-support-for-salary-cap -along-with-mets-bid-1234609420.

78   **Rodriguez sat down for an interview:** "Eye to Eye: A-Rod Speaks Out," *60 Minutes*, December 17, 2007, video, 2:13, https://www.youtube.com/watch?v=oVcqLt9sJLs.

79   **Rodriguez did come clean:** Jay Weaver, "Alex Rodriguez's DEA Confession: Yes, I Used Steroids from Fake Miami Doctor," *Miami Herald,* November 5, 2014, https://www .miamiherald.com/sports/mlb/article3578762.html.

79   **In 2009, researchers decided to test:** Jolene Simpson, "Does Nodding Cause Contagious Agreement? The Influence of Juror Nodding on Perceptions of Expert Witness Testimony," (PhD diss., University of Alabama, 2009), https://www .semanticscholar.org/paper/Does-nodding-cause-contagious-agreement%3Athe -of-on-Simpson/f1175810c56ddf6cf798cec9cf2c2935c9549fa9.

81   **women tend to nod more than men:** Marie Helweg-Larsen, Stephanie J. Cunningham, Amanda Carrico, and Alison M. Pergram, "To Nod or Not to Nod: An Observational Study of Nonverbal Communication and Status in Female and Male College Students," *Psychology of Women Quarterly* 28, no. 4 (December 2004): 358–61, https://doi.org/10.1111/j.1471-6402.2004.00152.x.

82   **In one episode of *Dating in the Dark*:** *Dating in the Dark Australia*, season 1, episode 7, aired January 19, 2011, on Fox8, video, 43:51, https://www.youtube.com /watch?v=bHvNBMSPyss.

83   **Universally, the eyebrow raise:** Karen L. Schmidt and Jeffrey F. Cohn, "Human Facial Expressions as Adaptations: Evolutionary Questions in Facial Expression Research," *American Journal of Physical Anthropology* 116, no. S33 (January 2001): 3–24, https://doi.org/10.1002/ajpa.20001.

83   **we also raise our eyebrows to show:** Chris Frith, "Role of Facial Expressions in Social Interactions," *Philosophical Transactions of the Royal Society B: Biological Sciences* 364, no. 1535 (December 12, 2009): 3453–58, https://doi.org/10.1098/rstb.2009.0142.

83   **When we're seeking confirmation:** María L. Flecha-García, "Eyebrow Raises in Dialogue and Their Relation to Discourse Structure, Utterance Function and Pitch Accents in English," *Speech Communication* 52, no. 6 (2010): 542–54, https://doi.org/10.1016/j.specom.2009.12.003.

83   **an eyebrow raise can be used:** Karl Grammer et al., "Patterns on the Face: The Eyebrow Flash in Cross-Cultural Comparison," *Ethology* 77, no. 4 (1988): 279–99, doi: 10.1111/j.1439-0310.1988.tb00211.x.

84   **Neil deGrasse Tyson even:** "Science and Communication: Alan Alda in Conversation with Neil deGrasse Tyson," 92nd Street Y, June 8, 2017, video, 36:54, https://www.youtube.com/watch?v=syIb73RQqVU.

85   **Here's something that won't:** Mark L. Knapp, Judith A. Hall, and Terrence G. Horgan, *Nonverbal Communication in Human Interaction,* 8th ed. (Boston: Wadsworth, Cengage Learning, 2014).

85   **Researchers put participants in:** Takashi Tsukiura and Roberto Cabeza, "Orbitofrontal and Hippocampal Contributions to Memory for Face-Name Associations: The Rewarding Power of a Smile," *Neuropsychologia* 46, no. 9 (2008): 2310–19, https://doi.org/10.1016/j.neuropsychologia.2008.03.013.

85   **Researchers found that smiling:** Beatrice Biancardi, Angelo Cafaro, and Catherine Pelachaud, "Analyzing First Impressions of Warmth and Competence from Observable Nonverbal Cues in Expert-Novice Interactions," *ICMI '17: Proceedings of the 19th ACM International Conference on Multimodal Interaction* (November 2017): 341–49, https://doi.org/10.1145/3136755.3136779.

86   **Researchers found that a smile:** Simone Schnall and James Laird, "Keep Smiling: Enduring Effects of Facial Expressions and Postures on Emotional Experience and Memory," *Cognition and Emotion* 17, no. 5 (September 2003): 787–97, https://doi.org/10.1080/02699930302286.

86   **And fake smiles aren't:** Ron Gutman, "The Hidden Power of Smiling," filmed March 2011, TED video, 7:10, https://www.ted.com/talks/ron_gutman_the_hidden_power_of_smiling.

86   **When we see someone else:** Barbara Wild, Michael Erb, and Mathias Bartels, "Are Emotions Contagious? Evoked Emotions While Viewing Emotionally Expressive Faces: Quality, Quantity, Time Course and Gender Differences," *Psychiatry Research* 102, no. 2 (July 2001): 109–24, https://doi.org/10.1016/S0165-1781(01)00225-6.

86   **In fact, researchers found:** Ulf Dimberg, Monika Thunberg, and Kurt Elmehed, "Unconscious Facial Reactions to Emotional Facial Expressions," *Psychological Science* 11, no. 1 (January 2000): 86–89, https://doi.org/10.1111/1467-9280.00221.

87   **Most people think of laughter:** Laura E. Kurtz and Sara B. Algoe, "When Sharing a Laugh Means Sharing More: Testing the Role of Shared Laughter on Short-Term Interpersonal Consequences," *Journal of Nonverbal Behavior* 41, no. 1 (March 1, 2017): 45–65, https://doi.org/10.1007/s109019-016-0245-9.

87   **laughing with someone is one of the best:** Marianne Sonnby-Borgström, "Automatic Mimicry Reactions as Related to Differences in Emotional Empathy," *Scandinavian Journal of Psychology* 43, no. 5 (December 2002): 433–43, https://doi.org/10.1111/1467-9450.00312.

88   **One group of researchers at UC Berkeley:** Scott Cacciola, "Dallas's Secret Weapon: High Fives," *Wall Street Journal*, June 9, 2011, https://online.wsj.com/article/SB1000 1424052702304392704576373641168929846.html.

88   **As we have learned, oxytocin:** Paul J. Zak, *The Moral Molecule: The Source of Love and Prosperity* (New York: Dutton, 2012).

88   **plays a complicated role:** Alberto Gallace and Charles Spence, "The Science of Interpersonal Touch: An Overview," *Neuroscience & Biobehavioral Reviews* 34, no. 2 (2010): 246–59, https://doi.org/10.1016/j.neubiorev.2008.10.004.

89   **Oxytocin also helps us:** L. Gebauer et al., "Oxytocin Improves Synchronisation in Leader-Follower Interaction," *Scientific Reports* 6, no. 1 (December 8, 2016): 38416, https://doi.org/10.1038/srep38416.

89   **Researchers wanted to know if a simple touch:** Michael Lynn, Joseph-Mykal Le, and David S. Sherwyn, "Reach Out and Touch Your Customers," *Cornell Hospitality Quarterly* 39, no. 3 (June 1, 1998): 60–65, https://doi.org/10.1177/0010880498039 00312.

90   **touch nuances are different:** Martin S. Remland, Tricia S. Jones, and Heidi Brinkman, "Proxemic and Haptic Behavior in Three European Countries," *Journal of Nonverbal Behavior* 15, no. 4 (December 1991): 215–32, https://doi .org/10.1007/BF00986923.

93   **humans begin to synchronize:** Erwan Codrons, Nicolò F. Bernardi, Matteo Vandoni, and Luciano Bernardi, "Spontaneous Group Synchronization of Movements and Respiratory Rhythms," *PLoS ONE* 9, no. 9 (September 12, 2014): e107538, https://doi .org/10.1371/journal.pone.0107538; Tamami Nakano and Shigeru Kitazawa, "Eyeblink Entrainment at Breakpoints of Speech," *Experimental Brain Research* 205, no. 4 (2010): 577–81, https://doi.org/10.1007/s00221-010-2387-z.

93   **Researchers from MIT tracked:** Alex Pentland, *Honest Signals: How They Shape Our World* (Cambridge, MA: MIT Press, 2008).

93   **researchers had an actor stop:** Ap Dijksterhuis, Pamela K. Smith, Rick B. van Baaren, and Daniel H. J. Wigboldus, "The Unconscious Consumer: Effects of Environment on Consumer Behavior," *Journal of Consumer Psychology* 15, no. 3 (December 2005): 193–202, https://doi.org/https://doi.org/10.1207/s15327663jcp1503_3.

94   **In one study, participants watched videotaped:** Robert W. Levenson and Anna M. Ruef, "Empathy: A Physiological Substrate," *Journal of Personality and Social Psychology* 63, no. 2 (August 1992): 234–46, https://doi.org/10.1037/0022-3514.63.2.234.

Chapter 5: How to Look Powerful

97   **Just weeks away from:** "The Kennedy-Nixon Debates," History, updated June 10, 2019, https://www.history.com/topics/us-presidents/kennedy-nixon-debates.

100   **Nixon had the nickname:** "The Kennedy-Nixon Debates."

100   **Before this debate:** Bill Newcott, "Behind the Scenes of the First Televised Presidential Debates 60 Years Ago," *National Geographic*, September 25, 2020, https://www.nationalgeographic.com/history/article/behind-scenes-first-televised -presidential-debates-nixon-jfk-1960.

103   **One 2016 study followed 144 speed dates:** Tanya Vacharkulksemsuk et al., "Dominant, Open Nonverbal Displays Are Attractive at Zero-Acquaintance," *PNAS* 113, no. 15 (April 12, 2016): 4009–14, https://doi.org/10.1073/pnas.1508932113.

103   **Here's a simple rule:** Dana R. Carney, "The Nonverbal Expression of Power, Status, and Dominance," *Current Opinion in Psychology* 33 (June 2020): 256–64, https://doi .org/10.1016/j.copsyc.2019.12.004.

103   **One study had participants:** John H. Riskind and Carolyn C. Gotay, "Physical Posture: Could It Have Regulatory or Feedback Effects on Motivation and Emotion?,"

Motivation and Emotion 6, no. 3 (September 1982): 273–98, https://doi.org/10.1007/BF00992249.

103   **using bigger screens inspires:** Maarten W. Bos and Amy J. C. Cuddy, "iPosture: The Size of Electronic Consumer Devices Affects Our Behavior," *Harvard Business School, Working Paper 13-097,* May 20, 2013, https://dash.harvard.edu/handle/1/10646419.

105   **We do this for:** Daniel H. Lee and Adam K. Anderson, "Reading What the Mind Thinks from How the Eye Sees," *Psychological Science* 28, no. 4 (February 2017): 494–503, https://doi.org/10.1177/0956797616687364.

106   **Then you're doing it right:** Fiona Ellis, "Will Ferrell: The Zoolander Look Was a Blue Steel from Pierce Brosnan," *Irish Sun,* February 13, 2016, https://www.thesun.ie/archives/bizarre/142684/will-ferrell-the-zoolander-look-was-a-blue-steel-from-pierce-brosnan.

109   **participants were shown pictures:** Linda Talley and Samuel Temple, "Silent Hands: A Leader's Ability to Create Nonverbal Immediacy," *Journal of Social, Behavioral, & Health Sciences* 12, no. 1 (2018), https://doi.org/10.5590/JSBHS.2018.12.1.09.

109   **In a study involving medical school teachers:** Andrew J. Hale et al., "Twelve Tips for Effective Body Language for Medical Educators," *Medical Teacher* 39, no. 9 (May 14, 2017): 914–19, https://doi.org/10.1080/0142159X.2017.1324140.

111   **Maria Konnikova had been:** "2018 PokerStars Caribbean Adventure: $1,650 National Championship," PokerNews, January 9, 2018, https://www.pokernews.com/tours/pca/2018-pca/1650-no-limit-holdem; Maria Konnikova, *The Biggest Bluff: How I Learned to Pay Attention, Master Myself, and Win* (New York: Penguin Press, 2020).

113   **Researchers asked participants:** Linda Talley and Samuel Temple, "How Leaders Influence Followers Through the Use of Nonverbal Communication," *Leadership & Organization Development Journal* 36, no. 1 (March 2015): 69–80, https://doi.org/10.1108/LODJ-07-2013-0107.

113   **Researchers found that liars:** Stephen Porter and Mary Ann Campbell, "A. Vrij, Detecting Lies and Deceit: The Psychology of Lying and Implications for Professional Practice," *Expert Evidence* 7, no. 3 (1999): 227–32, https://doi.org/10.1023/A:1008978705657.

113   **purposeful, confident gestures improve comprehension:** Geoffrey Beattie, *Visible Thought: The New Psychology of Body Language* (London: Routledge, 2003).

116   **Researcher Susan Goldin-Meadow:** William Harms, "Susan Goldin-Meadow on What Gesture Says about How Our Minds Work," American Association for the Advancement of Science, October 27, 2014, https://www.aaas.org/susan-goldin-meadow-what-gesture-says-about-how-our-minds-work.

116   **Taking off one's glasses:** Allan Pease and Barbara Pease, *The Definitive Book of Body Language* (New York: Bantam Books, 2006).

116   **Gesturing also helps us:** Susan Goldin-Meadow, *Hearing Gesture: How Our Hands Help Us Think* (Cambridge, MA: Harvard University Press, 2003).

117   **Researchers have found that:** Beattie, *Visible Thought*; David McNeill and Elena T. Levy, "Conceptual Representations in Language Activity and Gesture," in *Speech, Place, and Action: Studies in Deixis and Related Topics,* eds. Robert J. Jarvella and Wolfgang Klein (New York: John Wiley & Sons, 1982), 271–95; Geoffrey Beattie and Heather Shovelton, "What Properties of Talk Are Associated with the Generation of Spontaneous Iconic Hand Gestures?," *British Journal of Social Psychology* 41, no. 3 (October 2002): 403–17, https://doi.org/10.1348/014466602760344287.

118   **Some researchers have noted:** Beattie, *Visible Thought*; McNeill and Levy, "Conceptual Representations in Language Activity and Gesture"; Beattie and Shovelton, "What Properties of Talk Are Associated with the Generation of Spontaneous Iconic Hand Gestures?"

118 **Nicknamed Evita, at sixteen:** "Eva Peron's Final Speech (1951)," YouTube, April 2, 2012, video, 1:38, https://www.youtube.com/watch?v=Dr7ymWtnHWc.

120 **Researchers found that when:** Daniel J. Siegel, *Mindsight: The New Science of Personal Transformation* (New York: Bantam Books, 2010).

123 **Here are my favorite:** Vanessa Van Edwards, "How to Get Someone to Stop Talking to You, Nicely," Science of People, June 30, 2017, https://www.scienceofpeople.com /stop-talking.

126 **Researchers in 2014 studied:** Annick Darioly and Marianne Schmid Mast, "The Role of Nonverbal Behavior for Leadership: An Integrative Review," in *Leader Interpersonal and Influence Skills: The Soft Skills of Leadership,* eds. Ronald E. Riggio and Sherylle J. Tan (London: Routledge, 2014), 73–100.

Chapter 6: How to Spot a Bad Guy . . . and Not Be One Yourself

131 **On August 25, 2005:** "2005: Lance Armstrong Denies Doping," *Larry King Live*, CNN, aired August 25, 2005, video, 2:10, https://www.cnn.com/videos /sports/2011/05/20/vault.2005.lkl.armstrong.cnn.

134 **We've found that no one cue:** David DeSteno et al., "Detecting the Trustworthiness of Novel Partners in Economic Exchange," *Psychological Science* 23, no. 12 (November 2012): 1549–56, https://doi.org/10.1177/0956797612448793.

134 **"I am not a crook":** "Richard Nixon Associated Press Q and A Session 1973," Buyout Footage Historic Film Archive, video, quote at 35:08, https://www.youtube.com /watch?v=NqPAixaBFOQ.

135 **In one study, physical therapists were videotaped:** Nalini Ambady, Jasook Koo, Robert Rosenthal, and Carol H. Winograd, "Physical Therapists' Nonverbal Communication Predicts Geriatric Patients' Health Outcomes," *Psychology and Aging* 17, no. 3 (September 2002): 443–52, https://doi.org/10.1037/0882-7974.17 .3.443.

135 **Not only is this *super* rude:** James A. Roberts and Meredith E. Daniel, "Put Down Your Phone and Listen to Me: How Boss Phubbing Undermines the Psychological Conditions Necessary for Employee Engagement," *Computers in Human Behavior* 75 (2017): 206–17, https://doi.org/10.1016/j.chb.2017.05.021; Beth Elwood, " 'Phubbing' Study Finds Ignoring Others for Your Phone Screen Is Linked to Increased Anxiety and Depression," PsyPost, April 27, 2020, https://www.psypost.org/2020/04 /phubbing-study-finds-ignoring-others-for-your-phone-screen-is-linked-to-increased -anxiety-and-depression-56624.

137 **when people take a literal step back:** Severine Koch, Rob W. Holland, Maikel Hengstler, and Ad van Knippenberg, "Body Locomotion as Regulatory Process: Stepping Backward Enhances Cognitive Control," *Psychological Science* 20, no. 5 (May 2009): 549–50, https://doi.org/10.1111/j.1467-9280.2009.02342.x.

138 **Britney Spears is on *Dateline*:** "Dateline Special Interview with Britney Spears, Part 02," *Dateline*, NBC, aired June 15, 2006, video, 9:49, https://www.youtube.com /watch?v=-Q8dFKDeNjg.

138 **Research finds that we self-touch:** Elizabeth G. Shreve, Jinni A. Harrigan, John R. Kues, and Denise K. Kagas, "Nonverbal Expressions of Anxiety in Physician-Patient Interactions," *Psychiatry* 51, no. 4 (December 1988): 378–84, https://doi.org /10.1080/00332747.1988.11024414.

139 **women preen more than men:** John A. Daly et al., "Sex and Relationship Affect Social Self-Grooming," *Journal of Nonverbal Behavior* 7, no. 3 (1983): 183–89, https://doi.org/10.1007/BF00986949.

139 **Psychiatrists used thermographic cameras:** Lee Moran, " 'Pinocchio Effect': Lying Sends Nose-Tip Temperature Soaring, but Size Unchanged: Scientists," *New York*

Daily News, November 24, 2012, https://www.nydailynews.com/life-style/health/pin occhio-effect-lying-sends-nose-tip-temperature-soaring-scientists-article-1.1206872.

140 **Researchers Alan Hirsch and Charles Wolf:** A. R. Hirsch and C. J. Wolf, "Practical Methods for Detecting Mendacity: A Case Study," *Journal of the American Academy of Psychiatry and the Law* 29, no. 4 (December 2001): 438–44, http://jaapl .org/content/29/4/438.

140 **Study after study finds that comfort gestures:** Jehanne Almerigogna, James Ost, Lucy Akehurst, and Mike Fluck, "How Interviewers' Nonverbal Behaviors Can Affect Children's Perceptions and Suggestibility," *Journal of Experimental Child Psychology* 100, no. 1 (May 1, 2008): 17–39, https://doi.org/10.1016/j.jecp.2008.01.006; Erin A. Heerey and Ann M. Kring, "Interpersonal Consequences of Social Anxiety," *Journal of Abnormal Psychology* 116, no. 1 (March 2007): 125–34, https://doi.org/10.1037/0021 -843X.116.1.125; Randall A. Gordon, Daniel Druckman, Richard M. Rozelle, and James C. Baxter, "Non-Verbal Behaviour as Communication: Approaches, Issues, and Research," in *The Handbook of Communication Skills*, 3rd ed., ed. Owen Hargie (London: Routledge, 2006), 73–120, https://www.routledgehandbooks.com/doi/10.43 24/9781315436135-4.

140 **when speakers were fidgety onstage:** Tony W. Buchanan, Christina N. White, Mary Kralemann, and Stephanie D. Preston, "The Contagion of Physiological Stress: Causes and Consequences," *European Journal of Psychotraumatology* 3 (September 10, 2012), https://doi.org/10.3402/ejpt.v3i0.19380.

142 **We filmed a video of us:** "How to Conquer Your Fears with Kindness," Vanessa Van Edwards, November 11, 2016, video, 8:15, https://www.youtube.com /watch?v=l8ByY5-Po50.

144 **Rubbing the eyelids stimulates:** Katherine Gould, "The Vagus Nerve: Your Body's Communication Superhighway," Live Science, November 12, 2019, https://www .livescience.com/vagus-nerve.html.

144 **our blink rate speeds up:** Donald R. Meyer, Harry P. Bahrick, and Paul M. Fitts, "Incentive, Anxiety, and the Human Blink Rate," *Journal of Experimental Psychology* 45, no. 3 (March 1953): 183–87, https://doi.org/10.1037/h0058609.

145 **One researcher coded President Nixon's:** "Brain's Punctuation Marks: Blink Research Pioneer Says We Don't Blink at Random," *Washington University Record*, February 4, 1988, https://digitalcommons.wustl.edu/record/433.

146 **The city official and workmen:** "Ashton Kutcher vs. Allen Iverson, Jermaine O'Neal, George Lopez & Tyrese | Punk'd," *Punk'd*, season 5, episode 2, aired July 3, 2005, on MTV, video, 19:19, https://www.youtube.com/watch?v=ldPO09GXCUE.

146 **It is often accompanied by:** Jason P. Martens, Jessica L. Tracy, and Azim F. Shariff, "Status Signals: Adaptive Benefits of Displaying and Observing the Nonverbal Expressions of Pride and Shame," *Cognition & Emotion* 26, no. 3 (April 2012): 390–406, https://doi.org/10.1080/02699931.2011.645281; Carlos F. Benitez-Quiroz, Ramprakash Srinivasan, and Aleix M. Martinez, "Facial Color Is an Efficient Mechanism to Visually Transmit Emotion," *PNAS* 115, no. 14 (April 3, 2018): 3581–86, https://doi.org/10.1073/pnas.1716084115.

148 **This matters more than:** Alex Pentland, *Honest Signals: How They Shape Our World* (Cambridge, MA: MIT Press, 2008).

148 **Faces give us a wealth of information:** Chris Frith, "Role of Facial Expressions in Social Interactions," *Philosophical Transactions of the Royal Society B: Biological Sciences* 364, no. 1535 (December 12, 2009): 3453–58, https://doi.org/10.1098/rstb.2009.0142.

149 **One researcher had parents:** Andrew N. Meltzoff, " 'Like Me': A Foundation for Social Cognition," *Developmental Science* 10, no. 1 (February 2007): 126–34, https://doi.org/10.1111/j.1467-7687.2007.00574.x.

150   **A furrowed brow makes:** Sandra E. Duclos and James D. Laird, "The Deliberate Control of Emotional Experience Through Control of Expressions," *Cognition & Emotion* 15, no. 1 (2001): 27–56, https://doi.org/10.1080/02699930126057.

150   **Incredibly, research found that:** Michael B. Lewis and Patrick J. Bowler, "Botulinum Toxin Cosmetic Therapy Correlates with a More Positive Mood," *Journal of Cosmetic Dermatology* 8, no. 1 (March 2009): 24–26, https://doi.org/https://doi .org/10.1111/j.1473-2165.2009.00419.x.

150   **Researchers actually studied this:** Daniele Marzoli et al., "Sun-Induced Frowning Fosters Aggressive Feelings," *Cognition & Emotion* 27, no. 8 (2013): 1513–21, https://doi.org/10.1080/02699931.2013.801338.

153   **The Republican Party took:** Drew Westen, *The Political Brain: The Role of Emotion in Deciding the Fate of the Nation* (New York: PublicAffairs, 2008).

153   **"The smirk is causing much":** "George W.'s Smirk: A Chatterbox Investigation," *Slate*, December 8, 1999, https://slate.com/news-and-politics/1999/12/george-w-s-smirk-a -chatterbox-investigation.html.

153   **When researchers asked participants:** Linda Talley and Samuel Temple, "How Leaders Influence Followers Through the Use of Nonverbal Communication," *Leadership & Organization Development Journal* 36, no. 1 (March 2015): 69–80, https://doi.org/10.1108/LODJ-07-2013-0107.

154   **Research shows contempt is:** Aaron Sell, Leda Cosmides, and John Tooby, "The Human Anger Face Evolved to Enhance Cues of Strength," *Evolution and Human Behavior* 35, no. 5 (May 2014): 425–29, https://doi.org/10.1016/j.evol humbehav.2014.05.008.

154   **Dr. John Gottman is a:** John M. Gottman, "A Theory of Marital Dissolution and Stability," *Journal of Family Psychology* 7, no. 1 (1993): 57–75, https://doi .org/10.1037/0893-3200.7.1.57; John M. Gottman, *What Predicts Divorce? The Relationship Between Marital Processes and Marital Outcomes* (Hove, UK: Psychology Press, 2014; https://doi.org/10.4324/9781315806808); John M. Gottman and Robert Wayne Levenson, "How Stable Is Marital Interaction Over Time?," *Family Process* 38, no. 2 (June 1999): 159–65, https://doi.org/https://doi.org/10.1111/j.1545-5300 .1999.00159.x.

154   **most people have an expression:** Paul Ekman and Wallace V. Friesen, *Unmaking the Face: A Guide to Recognizing Emotions from Facial Clues* (New York: Prentice-Hall, 1975).

154   **it's a Danger Zone cue:** Lisa Feldman Barrett and Elizabeth A. Kensinger, "Context Is Routinely Encoded During Emotion Perception," *Psychological Science* 21, no. 4 (April 2010): 595–99, https://doi.org/10.1177/0956797610363547.

156   **Researchers even found that nonverbal ambivalence:** Naomi B. Rothman and Gregory B. Northcraft, "Unlocking Integrative Potential: Expressed Emotional Ambivalence and Negotiation Outcomes," *Organizational Behavior and Human Decision Processes* 126 (January 2015): 65–76, https://doi.org/10.1016/j.obhdp .2014.10.005.

158   **Research confirms that looking:** Barrett and Kensinger, "Context Is Routinely Encoded During Emotion Perception."

158   **For example, one researcher:** Gordon, Druckman, Rozelle, Baxter, "Non-Verbal Behaviour as Communication."

Chapter 7: Sound Powerful

165   **They're participants on Netflix's *Love Is Blind*:** *Love Is Blind*, season 1, episode 1, "Is Love Blind?," released February 13, 2020, on Netflix, https://www.netflix.com /title/80996601.

166   **We can tell a lot:** Anna Oleszkiewicz, Katarzyna Pisanski, Kinga Lachowicz-Tabaczek, and Agnieszka Sorokowska, "Voice-Based Assessments of Trustworthiness, Competence, and Warmth in Blind and Sighted Adults," *Psychonomic Bulletin & Review* 24, no. 3 (June 2017): 856–62, https://doi.org/10.3758/s13423-016-1146-y.

166   **Our voice is so indicative:** William J. Mayew and Mohan Venkatachalam, "The Power of Voice: Managerial Affective States and Future Firm Performance," *Journal of Finance* 67, no. 1 (January 2012): 1–43, https://doi.org/10.1111/j.1540-6261.2011.01705.x.

166   **An analysis of the vocalizations of Mixed Martial Arts:** Pavel Šebesta, Vít Třebický, Jitka Fialová, and Jan Havlíček, "Roar of a Champion: Loudness and Voice Pitch Predict Perceived Fighting Ability but Not Success in MMA Fighters," *Frontiers in Psychology* 10 (April 2019), 859, https://doi.org/10.3389/fpsyg.2019.00859.

167   **One study completely blew:** Nalini Ambady et al., "Surgeons' Tone of Voice: A Clue to Malpractice History," *Surgery* 132, no. 1 (July 2002): 5–9, https://doi.org/10.1067/msy.2002.124733.

167   **"Were you scared to face":** Alan Alda and Betty White, "Betty White and Alan Alda Fall Desperately in Love," *Clear+Vivid with Alan Alda*, podcast, 40:00, https://omny.fm/shows/clear-vivid-with-alan-alda/betty-white-and-alan-alda-fall-desperately-in-love.

168   **When we're nervous or stressed:** Gina Villar, Joanne Arciuli, and Helen Paterson, "Vocal Pitch Production During Lying: Beliefs about Deception Matter," *Psychiatry, Psychology and Law* 20, no. 1 (February 2013): 123–32, https://doi.org/10.1080/13218719.2011.633320.

168   **This is why our voice:** Timothy DeGroot and Stephan J. Motowidlo, "Why Visual and Vocal Interview Cues Can Affect Interviewers' Judgments and Predict Job Performance," *Journal of Applied Psychology* 84, no. 6 (December 1999): 986–93, https://doi.org/10.1037/0021-9010.84.6.986; Timothy DeGroot, Federico Aime, Scott G. Johnson, and Donald Kluemper, "Does Talking the Talk Help Walking the Walk? An Examination of the Effect of Vocal Attractiveness in Leader Effectiveness," *Leadership Quarterly* 22, no. 4 (2011): 680–89, https://doi.org/10.1016/j.leaqua.2011.05.008.

168   **This relaxes and expands:** L. A. McCoy, "The Power of Your Vocal Image," *Journal of the Canadian Dental Association* 62, no. 3 (March 1996): 231–34.

169   **participants unknowingly raised:** Villar, Arciuli, and Paterson, "Vocal Pitch Production During Lying."

169   **Babies prefer interacting with:** J. J. Kevin Nugent et al., *Understanding Newborn Behavior and Early Relationships* (Baltimore: Brookes Publishing, 2007).

169   **While we're uncomfortable listening:** Eric Bucy, "Nonverbal Cues," in *The International Encyclopedia of Media Effects*, eds. Patrick Rössler, Cynthia A. Hoffner, and Liesbet van Zoonen (West Sussex, UK: John Wiley & Sons, 2017); Casey A. Klofstad, Rindy C. Anderson, and Stephen Nowicki, "Perceptions of Competence, Strength, and Age Influence Voters to Select Leaders with Lower-Pitched Voices," *PLoS ONE* 10, no. 8 (August 7, 2015): e013377, https://doi.org/10.1371/journal.pone.0133779.

169   **Researchers find that lowering:** Mariëlle Stel et al., "Lowering the Pitch of Your Voice Makes You Feel More Powerful and Think More Abstractly," *Social Psychological and Personality Science* 3, no. 4 (July 2012): 497–502, https://doi.org/10.1177/1948550611427610.

169   **Elizabeth Holmes, the now-infamous:** Katie Heaney, "What Kind of Person Fakes Their Voice?," *The Cut*, March 21, 2019, https://www.thecut.com/2019/03/why-did-elizabeth-holmes-use-a-fake-deep-voice.html.

171 **Researchers find using the:** Michel Belyk and Steven Brown, "Perception of Affective and Linguistic Prosody: An ALE Meta-Analysis of Neuroimaging Studies," *Social Cognitive and Affective Neuroscience* 9, no. 9 (2014): 1395–403, https://doi.org/10.1093/scan/nst124.

171 **And when the question:** "The Unstoppable March of the Upward Inflection?," *BBC News,* August 11, 2014, https://www.bbc.com/news/magazine-28708526.

171 **"Do you believe me?":** Villar, Arciuli, and Paterson, "Vocal Pitch Production During Lying."

173 **Have you ever heard:** "Vocal Fry: What It Is and How to Get Rid of It," Science of People, September 14, 2018, https://www.scienceofpeople.com/vocal-fry.

173 **Research finds that using:** Rindy C. Anderson, Casey A. Klofstad, William J. Mayew, and Mohan Venkatachalam, "Vocal Fry May Undermine the Success of Young Women in the Labor Market," *PLoS ONE* 9, no. 5 (May 28, 2014): e97506, https://doi.org/10.1371/journal.pone.0097506; Lesley Wolk, Nassima B. Abdelli-Beruh, and Dianne Slavin, "Habitual Use of Vocal Fry in Young Adult Female Speakers," *Journal of Voice* 26, no. 3 (May 2012): e111–16, https://doi.org/10.1016/j.jvoice.2011.04.007.

175 **Research has backed it up:** Laetitia Bruckert et al., "Vocal Attractiveness Increases by Averaging," *Current Biology* 20, no. 2 (January 2010): 116–20, https://doi.org/10.1016/j.cub.2009.11.034.

175 **In one study called "How the Voice Persuades":** Alex B. Van Zant and Jonah Berger, "How the Voice Persuades," *Journal of Personality and Social Psychology* 118, no. 4 (April 2020): 661–82, https://doi.org/10.1037/pspi0000193.

177 **Another study asked participants to listen to:** Rachel Hosie, "Study Reveals the Most Annoying Filler Words British People Use," *Independent*, September 26, 2018, https://www.independent.co.uk/life-style/uk-british-slang-urban-dictionary-filler-words-a8555681.html.

178 **long pauses in conversation can hurt:** University of Gothenburg, "Pauses Can Make or Break a Conversation," PsyPost, September 30, 2015, https://www.psypost.org/2015/09/pauses-can-make-or-break-a-conversation-38070.

179 **Is speaking quickly the best:** Brown University, "Whether Our Speech Is Fast or Slow, We Say about the Same," PsyPost, January 17, 2017, https://www.psypost.org/2017/01/whether-speech-fast-slow-say-46941.

179 **A slower speaking pace:** Abdullah A. Khuwaileh, "The Role of Chunks, Phrases and Body Language in Understanding Co-Ordinated Academic Lectures," *System* 27, no. 2 (1999): 249–60, https://doi.org/10.1016/S0346-251X(99)00019-6.

179 **waiting five to seven:** Andrew J. Hale et al., "Twelve Tips for Effective Body Language for Medical Educators," *Medical Teacher* 39, no. 9 (May 14, 2017): 914–19, https://doi.org/10.1080/0142159X.2017.1324140.

181 **Psychological researchers Nick Epley:** University of Chicago Booth School of Business, "The Sound of Intellect: Job Seeker's Voice Reveals Intelligence," PsyPost, February 21, 2015, https://www.psypost.org/2015/02/the-sound-of-intellect-job-seekers-voice-reveals-intelligence-31900.

Chapter 8: Vocal Likability

184 **She was called the Iron Lady:** Max Fisher, "'Irony Lady': How a Moscow Propagandist Gave Margaret Thatcher Her Famous Nickname," *Washington Post*, April 8, 2013, https://www.washingtonpost.com/news/worldviews/wp/2013/04/08/irony-lady-how-a-moscow-propagandist-gave-margaret-thatcher-her-famous-nick name.

184 **"Physically she had a problem":** Anne Karpf, *The Human Voice: The Story of a Remarkable Talent* (London: Bloomsbury, 2006).

184　**She particularly struggled during Question Time:** "Question Time," UK Parliament, accessed September 16, 2021, https://www.parliament.uk/about/how /business/questions.

185　**This was the start of:** Karpf, *The Human Voice.*

185　**people determine how confident you are within:** Xiaoming Jiang and Marc D. Pell, "On How the Brain Decodes Vocal Cues about Speaker Confidence," *Cortex* 66 (May 1, 2015): 9–34, https://doi.org/10.1016/j.cortex.2015.02.002.

186　**in particular, how emotion:** "How to Speak with Confidence and Sound Better," Science of People, April 20, 2020, https://www.scienceofpeople.com/speak-with -confidence.

187　**There's a scientific reason:** Steve Ayan, "Nine Things You Don't Know about Yourself," *Greater Good*, June 4, 2018, https://greatergood.berkeley.edu/article/item /nine_things_you_dont_know_about_yourself; Rébecca Kleinberger, "Why You Don't Like the Sound of Your Own Voice," filmed November 2017, TED video, 12:42, https://www.youtube.com/watch?v=g3vSYbT1Aco.

191　**it takes just a tenth of a second:** Christer Gobl and Ailbhe Ní Chasaide, "The Role of Voice Quality in Communicating Emotion, Mood and Attitude," *Speech Communication* 40, no. 1–2 (April 2003): 189–212, https://doi.org/10.1016/S0167 -6393(02)00082-1; McGill University, "Human Sounds Convey Emotions Clearer and Faster Than Words," PsyPost, January 18, 2016, https://www.psypost.org/2016/01 /human-sounds-convey-emotions-clearer-and-faster-than-words-40283.

191　**Emotion is what captures:** Springer Select, "Words Have Feelings," PsyPost, December 12, 2012, https://www.psypost.org/2012/12/words-have-feelings-15507.

191　**When nurses used more vocal:** Fergus Lyon, Guido Möllering, and Mark Saunders, *Handbook of Research Methods on Trust,* 2nd ed. (Northampton, MA: Edward Elgar Publishing, 2016).

192　**Data scientists at Quantified:** Matt Abrahams, "A Big Data Approach to Public Speaking," Stanford Graduate School of Business, April 4, 2016, https://www.gsb .stanford.edu/insights/big-data-approach-public-speaking.

199　**One study examined vocal mirroring:** Jared R. Curhan and Alex Pentland, "Thin Slices of Negotiation: Predicting Outcomes from Conversational Dynamics Within the First 5 Minutes," *Journal of Applied Psychology* 92, no. 3 (June 2007): 802–11, https://doi.org/10.1037/0021-9010.92.3.802.

201　**This ridiculous exercise was an:** Rebecca K. Ivic and Robert J. Green, "Developing Charismatic Delivery Through Transformational Presentations: Modeling the Persona of Steve Jobs," *Communication Teacher* 26, no. 2 (January 2012): 65–68, https://doi .org/10.1080/17404622.2011.643808.

202　**Find a private space:** Vanessa Van Edwards, "5 Vocal Warm Ups Before Meetings, Speeches and Presentations," Science of People, January 25, 2019, https://www .scienceofpeople.com/vocal-warm-ups.

Chapter 9: How to Communicate with Charisma

210　**Dr. Frank Luntz found:** Frank Luntz, *Words That Work: It's Not What You Say, It's What People Hear* (New York: Hachette Books, 2007).

210　**"Eighty percent of those":** Adam L. Penenberg, "PS: I Love You. Get Your Free Email at Hotmail," *TechCrunch*, October 18, 2009, https://social.techcrunch .com/2009/10/18/ps-i-love-you-get-your-free-email-at-hotmail.

210　**Turns out the resounding:** Varda Liberman, Steven M. Samuels, and Lee Ross, "The Name of the Game: Predictive Power of Reputations versus Situational Labels in Determining Prisoner's Dilemma Game Moves," *Personality and Social Psychology*

Bulletin 30, no. 9 (October 2004): 1175–85, https://doi.org/10.1177/014616720 4264004.

210 **One study found that customers:** Penn State, "Emoticons May Signal Better Customer Service," PsyPost, May 21, 2015, https://www.psypost.org/2015/05 /emoticons-may-signal-better-customer-service-34525.

228 **Servers who repeat orders:** Roderick I. Swaab, William W. Maddux, and Marwan Sinaceur, "Early Words That Work: When and How Virtual Linguistic Mimicry Facilitates Negotiation Outcomes," *Journal of Experimental Social Psychology* 47, no. 3 (May 2011): 616–21, https://doi.org/10.1016/j.jesp.2011.01.005.

228 **negotiate via virtual chat:** Kate Muir et al., "When Asking 'What' and 'How' Helps You Win: Mimicry of Interrogative Terms Facilitates Successful Online Negotiations," *Negotiation and Conflict Management Research* 14, no. 2 (2021), https://doi .org/10.1111/ncmr.12179.

229 **Here are just the first four seconds:** "Jennifer Aniston's First Text During Her Plane Scare Was from Ellen," *Ellen DeGeneres Show*, NBC, aired June 5, 2019, video, 6:48, https://www.youtube.com/watch?v=NUjlpiEF9DE.

230 **"thanking a new acquaintance":** Lisa A. Williams and Monica Y. Bartlett, "Warm Thanks: Gratitude Expression Facilitates Social Affiliation in New Relationships via Perceived Warmth," *Emotion* 15, no. 1 (February 2015): 1–5, https://doi.org/10.1037 /emo0000017.

Chapter 10: Creating a Powerful Visual Presence

235 **When researchers asked participants:** Richard E. Nisbett and Timothy D. Wilson, "Telling More Than We Can Know: Verbal Reports on Mental Processes," *Psychological Review* 84, no. 3 (March 1977): 231–59, https://doi.org/10.1037/0033 -295X.84.3.231.

236 **Everyone's neural maps:** Allan M. Collins and Elizabeth F. Loftus, "A Spreading-Activation Theory of Semantic Processing," *Psychological Review* 82, no. 6 (November 1975): 407–28, https://doi.org/10.1037/0033-295X.82.6.407.

238 **From the beginning, the founders:** Rebecca Adams, "The Story of How Two Candy Lovers Found Business Partners (and Love) on Match.com," *HuffPost*, April 28, 2014, https://www.huffpost.com/entry/sugarfina-candy_n_5191870.

240 **people ascribe emotional:** Elisabeth Donahue, "Font Focus: Making Ideas Harder to Read May Make Them Easier to Retain," Princeton University, October 28, 2010, https://www.princeton.edu/news/2010/10/28/font-focus-making-ideas-harder-read -may-make-them-easier-retain; Aditya Shukla, "Font Psychology: New Research & Practical Insights," *Cognition Today,* May 28, 2018, https://cognitiontoday.com /font-psychology-research-and-application.

241 **a story about a fictional alien creature:** Connor Diemand-Yauman, Daniel M. Oppenheimer, and Erikka B. Vaughan, "Fortune Favors the **Bold** (*and the Italicized*): Effects of Disfluency on Educational Outcomes," *Cognition* 118, no 1 (2011): 111–15, https://doi.org/10.1016/j.cognition.2010.09.012.

241 **assemble puzzle pieces that were:** Joshua M. Ackerman, Christopher C. Nocera, and John A. Bargh, "Incidental Haptic Sensations Influence Social Judgments and Decisions," *Science* 328, no. 5986 (June 25, 2010): 1712–15, https://doi.org/10.1126 /science.1189993.

242 **Research finds that cold temperatures:** Eric W. Dolan, "Cold Temperatures Make People Cold-Hearted, Study on Moral Judgments Finds," PsyPost, October 8, 2014, https://www.psypost.org/2014/10/cold-temperatures-make-people-cold-hearted-study -moral-judgments-finds-28614.

243 **If you image yourself sunbathing:** Judith Simon Prager and Judith Acosta, *Verbal First Aid: Help Your Kids Heal from Fear and Pain—and Come Out Strong* (New York: Berkley Books, 2010), 13.

244 **Our brain can identify images:** Anne Trafton, "In the Blink of an Eye," MIT News, January 16, 2014, https://news.mit.edu/2014/in-the-blink-of-an-eye-0116.

244 **some phone operators read scripts:** Robert B. Cialdini, *Pre-Suasion: A Revolutionary Way to Influence and Persuade* (New York: Simon & Schuster, 2016).

244 **In one fascinating dive:** Elizabeth Segran, "Netflix Knows Which Pictures You'll Click On—and Why," *Fast Company*, May 3, 2016, https://www.fastcompany .com/3059450/netflix-knows-which-pictures-youll-click-on-and-why.

244 **In a YouTube video of a virtual interview:** "Kevin Hart on Quarantine with Pregnant Wife & Backyard Camping with Kids," *Jimmy Kimmel Live*, ABC, May 22, 2020, video, 6:44, https://www.youtube.com/watch?v=WzpXypS1ihs.

244 **students learn best when presented:** Richard E. Mayer, "Applying the Science of Learning: Evidence-Based Principles for the Design of Multimedia Instruction," *American Psychologist* 63, no. 8 (November 2008): 760–69, https://doi .org/10.1037/0003-066X.63.8.760.

246 **Benjamin Franklin was sent:** James C. Humes, *Speak Like Churchill, Stand Like Lincoln: 21 Powerful Secrets of History's Greatest Speakers* (New York: Crown, 2002).

248 **the late U.S. senator Robert Byrd:** Johanna Neuman, "Robert Byrd Dies at 92; U.S. Senator from West Virginia," *Los Angeles Times*, June 29, 2010, https://www.latimes .com/archives/la-xpm-2010-jun-29-la-me-byrd-20100628-story.html.

248 **the mere presence of a backpack or briefcase:** Travis J. Carter, Melissa J. Ferguson, and Ran R. Hassin, "A Single Exposure to the American Flag Shifts Support Toward Republicanism up to 8 Months Later," *Psychological Science* 22, no. 8 (July 2011): 1011–18, https://doi.org/10.1177/0956797611414726.

248 **award-winning television producer:** "Lee Tomlinson—Cancer Survivor Sparking the C.A.R.E. Effect Movement," speech at Eagles Talent Speakers Bureau, February 23, 2018, video, 3:33, https://www.youtube.com/watch?v=48DHHBTljA4.

250 **Research finds women rate:** Eric W. Dolan, "Women Rate Men as Less Masculine and Less Dateable When They've Got a Cat in Their Lap," PsyPost, August 19, 2020, https://www.psypost.org/2020/08/women-rate-men-as-less-masculine-and-less -dateable-when-theyve-got-a-cat-in-their-lap-57738.

251 **They call these colors:** Darren Bridger, *Neuro Design: Neuromarketing Insights to Boost Engagement and Profitability* (London: Kogan Page, 2017).

251 **people make up their minds within 90 seconds:** Satyendra Singh, "Impact of Color on Marketing," *Management Decision* 44, no. 6 (July 2006): 783–89, https://doi .org/10.1108/00251740610673332.

251 **Color psychology is:** Andrew J. Elliot, "Color and Psychological Functioning: A Review of Theoretical and Empirical Work," *Frontiers in Psychology* 6 (April 2, 2015): 368, https://doi.org/10.3389/fpsyg.2015.00368.

251 **For example, in one:** Anton J. M. de Craen et al., "Effect of Colour of Drugs: Systematic Review of Perceived Effect of Drugs and of Their Effectiveness," *BMJ* 313, no. 7072 (December 1996): 1624–26, https://doi.org/10.1136/bmj.313.7072.1624.

252 **MSNBC, a liberal network:** Qiao Wang (@QwQiao), "Notice that on Fox the 'presidential' in 'presidential debate' is red, and on MSNBC the 'presidential' is blue," Twitter, October 22, 2020, https://twitter.com/qwqiao/status/1319453677434904579.

252 **This happens across cultures:** Danielle Levesque, "Psychology Research Reveals the Connection between Color and Emotion," PsyPost, January 30, 2016, https://www .psypost.org/2016/01/psychology-research-reveals-the-connection-between-color-and -emotion-40586.

252   **One research team:** Andrew J. Elliot and Markus A. Maier, "Color Psychology: Effects of Perceiving Color on Psychological Functioning in Humans," *Annual Review of Psychology* 65, no. 1 (January 2014): 95–120, https://doi.org/10.1146/annurev-psych -010213-115035.

252   **our cave-dwelling ancestors were foraging:** Michael Price, "You Can Thank Your Fruit-Hunting Ancestors for Your Color Vision," *Science*, February 19, 2017, https://www.science.org/content/article/you-can-thank-your-fruit-hunting-ancestors -your-color-vision.

253   **Anecdotal evidence also:** Lu Ann Ahrens, "Color Psychology: Does It Affect How You Feel?," *Lu Ann Ahrens* (blog), April 17, 2018, https://luannahrens.com/color -psychology-does-it-affect-how-you-feel.

253   **suggests that blue:** Zena O'Connor, "Colour Psychology and Colour Therapy: Caveat Emptor," *Color Research & Application* 36, no. 3 (June 2011): 229–34, https://doi.org/10.1002/col.20597.

253   **In the business world:** Lauren I. Labrecque and George R. Milne, "Exciting Red and Competent Blue: The Importance of Color in Marketing," *Journal of the Academy of Marketing Science* 40, no. 5 (September 2012): 711–27, https://doi.org/10.1007 /s11747-010-0245-y.

253   **This has been reported in:** Elliot, "Color and Psychological Functioning."

254   **Researchers found that using:** University of Oregon, "Research Suggests Color Affects Ethical Judgments of Brands," PsyPost, December 3, 2015, https://www .psypost.org/2015/12/research-suggests-color-affects-ethical-judgments-of-brands -39676; Aparna Sundar and James J. Kellaris, "How Logo Colors Influence Shoppers' Judgments of Retailer Ethicality: The Mediating Role of Perceived Eco-Friendliness," *Journal of Business Ethics* 146, no. 3 (2017): 685–701, https://doi.org/10.1007 /s10551-015-2918-4.

254   **Other researchers have found:** Walid Briki and Olivier Hue, "How Red, Blue, and Green Are Affectively Judged: Affective Judgments of Colors," *Applied Cognitive Psychology* 30, no. 2 (2016): 301–4, https://doi.org/10.1002/acp.3206.

254   **Researchers also find that:** Briki and Hue, "How Red, Blue, and Green Are Affectively Judged."

255   **In a comprehensive study of the color yellow:** Domicele Jonauskaite and Christine Mohr, "A Commentary: The Sun Is No Fun Without Rain: Reply to 'The Sun and How Do We Feel about the Color Yellow? Methodological Concerns,'" *Journal of Environmental Psychology* 67 (February 1, 2020): 101379, https://doi.org/10.1016/j .jenvp.2019.101379.

255   **It's one of the most difficult colors:** Kendra Cherry and Amy Morin, "The Color Psychology of Yellow," Very Well Mind, March 25, 2020, https://www.verywellmind .com/the-color-psychology-of-yellow-2795823.

256   **Sadly, researchers found that fictitious résumés:** Kizza Chadiha, "State of Science on Unconscious Bias," UCSF Office of Diversity and Outreach, https://diversity.ucsf .edu/resources/state-science-unconscious-bias.

257   **science faculty rated male applicants:** Corinne A. Moss-Racusin et al., "Science Faculty's Subtle Gender Biases Favor Male Students," *PNAS* 109, no. 41 (October 9, 2012): 16474–79, https://doi.org/10.1073/pnas.1211286109.

257   **One study found that people with stereotypically:** "People with 'Gay-Sounding' Voices Face Discrimination and Anticipate Rejection," *Academic Times,* February 11, 2021, https://academictimes.com/people-with-gay-sounding-voices-face-particular -discrimination.

257   **It's called the beauty premium:** Eric W. Dolan, "Women Viewed as More Trustworthy When Wearing Makeup—and Receive Larger Money Transfers in an

Economic Game," PsyPost, May 3, 2020, https://www.psypost.org/2020/05/women
-viewed-as-more-trustworthy-when-wearing-makeup-and-receive-larger-money
-transfers-in-an-economic-game-56679.

257 **Black women with natural hairstyles:** Christy Zhou Koval and Ashleigh
Shelby Rosette, "The Natural Hair Bias in Job Recruitment," *Social Psychological and
Personality Science* 12, no. 5 (May 2021): 741–50, https://doi.org/10.1177/1948550
620937937.

257 **Research finds unconscious biases:** Nilanjana Dasgupta, "Implicit Attitudes and
Beliefs Adapt to Situations," *Advances in Experimental Social Psychology* 47 (December
2013): 233–79, https://doi.org/10.1016/B978-0-12-407236-7.00005-X.

257 **Researchers tested whether clothing:** Regan A. R. Gurung et al., "Can Success
Deflect Racism? Clothing and Perceptions of African American Men," *Journal of Social
Psychology* 161, no. 1 (2021): 119–28, https://doi.org/10.1080/00224545.2020.1787938.

Conclusion: Cues Best Practices

261 **He first conclusively demonstrated:** The Editors of Encyclopaedia Britannica, "Radio
Wave," accessed September 16, 2021, https://www.britannica.com/science/radio-wave;
"Heinrich Rudolf Hertz," Hebrew University of Jerusalem, updated July 30, 2004,
https://web.archive.org/web/20090925102542/http://chem.ch.huji.ac.il/history
/hertz.htm.

262 **Researchers found that the more trusting:** Nancy L. Carter and J. Mark Weber,
"Not Pollyannas: Higher Generalized Trust Predicts Lie Detection Ability," *Social
Psychological and Personality Science* 1, no. 3 (July 2010): 274–79, https://doi
.org/10.1177/1948550609360261.

Index

Read more from Vanessa Van Edwards

Translated into over sixteen languages!